Media and the Experience of Social Change

Media and the Experience of Social Change

The Arab World

Tim Markham

ROWMAN &
LITTLEFIELD
INTERNATIONAL
London • New York

Published by Rowman & Littlefield International Ltd.
Unit A, Whitacre Mews, 26–34 Stannary Street, London SE11 4AB
www.rowmaninternational.com

Rowman & Littlefield International Ltd. is an affiliate of Rowman & Littlefield
4501 Forbes Boulevard, Suite 200, Lanham, Maryland 20706, USA
With additional offices in Boulder, New York, Toronto (Canada), and Plymouth (UK)
www.rowman.com

British Library Cataloguing in Publication Data
A catalogue record for this book is available from the British Library

ISBN: HB 978-1-78660-421-7
PB 978-1-78660-422-4

Library of Congress Cataloging-in-Publication Data Available

ISBN: 978-1-78660-421-7 (cloth : alk. paper)
ISBN: 978-1-78660-422-4 (pbk. : alk. paper)
ISBN: 978-1-78660-423-1 (electronic)

Printed in the United States of America

Contents

Chapter One

Introduction

This book begins from a well-observed conundrum (Bourdieu, 2001) about journalism's conflicted role as writer of the first draft of history. On the one hand, journalists are fixated by change, obsessively looking for those day-to-day shifts in politics, economics and anything else, shifts that constitute news. In many ways the rise of data journalism and non-professional media production has diminished the centrality of the classic job of reporting what has happened in the immediate past, with many journalists and commentators more often engaged in predicting the future: spotting trends, identifying directions of travel and speculating about probable outcomes. On the other hand, though, journalists and commentators have a fairly dismal record when it comes to apprehending – let alone predicting – political and social changes that are more systemic and take time to gestate: few predicted the financial crisis of 2008 (Fraser, 2009) or the uprisings that erupted in Iran in 2009 and the Arab world towards the end of the following year (Cottle, 2011); most were surprised by the outcome of Britain's EU referendum and the election of Donald Trump in 2016. The fault lies not just with media practitioners, however, but also with political scientists collectively overstating the resilience of authoritarian regimes (Stoker et al., 2015) and academic economics departments roundly accused of tunnel vision when it comes to the historical context in which neo-liberal capitalism operates (Colander et al., 2009). And more widely than that, it is arguable that one of the conditions of contemporary life for most of us, experts and amateurs alike, is that we experience things in a bubble of the present, pushed this way and that by a constant stream of stimuli that leaves us insensible to the broader sweep of history (Stiegler, 1998). Philosophers have identified such temporal blindness as a symptom of life lived inauthentically, but this book wants to push back against that accusation along with all of the associated claims about our superficial, distracted and fickle engagement with the world around us. In doing so it foregrounds the role that media play in this lived experience of change and continuity – media we consume, produce and just live among – since it is media saturation that is often said to foster this inauthentic way of being in the world. Further, the specific focus on media practitioners that opens up an opportunity to explore precisely how change is experienced when engaging with the world is ostensibly the core of one's personal principle and professional ambition. Above all else what becomes clear is that substantive engagement is not all or nothing, and certainly never constant – seen under the microscope it is uneven, contingent and provisional, though no less real than any pious proclamation of solidarity with global others. And if that is true for the professionals, might it not also be so for the rest of us?

Thinking about the experience of continuity and change, big and small, in everyday life (Back, 2015; Neal, 2015) is the lodestar of the phenomenological tradition, whose lineage can be traced back through Merleau-Ponty and Schutz to Husserl, Kierkegaard, Marx, Hegel and, ultimately, Kant. Phenomenology has continued to evolve and mutate, but much contemporary research still takes its cue from Martin Heidegger's *Being and Time*, originally published in 1927. Among its many innovations is the provocative claim that *thinking* is not really the point. You can only understand being in the world by acting in it; you do not grasp the meaning of a tool by reflecting on it but by picking it up and using it, its meaning consisting not in the conscious awareness of what you are about to do with it but the fact that everything you could do with it and how to do it is activated by you reaching out to pick it up. This is at-handness, an idea that drives beyond experience and expertise – knowing how to do things with objects – to the way that whole worlds of possibility and meaning are effortlessly invoked by a tool's being not simply there but just-pick-upable. How does such a state of affairs come to pass, an experience in which plenitudes of actions and ideas are seamlessly summoned as we go about our daily routines? Habituation and taking things for granted is the norm, but what becomes habituated and accepted as given is heavily, historically contingent. Heidegger writes about how our being in the world is always simultaneously oriented in relation to the past, present and future – and that to live authentically entails fully grasping the significance of each. Now, this could be interpreted as saying that it is incumbent upon us to know how we got to where we are, as individuals and collectively – and this would certainly fit some post-Marxist calls for an archaeological approach (Foucault, 1972) to political and cultural analysis, digging through layers of determination that made the status quo possible. But Heidegger has something else in mind: not so much the determination of symbolic superstructure by economic base as the preconditions for everyday experience being just liveable, what makes it possible to just be and do in the world, usually without reflection.

This is the core principle of all phenomenology – seeking to understand what makes so much of what we do instinctive, and instinctively meaningful – and it will be seen that far from committing ourselves to cataloguing the banal, it is at this level that political insight is at its most acute. Likewise, Heidegger's appeal for us to stand in full recognition of the future is taken in more psychologizing readings (Mulhall, 2005) to mean a reconciliation with mortality and in historical ones (Farías et al., 1989) as foreshadowing the disastrous embrace of national destiny. But there is a much more practical application of his understanding of time to come, in being aware of the stakes in whatever situation we find ourselves thrown into, knowing how it could play out and accepting responsibility accordingly.

The fact that we for the most part fail to grasp how the past and future inform our experience of the present need not trouble us overly, since the last thing this book aims for is advice on how to live more fully in the present. Instead, the objective is to set out how we experience, often through media, the past, present and future, and with what implications (Barker, 2009). Thinking about the way that the future emerges to consciousness is then not about prediction but about assessing what it tells us about our experience of the present – it is about temporal orientation. Dire predictions about the death of news, for instance, tell us much more about what journalism means to us now, not least to journalists, than it can actually foretell what the future has in store. Or if our imaginings of future forms of politics are unencumbered by history or parties, manifestos or leadership, then this reveals much about our current relation to all things political and what we think is at stake. The distinctive experience of media *as new* (Rantanen, 2009), as constantly ushering in new futures, points to potentially profound insights not just about our attitudes towards technology but also about what we understand by concepts like identity, cultural value and citizenship. As for the past, we will see in chapter 6 that the way it appears to consciousness is *functional* more than anything else, in that it often serves little more purpose than to rationalize what people do day in, day out. More importantly, it will become clear that it appears in ways that are decontextualized, atemporal or just at odds with an understanding of historical change as necessarily incremental, non-linear and, above all, generative of contingent modes of thinking and behaving. The upshot is much more significant than a time lag between historical change and the way we see the world (Bourdieu, 1984): while significant shifts are taking place around us, shifts which will also leave their mark on our own subjectivities, we are thrown backwards and forwards or simply out of time, enacting mislearned schema and wishful projections in order to navigate each encounter in the world as it appears to us.

But before proceeding, it is worth making a few caveats clear. The intention of this book is not to diagnose false consciousness that leaves us blind to what is 'really' going on. Against Heidegger's notion of living authentically, fully cognizant of past and future and the passing of time in between, the aim here is to understand how change is experienced, as opposed to how it should be experienced. Much can be gleaned from the starting point that while upheaval apparently swept the Middle East in the early years of this decade, for many of those interviewed for this research, the daily rituals of being woken by an alarm set on a mobile phone, grabbing a hurried bite to eat and taking a bus or driving a car to work went more or less unchanged. This is not to render political turmoil mundane but to counsel against imagining it as something ethereal. Likewise, this book does not set out to *blame* the media for surrounding us in a fog of stimuli and distraction (Poster, 2001) – in this regard it is in line with much current thinking that resists reducing analysis to what media do to people (see, for instance, Bird, 2003). It is important to appreciate the extent to which habituated media encounters – whether conscious or barely registered – contribute to the seamlessness and continuity of everyday experience, even or especially when our attention is repeatedly drawn to the apparently novel. But media are not extrinsic to subjectivity; they sit alongside all the other determinants of conscious experience, none of which we could easily call unmediated. Everyday encounters demand individually internalized habits and collective cultures of practice. The book sets out how those habits and cultures rub against transformations taking place in the world and sheds light on our relation to historical change – whether it is engaged or fantastic, ambivalent or indifferent.

PHENOMENOLOGY AND POLITICS

The aim, then, is to investigate the myriad media practices people enact as they navigate the world temporally, amid the routines and taken-for-granted realities of everyday life. Those practices obviously include media consumption and production, though just living among media is not a passive state of being but something achieved practically: reacting to, adjusting to and ignoring media are as much practices as commissioning, curating or managing it. And that world being negotiated a mile a minute as we adapt to its vicissitudes by learning to embody habits and strategies is no flat backdrop but a complex configuration of environments that threatens to overwhelm and demands to be apprehended at every turn. How we do that apprehending changes over time and space, and scholars disagree about how well we and others understand what is going on out there, often through the media we use and are exposed to. It is also a particular kind of world in historical terms, threaded through with all manner of continuities and long-term trends but also vivid and maybe transformative events: financial crises, environmental chaos and an outbreak in the early 2010s of uprising and protest across the world that the journalist Paul Mason (2012) described as 'kicking off everywhere'. The years 2010 and 2011 saw eruptions of protest in the Middle East, Spain, Greece and Israel as well as the spread of the Occupy movements from Zuccotti Park around the globe (Benski et al., 2013; Tejerina et al., 2013). As well as proliferating like a blithe kind of global contagion, there seemed to be something about these nascent political cultures that was capable of anything: overthrowing dictators, resisting the remorseless march of capitalism and so on. Soon we started asking whether the way the political groupings organized themselves and their activism through new kinds of networked media was what lay behind their unique potency (Castells, 2012), though this book starts from the consensus that congealed in the following few years, these were not Facebook revolutions; social media were important but not causal (see, for instance, Dencik & Leistert, 2015; Uldam & Verstegaard, 2015). Rather than take on all of those diffuse political phenomena, the book frames its analysis specifically around the uprisings in the Arab world no longer known as the Arab Spring, in the light of subsequent reversals and stagnation in many countries of the Middle East and North Africa (Moghadam, 2013).

What role have different forms of media, as well as the more generalized condition of living in an age of media abundance and convergence, played in how individuals have lived through the political turmoil as citizens, media practitioners, activists and audiences? That many of those watching and interpreting the Arab uprisings were not from that part of the world – often with a limited understanding of its histories, cultures and languages – presents clear problems. Are clueless distant spectators chipping in with their view on events in Tahrir Square on Twitter somehow worse than those who do not engage at all (Alterman, 2011; cf. Žižek, 2011)? Are Western academics and journalists commenting on developments in the region inevitably complicit in the neocolonial subjugation of its peoples, however pure their intentions (Newsom et al., 2011)? We have been here before, needless to say. Edward Said (1978) pushed beyond doubt the fact that the Middle East of the West's imagining cannot escape centuries of exploitation, bloodshed, literature and tourism. And yet to posit the insuperability of orientalism as a Foucauldian sort of always-everywhere discourse, while politically compelling, does us little good as we seek better ways to understand and engage with the wider world. Just as problematic is the refusal of critical academic engagement, instead framing historic events as the expression of some authentic Arab culture – or worse yet, Arab street (for a critical view, see Lynch, 2003) – as though such an embodying, reductive essence existed. Like everything else we encounter in the world, the people, places and events of the Arab world appear to us as objects – of journalism, international relations, travel and so on. Objectification is a given; the phenomenologist's task is to unpack how it proceeds and on the basis of what assumptions, always motivated by the Hegelian imperative of apprehending the full subjectivity of that objectified other, a subjectivity for which we in turn *are* other (Miller, 2016).

Recognition of the subjective other (see especially Taylor, 1994; Fraser & Honneth, 2003; Mark, 2014) is no small feat, still less embedding recognition in professional practice and institutionalizing it in mission statements and codes of practice. Lois McNay (2008) makes a compelling case that all recognition is essentially misrecognition, deriving from the phenomenological tenet that perception always begins with intention; intentive recognition always comes from the recognizer, not the recognizee (see also Klikauer, 2016). Judith Butler (1993) makes this point more sharply political, arguing that the act of recognizing amounts to the incited performance of subjectivity on the part of the recognized: it is not just that we do not see them for who they are, we also require them to be the selves that we see. Both tie into more widespread angst about a contemporary crisis of recognition. Whether it is because of galloping narcissism (Lasch, 1978), the commodification of everything (Lash, 2010) or the inexorable pervasiveness of mediated representation (Baudrillard, 1983), there is something fundamentally lacking in the relations that unknown others have with each other. This is not simply about solipsism, since the inability to grasp the reality of others prevents us from understanding the profundity of change and continuity in the world we inhabit on a daily basis. For Hegel (Hegel, 1979 [1807]) this is much more than a belief that people should try to imagine walking in another's shoes; it is how subjectification works, the dialectic through which individually and collectively we perceive and act in the world around us as we are perceived and acted on by it.

If there is a crisis of recognition, then it is one of self-identity as well as global citizenship. The selves we instinctively see and the worlds they invoke when we watch the news are insuperable stereotypes, while the selves we snap into becoming as we watch are short-circuited, stunted. Worse yet, the collective act of watching amounts to subjugating others to our regimes of recognition, while those subjects that we snap into becoming are not our own. What if each is not just an accident of history but the expression of economic and political logics embedded in cultural norms, industries and the very architectures of the technologies that mediate between us all? How can we make people more aware not only of the lives of others but also of the sheer contingency of our own lived presents, the historic *evitability* that what is experienced as utterly normal and unremarkable would actually come to pass? And, finally, how can we ensure apprehension by audiences and publics of what is at stake in how things unfold from here? An important starting point is to disentangle what is at stake in the playing out of history and what is at stake in each encounter – everything in the case of the former, not so much in the latter. Rowing back from the idea that particular mediated encounters between distant others matter makes the question of solidarity one of ongoing work, work that does not have to be continuous, intense and focused. This changes the game for journalists, humanitarian campaigners and academics, from one in which the agreed goal is to produce critical encounters that break through habituated experience to something less intense but more protracted and able to underpin a more generalized and dispersed orientation towards subjective recognition.

The same logic applies to those selves summoned when we pay attention to media. It is true that at the moment of activation, media demands that we apprehend it as a fully formed, always-already world and that this apprehension necessitates a particular apprehending self (Scannell, 1996). As with Heidegger's tools, media calls forth not just particular competences and skills but also whole ways of being. And yet, these are not as enveloping or overdetermining as they seem; after Scannell (see also Friedman, 2016, on the 'habitus clivé', and Silva, 2016, on the fragmented habitus), they are only *partially* implicated selves. This is not because of some innate resistance to coerced subjectification but rather because we are being simultaneously summoned by different worlds all demanding to be encountered as they are. Over time, dominant modes of subjectification emerge that cut across different kinds of interaction and experience – we are historical creatures after all – but we are not overwhelmed or incited towards replete subjective enactment every time we switch on one of our media devices. In Butler's (1993: 121) terms, interpellation may be formative. But against Butler, this need not amount to complete subjectification: users of social media are not invoked fully formed when they participate in their favourite platforms (cf. Hay, 2011; Andrejevic, 2011) – other things are going on. Users may be called forth in particular ways and asked to be certain kinds of self, but this is not the same as being annihilated or rent asunder by the logics of these platforms – their architectures, their algorithms, their profit-seeking business models.

PRINCIPAL AIMS AND CLAIMS

In its concluding pages this book makes a case for journalists, professional or otherwise, playing an integral role in future public life by acting as agents of dissensus. The term is Rancière's, and in our context it can be simply explained: What if journalists, beyond acting as intermediaries and translating different groups to each other, focused on explicating that which is untranslatable? The underlying argument is that if we are to properly grasp social change at its most profound and nuanced, which means recognizing the stakes in the various presents we find ourselves in, we need to constantly work at making clear the limits of intelligibility of our conscious experience of everyday life. Chapter 2 begins to make this case by positing that journalists are well placed to perform this function, equipped with a particularly epistemological relation to the world around them. This is not about journalists knowing more than others or possessing an ethereal sense of what is important, but a basic anticipatory framework that methodically sizes up all encounters big and small and refuses to take them at face value. The way that journalists often operate according to gut instinct (Schultz, 2007), effortlessly turning everything they see into copy that cleaves to stale convention, is rightly critiqued (Johnson-Cartee, 2005). The same can be said about the constant quest for novelty, wilfully blind to less sensational but more meaningful longer-term trends. But there is something else in the journalistic disposition that only grows in salience as media converges and proliferates, a sceptical curiosity that resists the urge to think that whatever is present is always-already the way things are now.

That sceptical, curious professional bearing towards the world opens up new ways of thinking about how change is experienced – by journalists as well as the rest of us. We are creatures of habit, and our habituated orientations towards the world we inhabit have the tendency to reproduce the status quo in that world. At the same time, however, we are constantly being reminded that we are living in times of ever-escalating flux, with the comforting continuities as well as durable iniquities of the past about to be swept away by whatever comes relentlessly next. For journalists this often takes the form of the death of the trade itself, rent asunder by massively networked communication, redundant economic models and algorithmic automation. The reality, though, is that most journalists neither have their head in the sand when it comes to questions of systemic change nor do they accept claims of the imminent arrival of an unprecedented, unrecognizable future with wide eyes and gaping mouths. So how exactly are the profundity of historic change and the mundanity of work routines reconciled in everyday life? And what can we extrapolate from the journalistic experience to that of people more broadly? That is the task this book sets out to achieve, following Tilly's (2007) commitment to 'developing theoretically sophisticated accounts of social processes somewhere between the stratosphere of global abstraction and the underground of thick description'. It trains its empirical gaze on the Middle East in part as a small corrective to the dominance by the global North and west of the academic literature in the disciplines of journalism, sociology, cultural studies and philosophy. But this focus is particularly apt given recent events in the region. Historically, our models for analysing media and politics under authoritarian regimes were skewed heavily towards continuity, with dysfunctional institutions and social injustice tending towards sclerosis rather than revolution. Suddenly, in the years after 2010, it seemed as if radical change was not just possible but inevitable – all fuelled by the media contagion afforded by social networks that bypass dominant media and political institutions. Reporters in the Arab world have historically been much maligned as ineffectual and corrupt (see especially Sakr, 2010; Pintak, 2011), not up to the job of holding power to account and deaf to the voices of the young and marginalized. There is a temptation to rebalance this by telling the story of valiant hacks persevering in the face of enormous obstacles and malign forces. The reality is far more complex, and the book asks what we can learn from the experience of those living through and reporting on historic shifts that are in equal measure inspiring, troubling, conflicted, ambiguous and disappointing.

Chapter 3 begins the empirical work of this endeavour by investigating the tweets of Arab journalists in relation to significant political events in the aftermath of the uprisings in Egypt and the then nascent civil war in Syria. With the caveat that this kind of content cannot be interpreted as standing for what the political is now firmly in place, an epistemological journalistic orientation starts to take shape. The discourse on display here is variegated and messy, and a lot of it apparently signifies very little indeed, and yet an instinct to methodically size up and make sense of whatever is unfolding, however momentous or trivial or unpredictable, is clear enough. Alongside the transparently reportorial and political there is much bitchiness and silliness to be seen, too. And the chapter makes clear that this is not the dross that needs to be waded through to access what really matters. The apparently banal aspects of personal interactions matter, revealing the importance of routine affect to the experience of continuity and thus to the viability of subjective agency across time. Some of the sample are more at home on Twitter than others, but for most there is a palpable sense of delight at getting stuck into colleagues, engaging in slanging matches with unknown others and cracking jokes that on the surface seem to undermine the seriousness of their enterprise. The point, though, is that the sincerity of their political engagement does not persevere in spite of their lapses of human frailty; it is predicated on those very practices that on the face of it look puerile and irreverent.

It is in chapters 4 and 5 that these themes emerge fully fledged. The twenty journalists interviewed – ten in each of Cairo and Beirut – span generations, specialisms, faiths and political commitments, and each reveals something distinct about living through times of enormous political and professional change. Corruption in politics as well as the media, and indeed the unhealthy closeness of those two worlds, is a constant theme. Factionalism recurs too, in Egypt in the growing polarization between Salafism and the Muslim Brotherhood, in Lebanon in the war next door and the inevitable failure at home of consociationalism. Among these are the indelibly human stories, the victims of war and political violence, domestic violence and sexual assaults in public spaces, the lack of education for Palestinian children growing up in Lebanese refugee camps, social injustice as it is lived under authoritarian regimes – high-handed officials, suspect colleagues, state indifference. But there was also a pervasive sense that these journalists love their work. Part of this comes down to a laudable determination to persevere in the face of all the obstacles and risks they face, motivated by personal principles and dreams of a better future. But it is important not to conflate the meaningfulness of someone's vocational mission and the meaningfulness of everyday routines – what makes it instinctively meaningful to get up in the morning and do *this* again, day in, day out. As well as soliciting views on history unfolding and the changes wrought by technology, participants were regularly prompted to talk about the small stuff: commuting, email inboxes, phones to be charged, meals taken and so on. They were also pushed to contextualize their lives relationally by talking about their colleagues, friends and families – not only their political views but their gossip too, what they got up to in their spare time, what journalists talk about when they talk about work. This is the core of the phenomenological approach to human research (Smith et al., 2009), understanding how things come to be experienced as mainly routine and given, even when times are tumultuous. Even with systemic change taking place around someone, experience proceeds iteratively, often oriented by underlying continuities.

Four main conclusions are drawn from this analysis. First, affect matters when it comes to political engagement (Clough & Halley, 2007; Gregg & Seigworth, 2010). This is distinct from well-established calls (Arendt, 1958; Fraser, 1990) for politics to be more inclusive of human experience, and especially human emotion, and speaks instead to a sense of affect which is more often than not meant pejoratively – that which is merely felt rather than fully apprehended, the small pleasures and annoyances experienced amid everyday routines (Leys, 2011). Second, in quotidian contexts being political is as much or more about social capital as it is about solidarity with protestors and victims. Social capital here is meant in the Bourdieusian (1984) sense, not just the glue that binds groups together but also the often unspoken games people play to pursue power and status. Most of these journalists were fiercely competitive, despite feeling loyalty towards their professional tribe, and they loved the authority that they were perceived to possess by their followers, clearly delighting in their ability to educate, persuade and lead. While this runs counter to the leaderless ideals of many contemporary protest movements (Krastev, 2014), the point is that game-playing and principle are not mutually exclusive – indeed, the former might sustain the latter. More broadly, the third conclusion is that while principle is a demonstrable motivation across these two groups, it is not about heart-on-sleeve piety or the expression of a true inner self but about ongoing work – work that is needed to achieve political and professional aims but also concerned with self-maintenance.

Political engagement happens in fits and starts; sometimes it appears to be all-consuming, and at others it is the punchline to a self-deprecating joke or wry aside. And this is precisely the point: political engagement is not about the externalization of some deep or authentic political subjectivity but part of the never-ending labour of political subjectification. The fourth insight follows directly from the third: that the experience of profound social change is not about critical moments of epiphany, but, like all experience, a matter of habitual orientation.

Chapter 6 takes a step back in order to map the global contexts of the historical epoch we are living through. Every protest movement, democratic uprising and civil conflict is in part sui generis, fully explicable only by way of deep immersion in the history and culture of a particular city or nation. And yet there seems to be something that links these very disparate phenomena, whether that something is ideology, a way of organizing and mobilizing political activism, or communication technology. The three are often elided so that new social media platforms are presumed to be inherently politically progressive (see, for instance, Loader & Mercea, 2012) or an anti-establishment ethos is held to be more politically authentic than a commitment to a political party (Barr, 2009). On the other side of these debates, social media and populism are cast as expressions of the same global force: neo-liberalism (Fuchs, 2014). This is well-trodden ground, emerging out of historic arguments that all forms of commercial popular culture are at base mechanisms of hegemonic reproduction, disciplinary regimes that manufacture wants and anxieties and ultimately selves according to the logic of late capitalism. There may well be a link between macroeconomic structures and the observable norms and practices of everyday life but not a one-to-one correspondence: any relationship between the macro and micro is inevitably uneven, haphazard and discontinuous. It is easy enough to fall into the line of thought that the embodied habits that sustain the overwhelming givenness of ordinary experience must be politically implicated in sustaining the status quo – most obviously by ensuring that the contingency of our presents remains hidden from consciousness, foreclosing the very thinkability of resistance and transformation. But this can only be conjecture and does not stand up to scrutiny in the banal contexts of everyday experience.

In politics, the upshot is that while populism might not amount to a radically democratic alternative to the congealed political institutions of yore, nor does it represent a historic shift towards Deleuzian regimes of control (Lash & Lury, 2007), of power ever more dispersed and ever more effective in constraining and orientating our thoughts and deeds. It is certainly an abandonment of politics as we know it, for better or worse, which amounts to a change in the conditions of meaningfulness in politics. That is, rather than representing a new way of pursuing historic political values, goals and agendas, many people simply expect something different out of politics now – something that reflects their identity, often couched in terms of specific issues and campaigns. Debates about identity politics in popular culture, then, are not simply the new politics, where the political is to be found now, but nor are they direct evidence of governmentality (Clifford, 2001), of subjects disciplined by the constant invidious prompts of mainstream media. A similar analysis applies to social media, chipping away equally at the competing claims that the network architectures of these platforms transform relations between global citizens by stripping away the mediating influence of stale institutions and obsolete authorities (boyd, 2011) and that social media effectively dupe people into relationships with others that feel unforced and organic but are in fact nothing more than debased commodities (Andrejevic, 2011). A closer look at how trust works in social media shows that neither is the case: social media are not radically new ways of shepherding and nurturing trust, but nor are they means to lure people into false trust ripe for exploitation. Trust, as it appears as a phenomenal object in ordinary circumstances, is simply not so heavily implicated; in day-to-day social media encounters it is above all else functional. This is not to say that social media are innocuous or disconnected from historical forces. But to interpret the shift away from old media and political institutions as a shift towards ever more embodied, less visible governmentalities is a normative claim grounded in the assumption that power tends to transform over time from the monolithic and explicit to the internalized and insidious.

The body is always at the core of phenomenological analysis (Blackman, 2008; Crossley, 2014; Wacquant, 2014; Wehrle, 2016), as it is one's corporeal being in the world that is the basis of all conscious experience. We know that bodies are not politically neutral, just serving up dumb-sense data that our individual and collective minds make sense of. The reason is, again, that perception is intentive, it begins with oriented projection that is physiological and muscular but also inculturated and historical. Here too – though we face a choice between celebrating the way we learn to manipulate new devices, effortlessly adapting them towards political and other ends, or pathologizing the way we unthinkingly adapt to them – the identical gestures our bodies make in swiping left and right on a touchscreen speak to corporeal incitement (see especially Wajcman, 2004). The body is also central to political claims made about media saturation, with technologies once visited and physically addressed now carried around and embedded in life's humdrum paraphernalia (Phillips & Speed, 2012). Media saturation is about the dissolution of the distinction between mediated and unmediated experience (McCarthy, 2001) but also the sheer amount of media to which we are exposed. And it relates directly to the experience of change since, the argument goes, constant inundation by new stimuli distracts us from longer-term transformations, demanding our attention in ways that leave us feeling like we are always barely keeping up with the novel, and all at sea in the bigger scheme of things (Virilio, 2012). As Stiegler (1998) puts it,

> Today, we need to understand the process of technical evolution given that we are experiencing the deep opacity of contemporary technics; we do not immediately understand what is being played out in our technics, nor what is being profoundly transformed therein, even though we unceasingly have to make *decisions* regarding technics, the consequences of which are felt to escape us more and more. And in day-to-day technical reality, we cannot spontaneously distinguish between the long-term processes of transformation from spectacular but fleeting technical innovations.

But in line with other empirical research (Best, 2010) this book finds that for most people the daily experience of media, social and otherwise, is not one of inundation. The journalists who participated in this project all spoke of being very busy, with emails always piling up and social media profiles to be maintained, but this is categorically different from deluge or discombobulation. And this goes further than an observation about what kinds of effects the proliferation of media content and technologies is having on us all, or not. We increasingly think of the experience of media in terms of flow (Sutherland, 2013), with all of the associations of liquidity that carries (Bauman, 2000). However, this too is a normative call rather than one derived from the experience of everyday life. A world devoid of modern media is nonetheless sufficiently complex and dynamic to be thought of along similar lines, surrounding us and presenting us with more stimuli than we could ever hope to attend to individually, let alone apprehend and respond reflexively. Flow, though, is not the same thing as *seamlessness*. All habituation is geared towards maintaining seamless conscious experience, and it is only right that we should investigate and unpick that which has become automated and normalized without much in the way of reflection or questioning. Unthinking adaptations matter, but learning how to process reams of stimuli efficiently is not the same thing as blindly adapting to political or economic regimes. Again, they may be linked, but as we will see in chapter 6, the flow metaphor makes too quick a leap from inundation to submission. Seamlessness is less obviously politically freighted simply because it characterizes the experience of all environments, nefarious and benign alike. More specifically, experience can be largely seamless and yet *iterative*, a more or less continuous series of encounters rather than an always-already, overwhelming, all-or-nothing subjective ultimatum. It is this dissection of conscious experience as iterative rather than fluid that allows for a conception of specific encounters in which everything is not at stake, experiences that are provisional or ambivalent. The relationship between such experiences and one's orientation towards larger-scale change is thus complicated, conflicted and potentially reflexive; quotidian experience is neither disconnected from historical shifts nor simply implicated in them.

Heidegger's model of thrownness is also open to interpretation in different directions, across his own writing as well as that which draws on it (see especially Gunkel & Taylor, 2014). Thrownness as constant, radical disruption set against a hardwired tendency towards experiential equilibrium can either make the navigation of everyday life seem a heroic triumph or something achieved only through giving oneself over to ways of being, thinking and acting that are alien, even corrupting. From this perspective if someone reports that they feel at home in a given environment, it is only because they have adapted themselves to its every contingency, not because they have attained self-mastery. However, such a view posits an anterior stable subject who is subsequently either unsettled by thrownness and left feeling all at sea or who is unsettled and submits to exterior adaptive mechanisms – mechanisms implicated in coercive relations of power. And the subject is no such thing but an ongoing unfolding of subjectifying practices: that is, the self emerges through and not in spite of thrownness and one's learned responses to it. The conditions of subjective emergence warrant investigation, but as a means of understanding how selfhood is enacted and experienced rather than the things that are done to the self by exogenous forces. If, as appears to be the case, a lot of people do not feel constantly thrown – a persistent state of edginess stuck in a precarious present, anxious about the future – then to respond along the lines that this can only be because they have submitted utterly to the logics of the worlds they find themselves in is disingenuous. Seen at the level of iterative encounters, while stimuli might demand a response, that response might be an ambivalent shrug or blithe indifference – remembering that in perceptive terms ignoring a prompt is intentive, not passive. Responding to being constantly thrown into replete worlds is both more and less than the recitation of internalized templates for action, or the clinching of fully fledged selfhood. Thrownness is a state of becoming, not the constant undermining of selves that would be unproblematically stable if only they were left alone.

If chapter 6 establishes a limit beyond which interpretations of the way people experience or fail to apprehend change can only be normative or conjectural in nature, the following chapter shows how this opens up ways of unpacking observed mediated orientations to the world. In the broadest terms this means going beyond conventional accounts of how representations of protest, for instance, variously spectacularize, dehumanize or delegitimize it, to ask precisely how protest and protestors appear as objects to consciousness. More specifically, it allows us to instigate more nuanced debate around the question of slacktivism, the concern shared by many (Christensen, 2011; cf. Vie, 2014; von Engelhardt, 2015) that there is something about mediated engagement by western audiences in particular with faraway protestors and victims of violence and injustice that is fundamentally superficial, emotional and self-serving. What phenomenology allows for is that all practices, including practices of recognition, are in part oriented towards the maintenance of the seamless experience of the self – not necessarily because of deep-seated narcissism, but simply how one navigates one's way through the world. Rather than the ostentatious performance of compassion (Bennett, 2012; Ibrahim, 2015; Koffman et al., 2015; Mason, 2016), engagement with distant others through routinized media practices will tend to reaffirm one's sense of self in an instinctive, affective manner – not as self-discovery or a jarring reminder of who you really are as opposed to who you think you are but, usually, a more or less continuous experience of liveability with oneself and one's place in the world.

This call to apprehend the lack of intensity of most mediated encounters, and to resist the pathologization of that lack, in an important sense draws on Couldry's (2003) myth of the mediated centre – since remodelled (2015) as a 'myth of us' to warn against presuming that social media are where the real social now resides. A lot of the early academic writing on the Arab uprisings certainly popularized the notion that social media are where politics happens now, and chapter 8 offers a broader contextualization of this turn in the literature. It is straightforward enough to argue against technologically deterministic readings of political change, though when pulled apart carefully it becomes clear that many of the more celebratory readings of the role that social media played in the Middle East and elsewhere are motivated by more than a naïve faith in liberation technology (Diamond & Plattner, 2012). First, the widespread use of ecological and biological metaphors to describe social media speaks to a yearning for a new kind of political agency that is incorruptible by individuals, ideology and institutions. The grammatical presentation of such agency is telling: it is not something that is practised, thought or enacted, but rather something that emerges with a vitality of its own. Where it emerges is also significant; there are spaces and imaginaries in which unsullied agency can take shape, but as there is a keenness not to prescribe what this agency should look like these spaces too are defined only negatively. Specifically, this means spaces that are structureless, in which ideas can appear and develop weightlessly and individuals can participate without fear of compromising their own subjectivity in the process. In part this reflects disillusionment with the failures and overfamiliarity of progressive politics, a sense that we have exhausted our ideas for collectively effecting social transformation, that our best hope lies in creating contexts in which something radically different might come to light and that in the meantime our priority should be treating individuals with respect (see, for instance, Cammaerts et al., 2013). There is much to be said for this approach, not least the possibilities of a political culture predicated not on fulsome commitment and sacrifice but something much more provisional and discontinuous. Its deficiencies, however, boil down to an excessive deference to those individuals: rather than conceding that individual engagement might be fickle and yet underpin political solidarity over time, everything that a protestor or victim does is read as dissent or resistance. This, finally, rests on a teleological proposition, that there is just something about protest cultures, or about social media, that gear them towards political transformation – rather than transformativity being something temporally contingent, viable only through embedded practices of work, organization and compromise.

The book's final chapter weaves all of these themes together using a simple claim as its thread: Because subjectivity is always work in progress, there are always stakes involved in how it develops over time. One's sense of self, as well as how one is seen by others, is provisional and unresolved – perhaps not often liable to radical disruption or metamorphosis, but nonetheless temporally contingent. This means that observed practices of media consumption that appear superficial cannot be read as direct evidence of a lack of engagement or recognition of subjective others; those latter qualities are worked on over time, not achieved in particular encounters. This is not to suggest that however people view others through media is fine, but it means rethinking how recognition works. It is not about recognizing the humanity of this or that individual, but nor is it blanket recognition of humanity in general, because encounters remain iterative rather than fluid. Recognition is enacted in relation to particular stimuli, but in isolation such practices will appear stunted and partial or just ill-informed. Insofar as these iterative encounters underpin conscious experience that is largely seamless, however, they can sustain a temporally stable subjectivity over time that is liveable – while I might not understand everything that is going on and while I might often be distracted, I am nonetheless compassionate – and which may also amount to solidarity (see also Chari, 2016). Failing to pay proper attention to a news item about distant protests or war, or failing to take action in relation to such an item, will rarely undermine a sense of self as caring and principled; that is something achieved over the long haul. When scrutinized longitudinally it may or may not meet the standards expected of engaged global citizens, but if it is a kind of engagement experienced as satisfactory and coherent by mediated publics then it suggests that our conventional notions of global citizenship need rethinking.

This has practical implications regarding the representation of distant others and what it should aim to achieve. The spectacularization thesis (Debord, 1970) – simply put, that spectacle goes all the way down, so that there can never be substantive recognition of mutual subjective others – is a counsel of despair, gloomily concluding that there is nothing that can be done to break through the fog of media and consumerism in which western audiences are wrapped. Much thought has gone into devising ways of shaking viewers out of their complacency (see especially Chouliaraki, 2006; Seeck & Rantanen, 2015), though there is always the counterargument that more mediated representation, however creative or counter-intuitive, will ultimately reduce the scope for substantive recognition (Tester, 1994). This, though, rests on the assumption that the subjectivities of those western audiences have become atrophied through comfort, smugly impervious to disruption, protected by impenetrable layers of affective pleasures and distractions. And complacency may well be endemic, but nonetheless subjectivity never just is – how it unfolds temporally is always to some degree up for grabs. That means there is an interest in ongoing subjectifying labour that might not look like much in observed behaviour but is real enough when one considers what is at stake: a self that is liveable with. Audiences might respond to faraway events through the at-hand tropes of melodrama, but an argument will be built on the back of the working lives of the participants in this research that substantive recognition and compassion can emerge through and not in spite of such affective entanglements. There is an echo here of Chouliaraki's (2013) claim that while we tend to think of irony as a cultural pall precluding real engagement between mediated others, maybe it is precisely the scepticism that ironic viewing entails which enables solidarity to develop over time. Representation still matters, and we should be quick to call out narratives and images that dehumanize (Boltanski, 1999; Rancière, 2009), but to aver that the wrong kinds of representation cause disengagement is as wide of the mark as holding on to the idea that the right representations will fix it.

Finally, and crucially, an orientation to the everyday world experienced affectively and habitually does not trap an individual in a self-contained, eternal present. Indeed, it is, or at least can be, the routines and felt experiences of daily life that afford an awareness of what is up for grabs and what is at stake for oneself, one's profession and one's society. This does not happen automatically, and it has been suggested that journalists might be well placed to worry at the edges of intelligibility, to elaborate that which appears unmoveable but is deeply contingent. Apathy and fatalism are real among publics and audiences in many parts of the world (Scott, 2015), and yet against this kind of stasis, subjectivity by definition lacks foreclosure: it is an ongoing process in whose unfolding individuals and collectives have an interest. Engagement with the world is not all or nothing but enacted haphazardly through the minutiae of life. It might not be the case that left to our own devices we are all equally disposed towards developing an orientation to the world built around solidarity with others, but we are inclined towards developing an orientation that is liveable. And what makes our selves just liveable – having a consistent sense of who we are and how we are seen – in everyday contexts may, while in situ we might look disengaged, distracted or self-regarding, over time congeal into something more substantive: an orientation to the world that is generalized enough that the self is not in jeopardy in each encounter with actual others but is nonetheless able to recognize the profundity of the subjectivity of others.

Across the different contexts that it maps out, this book's thesis is that everyday failures to apprehend social change around us, as well as to recognize the full subjectivity of mediated distant others undergoing transformations of their own, not to mention our own complicity in all of this, do not preclude a life lived authentically – that is to say, with an intuitive, at-hand grasp of what is unfolding and the ethical dimensions of our relation to others encountered in everyday contexts. That is because understanding our place in the world into which we find ourselves constantly thrown is not a matter of revelation, of breaking through to a higher level of consciousness. It is grasped as we go about merely doing, thinking and feeling things. Those acts present themselves as easy targets for scorn in their mundanity and insularity, especially media habits that appear distracted, self-serving or simply affective, or work routines which are just that – routine. But this overlooks their temporal aspect, and awareness of social change and our place in it is not clinched in critical moments; it is about orientation over time and can be sustained precisely through and not in spite of the repetitive little merely-felts of everyday life. As regards the journalistic trade, the lesson from this is that we should move on from the notion that journalists cannot see the wood for the trees, too ensconced in the trivial mechanics of their professional lives to see the bigger picture. This in turn means being open to this possibility that the same applies to those not employed to document change in a professional capacity. The failure of ordinary citizens to achieve ecstatic recognition of social change in our quotidian worlds is normal, not lamentable. It might be indicative of a life lived narcissistically and without empathy – but it also might not, since there are stakes for each subject in what kind of object we are to the world.

Chapter Two

Professional Media amid Change and Hysteresis

For all its faults, journalism has historically been one of the dominant means by which publics track change and continuity. The opening chapter trailed the possibility that it may actually be precisely the journalistic focus on news that precludes a better understanding of more profound change in society, but the news industries have nonetheless played a central role, for better or worse, in presenting audiences with new realities after significant political and economic shifts. Further, journalism itself has changed in many ways, most notably with the rise of digital and networked media and all the implications that it has for professional practice, but also with the advent of what is normatively referred to as citizen journalism but more correctly should be described as non-professional media production – both the citizen and journalism aspects of this terrain are debatable. If we are going to make sense of the role that media plays in the everyday experience of structural transformation, then it is necessary to take into account cultures of media production and consumption, and potentially media texts themselves, if a complete picture is to be rendered.

To situate this in the context of the Arab uprisings is easily done. First, coverage of the series of pro-democracy or anti-authoritarian movements at least briefly captured the imagination of many news consumers around the world, and by broadcasting what was going on within the region it may also have encouraged further movements to mobilize and surge. It is also possible, conversely, that news about the uprisings in Egypt and Tunisia variously cooled protest cultures in other parts of the Middle East, such as Algeria and Jordan, reduced events in Western media to simulations of prior or idealized democratic revolutions (Aouragh, 2012; Bady, 2012) or othered the peoples and cultures of the Arab world in popular and academic discourses (Newsom et al., 2011). Mainstream representations of distant protest and conflict are addressed in chapter 7, and it bears emphasizing that whatever the politics of mediated suffering and the recognition of global others, it is important not to overstate the propensity of global, corporate media to systematize their representations of particular parts of the world to serve particular political ends. Dominant Western/Northern cultures of production and reception there may be, but media production is complicated, with conflict endemic within and between institutions, flows of labour and capital subject to rapid change and audiences sometimes utterly predictable but at other times, strikingly, not. In line with structuration theory, individual journalists are a little more than the structured determinations of their professional and economic context: the endurance of those contextual structures also relies on individual and collective habits, neither the continuity nor consequences of which can be neatly mapped. To put it in more concrete terms, while it remains important to assess the content of mainstream, global news in political as well as journalistic terms, it is also imperative to consider how media industries are changing. One notable feature in our context is the rise of freelance conflict reporting, with usually young and often uninsured reporters seeing Middle Eastern war zones as rare opportunities for professional advancement (Palmer, 2015). It is also striking how the traditional gender imbalance in war reporting has shifted in coverage of the Arab Spring, though Francesca Borri (2013) reminds us that this too could be explicable by a precarious labour market as much as feminist or cultural factors. If professional desperation is shaping labour flows in the news industry, this is likely to be as important to our understanding of events in the region as professional norms and standards. The decline of permanently stationed foreign correspondents has been widely remarked upon (Archetti, 2012), but the broader implications of news budgets reduced as a result of falling circulation figures and advertising revenue are as yet unclear. It will be seen below that within the Arab journalistic field, the role played by all kinds of media amateurs in recent developments has been something of a short, sharp shock: professional journalists across the region, but nowhere so dramatically as in print journalism, have been broadly accused of being unfit for purpose, relics amid the new politics and technologies of the twenty-first century.

JOURNALISM'S PERENNIAL CRISIS

All of this leads to a question that has been the subject of a plethora of conference panels, journal special editions, public debates and academic research: Is journalism in crisis? With so much already written and spoken about this (Barnett, 2002; McChesney, 2003; Franklin, 2010; Hirst, 2011; Reinardy, 2011; Gleason, 2015; Nerone, 2015; Russial et al., 2015), there is hardly a need to rehearse the various arguments and predictions that have been put forth. But it is useful to consider in a second-order manner what this discursive focus on the possible futures of journalism – or its future non-existence – tells us about the cultural and political status of journalism, past and present. For instance, the future financial unsustainability of professional news production cannot be considered in an economic or technological vacuum. It is easy enough to trace the line of argument about the proliferation of free sources of information to the impact this is having on professional production in journalism as much as the music and video industries, but this does not hold water as a causal relationship; it is only with the concomitant loss in cultural status that professional journalism is unable to compete with non-professional media production. For some (Franklin, 2011), it is economic pressure that has led to an inability to perform the fundamental function of holding power to account that has produced the crisis in journalism; for others (Curran & Seaton, 2010), it is the abnegation of that scrutinizing role that has degraded its unique status and left it floundering among entertainment and sharing markets it little understands. Tracing the origins of the democratic deficit in journalism reduces to a chicken-and-egg weighing up of blame and response, which ultimately reveals little. However, to tease out the implied stakes of a crisis as perceived by journalists and others is potentially illuminating. For example, consider those (Marlière, 1998; 2001) who lament, not without reason, the commercial assault that many journalistic fields have faced in recent decades, among the consequences of which are public broadcasters being audited against popular criteria for success (Born, 2011). This speaks of a nostalgia for a time when the civic value of journalism did not have to be popularly validated but was confidently asserted by those within the field and acknowledged by those in positions of power (Curran & Seaton, 2010: 66–99). Similarly, the predictions of there being no professional journalists in the future, just an endless army of bloggers and trolls, evinces a yearning for a time when journalists were regarded as having personal integrity, trusted in the manner of a medical practitioner to act as gatekeeper to specialist or overwhelming information, signaller of relative importance and trustworthy provider of necessary context. Or, finally, think of those fears often voiced about journalists and editors being replaced by drones (Tremayne & Clark, 2014) and algorithms (Thurman et al., 2016). This speaks first to a belief that journalists are, or should be, above all producers of knowledge, not simply its wranglers; second, and more broadly, it suggests that there is something fundamentally human about the social role of the journalist that we should be minded to protect – that there is something visceral or reflexive about this profession, whose loss would be critical.

There are merits to all of these arguments, but also two downsides. The first is that they define journalism's role in society negatively, as something we would miss if we did not have it. The second is that it absolves journalists themselves of responsibility for that which has changed – this tends to be the nature of diagnosed crises, encountered as decontextualized and immediate rather than change that is usually incremental and explicable. It is not that there is an absence of journalists blaming journalists for the state they are in, but such accounts tend to be narrowly focused: on the unwillingness of journalists to stand up to editors, editors to proprietors and news organizations to political and corporate elites (Skovsgaard, 2014); on the inability to resist the siren call of popularity and commercial success (Picard, 2004); on the degradation of journalistic ethics (Örnebring, 2013); on the decline of professional, tribal identity (Deuze, 2008; Wiik, 2010). But there is more to this story, specifically a culpability that is detectable at the level of journalistic cultures writ large but in theory at least resistible by self-aware professionals. Journalists are often accused of cynicism (Cappella & Jamieson, 1997; Brants et al., 2010), worn down through inherited histories and their own experiences not to trust anything said by anyone in a position of power. Such a resistant disposition is entirely understandable given the prevalence of spin and strategic communication, even if one countered that it is the tendency towards exaggeration and selective attention amongst journalists that has predicated the rise of these dark arts. But it is also something of a red herring. Cynicism often makes sense as a professional strategy, and indeed that is how it is seen by many practitioners – not as an affliction that renders good journalism impossible but something to be wielded as required. Cynicism rarely goes all the way down (Markham, 2011b). This is not to suggest that its presence is an affectation but rather a part of the journalists' armoury that can be picked up and put down again.

Something which is less easily cast off is the epistemological relation of journalists to the objects of their work. This is a kind of ironized distance (Glasser & Ettema, 1993; Ettema & Glasser, 1994), one which is seen in all manner of professions but which has particular implications here. It is also something that goes beyond the stereotype of the journalist as irreverent, unable to take anything seriously. But it does indicate an instinctive recognition of everything – events, people, phenomena, trends – primarily as journalistic objects, effortlessly rationalized and categorized, and thus managed or dismissed. Now, there is no call in this book for journalists to escape the mechanized processing (Becker & Vlad, 2009) that comes as second nature to them and to engage authentically with the world and recognize the uniqueness of each event. But ironized distance as a default orientation to the world among journalists is part of a broader trend to which they have contributed and from which they would benefit from extracting themselves periodically. On the one hand this distance can be explained away as professional self-presentation, a way of performing experience and wisdom. But on the other it is part of a social positioning which rationalizes disengagement from issues of collective concern, which ascribes cultural value to disaffection. We will return to this question and its implications in the final chapter.

There is a debate that extends well beyond the confines of these pages (McNair, 2000) about journalism's role in facilitating and encouraging an active public sphere. The view underpinning the argument developed here is that while journalists play a vital role in facilitating public deliberation, it is not their job to mobilize or politicize citizens. The flipside of this is that nor are journalists primarily responsible for public apathy. However, inasmuch as journalistic practice aims not just at disseminating information but giving people a voice, and given that despite evidence to the contrary discussed here the ideal of journalism as a public service remains widespread (Beam et al., 2009) – and this refers to journalists in the Middle East as it does to journalists in the Anglo-American context (Pintak, 2011) – the nature of this common cause between journalists and their publics is more conflicted than it appears (Brants & de Haan, 2010). At one level the self-identity of journalists is defined against establishment power and, potentially, establishment values; this means not only taking seriously journalism's accountability function but personally siding with audiences against those perceived to be in privileged positions. Journalists with an ironized distance to their work are thus acting strategically, aligning themselves with wider trends of knowing detachment. Again, this is different from journalists echoing public cynicism towards politicians or humanitarian campaigners; it is a valorization of perceived anti-establishment values that extend to all forms of knowledge production, from the cultural to the scientific. And this is disingenuous, on three grounds: First, the evidence marshalled for this research demonstrates a kind of long-suffering disdain, or in some cases pity, for those mass audiences for which journalists – some journalists – feel it is their role to speak. Second, there is no shortage of sociological evidence demonstrating that the majority of journalists in the countries under consideration here – Egypt and Lebanon (Watenpaugh, 2014) as much as the United Kingdom and the United States (Weaver et al., 2009; 2012) – are of the establishment themselves, in terms of their social origins and trajectories. Third, there is a growing body of ethnographic work that sets out in detail the ways in which professional journalists act to maintain their elevated status and the gates that keep others outside of this world – most notably in the way that non-professional content is regarded and dealt with (Singer et al., 2011). Together, these suggest that couching the crisis in journalism in terms of what the public stands to lose is at best artful and at worst narcissistic.

In purely sociological terms there is no deontological reason why journalism should be revered or even taken seriously, and this means that the cultural status of journalistic epistemology is directly linked to the cultural status of journalism as a field (Bourdieu, 1993; Benson & Neveu, 2005): if its principles for producing knowledge are seen as unserious or a kind of game-playing, then this will be reflected in how the profession is regarded. The opposite applies too, in that a journalism that takes itself too seriously, or that is overly deferential towards power, or wide-eyed in the face of every new phenomena, will also be regarded with derision by those in a position to have an opinion on the state of journalism. While for some this kind of state-of-the-union discourse is an irrelevance, it is established (Couldry et al., 2010) that there remains at least a residual duty to keep up with the news, though this is demographically inflected, and we can get a rough measure of the cultural status of knowledge produced by journalists not just by audience figures for mainstream media but the extent to which this has been specifically displaced by other, non-professional forms of media. Declining circulation on its own reflects a variety of factors including cost, time, civic engagement as well as perceived quality; a correlative rise in other forms of media suggests that the appetite for information or social connection might be relatively constant but that journalism is not flattered by comparison with the competition. In any event, the evidence (Mindich, 2005) suggests not that audiences do not perceive a coming crisis in journalism but that they do not regard the question of journalism's status or health as an apposite one.

JOURNALISM'S MULTIPLE FUTURES

However, beneath the sometimes grandiloquent claims made about the future of journalism lies something that journalists in general do not feel they should *have* to defend: their basic role as guardians of knowledge and a profession trusted to scrutinize various forms of institutional power in society as well as to give voice to those who would otherwise go unheard. These benchmarks instinctively seem anachronistic, and when these are further stripped back to the core principles of witnessing, documenting and perhaps empathizing, it is clear that for some time journalists have not enjoyed a monopoly on them. And yet we run the risk here of blithely dismissing all journalistic concern for the survival of the tribe, and for assuming that it speaks with one voice. To that end, it is worth considering how the coming crisis in journalism is perceived from different corners of the field, and James Curran (2010) sets out the terrain succinctly. First, there are industry leaders who, seemingly worldwide, share an ostrich-like denial of crisis and a firm faith that journalism has a future in spite of the death of mass advertising and declining print sales. Common but not universal in this part of the sector is an expectation that some means of charging for content, subscription or membership will sustain quality journalism in the longer term. Curran's view is that the movement of journalism online means that its future is essentially beyond the control of media management, which is both right and indicative of how change is experienced in this context. At the day-to-day level, uncontrollable change is more or less unthinkable to those whose job it is to manage organizations and industries; here, denial is not a matter of a dearth of strategic thinking as an instinctive orientation to the world of work they inhabit. If this sounds condescending, it is not intended to be; in any profession to be conscious of its potential obsolescence while engaged in everyday routines is not only difficult but impracticable. This is not to suggest either a psychological coping mechanism or a thoroughgoing historical materialist account in which to imagine beyond the scope of one's habituated phenomenal realm is by definition unthinkable. Rather, it makes more sense to think of subjectivity, the way one experiences the world as a discrete self, as something temporally and contextually specific. The upshot of this is that it is entirely possible that media managers placed in other contexts would be able to conceive of the fairly radical contingency of the world that they live in – though it is also probably true that academic conferences, away days and break-out meetings will themselves have become too much a part of habituated experience to enable such perspective. Likewise, it is common enough for various professionals to engage in light workplace humour about a future in which they are redundant, but a humour that is knowing and, again, ironic rather than destabilizing (Picard, 2015). Managers by this view are not blinkered people but people engaging in blinkered practices which may be pulled apart. And the basis on which the phenomenal world media managers' experience attains an unproblematic continuity is a belief, if not solely in their own intrinsic value as professionals, then in the often heard bromide that there will always be a market for quality journalism (Scheuer, 2008). There is undoubtedly truth in this in limited circles, in that for certain publications and broadcasters viability is predicated not on the size but the composition of the audience, but at the level of the mass market it cannot amount to more than a principle of faith.

Next up are the employees of the media managers, especially in the United States but elsewhere too, who see little point in faith in the face of overwhelming financial unsustainability. For this group of journalists, usually mid-level and mid-career, it is unthinkable that journalism can survive in anything like its present form. Again putting this in the context of everyday experience, such a view is reasonable given the fact of widespread job cuts, the closure of publications and broadcasters and individual burnout due to increased workloads (Reinardy, 2011). Collectively, however, this version of journalism in crisis is expressed in terms of what society stands to lose: already we are seeing courts and councils go unreported, and the future promises a steady erosion of transparency and accountability across the board. To use the same logic as was applied to the managers, but turned upside down, this could be explained as a rational response to the habituated practice of being forced to consider the inevitability of one's own redundancy. More pointedly, it could be seen as self-rationalizing or even self-righteous, though fighting one's corner by making visible what stands to be lost is reasonable enough. What is most interesting about this version of the crisis is the absence of irony, the fairly straight-faced avowal of journalism's importance to a functioning democracy. It is this that seems jarring, as though the threat to this kind of straightforwardly *good* journalism has come only from digital media and the disruption it has brought, rather than the slow morphing of most mainstream and local journalism into something more heightened, discursive, reflexive and playful (Thornburrow, 2010).

Curran next identifies a group in many ways the inverse of the doomsayers, though they are in agreement that all-consuming crisis is underway. These are the millennials, early-career and aspiring media professionals who see the old ways of doing journalism as both corrupt and corrupting and who welcome their demise. Curran is a little unkind in depicting how this cohort imagines the impetus for change – 'things will get better because they are getting worse' (2010: 466) – and it is in any case impossible to judge definitively on the comparative merits of this view without either reducing this set of employees to psychological profiles or professing the preferability of conservative versus radical philosophies of history, which is not our business here. To put things in phenomenological perspective, it is not being reductive to speculate that earlier on in one's immersion in a professional field, one's orientation is likely to be, temporally speaking, more future-facing (Bourdieu, 1993). It is a common misunderstanding of phenomenology that it has a *Groundhog Day* conception of conscious experience, consisting only of unchanging habits producing a seamless sense of being in the world, an always-already present. But change is a given, and while at the micro level encounters with the unfamiliar broadly proceed by way of anticipation and adaptation oriented towards continuity, this book takes seriously the Heideggerian proposition that our experience of change in the present is structured according to the pasts and futures it posits. In this case, rather than ascribing an optimistic outlook simply to generation, though this may well play a part, the millenarian perspective might be linked to a *temporal* orientation discussed in chapter 8, geared towards the valorization of events and objects according to their imminence rather than substantive principles. While this makes such a habitus seem essentially shallow and short-sighted, the intention is not to caricature an obsession with all things novel. It is consistent with the principle that change never just is – it demands responses that have real implications for individual and group subjectivity. It is true that in the phenomenological tradition reactions to the encounters into which we find ourselves thrown are conceived primarily as corporeal rather than knowing, incited rather than calculating. But this is in line with the claim that the experience of change as something to be continually navigated, negotiated or mastered is reasonable in the literal sense – of having reasons that are coherent and explicable. The millennials may be more confident than others in hurling themselves towards unknowable futures, but this does not make them starry-eyed.

Finally, Curran identifies those who instead of perceiving constructive crisis see crisis averted. For this group, which, it is claimed, includes most journalism educators, the advent of the digital era presented old-school journalism with a jolt, but one that has come to be experienced as a wake-up call. It has also brought with it many benefits, from the burgeoning accessibility of source material and the ability to engage in different kinds of journalistic investigation, such as data mining, to the growing scope for collaboration with peers across newsrooms and the globe as well as amateurs. The implications of this last point have been much discussed and are tackled, briefly, immediately below. For present purposes, however, it is necessary to deal with the alarming possibility that this kind of detection of a coming renaissance in journalism represents a kind of self-delusion – especially since in interviews, and this is backed up by other ethnographic research (Kian & Zimmerman, 2012; Hanusch, 2013; Pavlik, 2013), it is a widely held perspective. Many interviewees in the present research were quick to point out the benefits of audience participation, multi-tasking and the profession being kept on its toes by the pace of technological change. It is always conceivable that the dispositions that emerge in interviews are to a degree performative – an attempt to manage self-presentation by avoiding moaning or coming across as naïve. But there is also something rational in this sanguine orientation towards present and future as a professional norm: simply making the best of things. What is the alternative? This, though, brings us to a critical normative juncture at which we are observing individuals adapting to changes to which, one might want to argue, they should not adapt but find ways to resist – or, that professionals see much that is positive in an environment that sociologists are inclined to conclude is iniquitous for those same individuals. Who is in a better position to judge, after all?

This dilemma warrants closer attention, and chapters 3 through 5 present a detailed analysis of journalists and others working in the journalistic field undergoing systemic changes that could plausibly be labelled critical according to the discussion that has proceeded here. But in the broadest terms, what is at stake here is a reappraisal of what it means to experience change. Conventionally, we are used to thinking about being in the world as triply oriented: we face endless iterations of presents that insist on being responded to, and we do so by recourse to experience and anticipation. But endlessly demanding presents leave little room for contemplation of possible chains of causality and possibility, and nor does anticipation structured by narrow experience. The very condition of being in the world then blinds us to broader change, or at least there is a time lag between our ways of inhabiting the present and more profound shifts in sociopolitical structures which also produce the preconditions, in the longer term, of the ways in which we experience the world. There is nothing teleological about this; it is simply the consequence of needing to develop patterns of perception and acting that allow everyday life to be bearable (Withy, 2014). But there is a difference between learning to take physiological data for granted and doing the same with social and political cues. What if that which demands adaptation is an economic system? In phenomenological terms, Heideggerian thrownness captures the alienation of everyday experience from the brute force of the world and all it demands:

> This characteristic of Dasein's Being – this 'that it is' – is veiled in its 'whence' and 'whither', yet disclosed in itself all the more unveiledly; we call it the '*thrownness*' of this entity into its 'there'; indeed, it is thrown in such a way that, as Being-in-the-world, it is the 'there'. The expression 'thrownness' is mean to suggest the facticity of its being delivered over. (Heidegger, 1962: 174)

Thrownness is suggestive of finding oneself constantly in sink-or-swim crises in which it is achievement enough to survive each encounter and adapt as best one can to the way things seem to be heading, without the scope ever to be fully cognizant of the pasts leading to our present, or the true stakes of how things may play out in the future. And this is where thrownness translates relatively simply from a philosophy of existence to a critique of the modern world – and, for our purposes, the media saturation of contemporary life. And yet the empirical chapters that follow suggest something other than an experience of temporality which is simultaneously too close to apprehend and too profound to understand. In the interviews it will be seen that this is manifested in a relation to past and future, which is determined above all by the experience of *work* – and as such rationalized and instrumentalized, but not necessarily characterized as insistent, all-consuming and critical. And the discourse analysis of chapter 3 likewise points to a journalistic experience of media not as immersive and overwhelming but simply ever-present. Further, the variability of attention means that encounters are not all experienced as equally immediately demanding or subjectively implicating. Some stimuli pass us by, and to suggest that they are nonetheless threaded into the fabric that envelops our everyday lives can only be speculative. Other stimuli are acknowledged but barely attended to, and still others are met with a work-like orientation: sized up, compartmentalized and dealt with accordingly, rather than just reacted to as situations irresistibly insist. Possibly this also indicates a temporal aspect to being in the world aligned to logics of rationalization endemic to contemporary economic and cultural contexts, but the observed experience of it as something other than fraught, other than critical, may well be reasonable instead of complicit.

TEMPORAL PHENOMENOLOGIES: HOW JOURNALISTS EXPERIENCE CHANGE

Importantly, to ascribe reason to journalistic reactions to change, precariousness or crisis that are less than radical is not to explain away such behaviour. This is the main difference between descriptive and critical phenomenology. Descriptive phenomenology is most often associated with Husserl, though texts such as *The Crisis of European Sciences and Transcendental Philosophy* (1970) make it clear that there is more to his work than a philosophical kind of thick description of how the world appears to consciousness. *The Crisis of European Sciences* is firmly directed towards explaining the conditions of possibility of conscious experience; this will entail ascribing reasons which are not present to individuals in everyday routines or in interviews, and it will also attempt to explain how contexts which are manifestly contingent upon unique structural configurations, moments in time and space which from a critical distance seem distinctly odd, come to appear normal, if not unproblematic. While it neither excuses nor accuses, then, it is a perspective which asks how we arrived at such a kind of being in the world, and it poses the question of how different things could be. The mechanics of how change is experienced through a mode of being in the world geared towards anticipating and responding to everyday encounters such that continuity is usually maintained is set out in chapters 3 through 5. Now, however, it is possible to set out the principal questions – sociological, political and above all practical rather than philosophical – that such an analysis can answer.

The first is whether the failure to anticipate major social change demonstrates serious flaws in the professional cultures of journalists and other experts. Looking at the financial crisis, for instance, it has been argued (Fraser, 2009) that journalists' lack of foresight can be explained variously by their closeness to the financial world, their lack of education in economics beyond that underpinning the status quo and the pack mentality which decides newsworthiness. To these one could add the negative symbolic capital that attaches to being seen to be surprised by events. In front of each other, at least, journalists, analysts and editors tend to enact seen-it-all-before responses to events, even if to their audiences they routinely serve up shock and scandal on an unprecedented scale. In the case of the fall of the Berlin Wall, the consensus now is that reporters had drunk the Kool-Aid of U.S. neoconservative foreign policy, assuming the regimes of Eastern Europe to be ruthless and immovable, the world locked in a titanic stand-off without end (Kuran, 1991). It is easy to mock the way such a worldview was internalized by journalists and externalized in their work and important to hold up to scrutiny instances where it led to making excuses for or openly advocating particular policies. But it is also all too easy to forget how different the future looked twenty-five years ago, especially those contemporary realities it was assumed would continue as is or steadily progress or deteriorate.

What, then, are we to make of the fact that very few experts, and still fewer reporters, anticipated the Arab uprisings (Gause, 2011; Bellin, 2012)? One of the most straightforward explanations, widespread in the literature, is orientalism: whether we know it or not, we assume that oppression is an essential part of Arab culture. This means that beyond assuming that Arabs lack the political sophistication to oppose authoritarianism, we subconsciously posit that Arabs are somehow complicit in their own oppression. It should be pointed out here that while for some commentators this 'we' is unequivocally the West, or global North, for many it is all of us, with Arab political scientists and journalists also accused of orientalist tendencies. Chapter 8 challenges some of the propositions of the orientalism thesis, though to flag it briefly here the critique is, predictably, phenomenological: what is assumed to be embodied blanket prejudice is simply not manifest uniformly or unreflexively in everyday contexts of work, media production and consumption. Another explanation is more hermeneutic than cultural: journalists inhabit a world also peopled by authorities from academia, politics, consultancy and think tanks, for whom the at-hand conceptual toolbox is unimaginative, making predictions on the basis of equations in which too many variables are assumed to be constant. Such thinking could be labelled lazy or doctrinal, or else too much the product of positivistic social science, for which all behaviour is at root rational and the behaviour of complex systems can be extrapolated from observable data and historical precedents. It is certainly simpler to develop a model explaining the stability of authoritarian regimes than one that sets out the preconditions of their collapse.

The way that the Arab uprisings have taken shape in academic discourse has largely reflected the contours of discipline. Political science (Goodwin, 2011; Dalacoura, 2012; Inbar, 2013; Stepan & Linz, 2013) offers explanations based on historically derived authoritarian models of the state, with restrictions on political participation and organization, charismatic or despotic leadership, clientalism, nepotism, nationalism, vilification and suppression of internal and external dissent and militarization all offered up as rational grounds for medium-term political stability (see especially Wright & Escriba-Folch, 2013; O'Donnell et al., 2013). Against these, endemic corruption is generally considered a sufficient basis for mass unrest, as is a context in which the state is either unable to restrict popular political communication or it is counterproductive to do so. Other works (Hansen & Stepputat, 2001; Schatz, 2013) have been more receptive to the affective aspects of citizenship, which have made it possible, in this part of the literature, to avoid both the assumption that Arab publics are either complicit in or unaware of their own oppression and the belief that changing one or the other of the conditions of contemporary Arab life – exposing the misdeeds of state or ruler, spreading awareness of the freedoms enjoyed by citizens elsewhere, communicating international solidarity – will lead inexorably towards reform or revolution. Understanding the seamlessness of experience under authoritarian rule sheds light on how social and political structures are reproduced, without reducing the populations of such nations to the journalistic epithet 'benighted'. The same can be levelled at economic explanations of the Arab Spring (Campante & Chor, 2012), which often seek to identify tipping points of unemployment or income levels beyond which change is irresistible. What we have seen instead is the endurance of poverty and a lack of basic infrastructure and resources that, viewed telescopically, are beyond what most would call a tipping point and yet which are, at the everyday level, rational. The spark for several protest cultures has been economic but symbolically so: the retraction of subsidies for bread, for instance, subsequently overturned but to no quieting avail.

Next, it is plausible that contemporary Western journalistic discourse is heavily informed by modernist norms of rationalism, order and progress (Hallin, 1992) and that this would underpin a perspective in which the world order which provides the backdrop to endless cataclysm and sensation is itself relatively stable and comprehensible. Like other analysts and storytellers, journalists are in the business of imposing meaning on the world rather than simply relaying it, establishing broader norms and order even or especially while drawing attention to the bizarre and extreme. In light of the earlier discussion about the ironized distance journalists develop in relation to the objects of their work, the reality is that journalism is as much influenced by what previously would have been called postmodernism, meaning here an ambivalence towards notions such as truth, morality and cultural value. The postmodernist perspective is not the antithesis of modernism, though, but a partial inversion of some of its commitments, and an ambivalent orientation to the world does not presume endless flux in the world, simply less certainty about it. The valid question that remains is whether it is or should be the job of journalists to probe the long-term stability of the wider context of newsworthy events, and the final chapter of this book outlines what this might look like as a practicable professional ethos.

In daily professional life there is little to be gained by journalistic prognostication: columnists who proclaim 'I told you so' hardly gain in status, while the risk to reputation associated with predicting the fall of, say, the Jordanian or Algerian regimes in 2011 would have been very real. Beyond this, though, there is scant merit in arguing that journalists are only equipped to detect and make sense of day-to-day change. It is not as though there is a single journalistic habitus; there is the question of expertise, and also of experience, each of which structures orientation. Thus, while it is true that foreign correspondents tend not to be stationed in one place long enough to really get to grips with its culture and politics (Wizda, 1997; cf. Erickson & Hamilton, 2006), there is no shortage of media and other professionals who possess specialist knowledge of particular countries in the region, whether by dint of birth or life trajectory, a knowledge that extends beyond the factual to a grasp of how a culture works, how it got where it is and its possible futures. That sense of orientation towards possible futures is then not about speculation at all, or strictly speaking prediction, but Heideggerian authenticity: being cognizant of what is really at stake in the present we find ourselves in. It is, then, confidence in one's professional instincts.

But to elevate journalistic instinct is to mystify what it means to be a good journalist and what benefit, precisely, journalism provides to the rest of us (Markham, 2011b). The same presumably could be said of historians; in either case claims to possess the unique power to know history as it is being made are more likely assertions of authority than its work-like exercise. Ultimately, for journalists in Egypt, for instance, not to have foreseen the events of 2010–11 is not evidence that they were hopelessly out of touch with the state of the country, nor does it mean that their being in the world was inauthentic – or at least no more inauthentic than anyone else. This is not intended as invective against a whole era in which everyone lives inauthentically, rather to suggest that to be less than fully cognizant of one's temporal orientation while engaged in the everyday routines of work is normal. It does appear to be the case that too little attention was paid by many Arab journalists to the growing cultures of protest online and especially in social media; it is also likely true that more could have been learned from the research of economists and demographers. But as with the question of audience engagement, this volume takes the line that professional engagement in expert discourses is not something that is simply absent or present; it is inevitably sporadic, selective and often delegated. The ideal of an individual or group of individuals with their finger uniquely on the pulse of a whole nation or region does not tally with the way that attentive work is necessarily parcelled out. This could be seen as evidence of the over-rationalization of knowledge production, the reduction of a noble art to something task-based and clock-led, or indeed the alienation of the creative worker from the substance of her work. It is not proof, however, that Egyptian journalists in late 2010 and early 2011 were simply incompetent and outmoded with their heads in the sand.

Still, for others it is not the rationalized form that journalistic work has assumed but the attitude of journalists in Egypt and elsewhere that have led to a blindness to what is really going on. Specifically, it has been noted here that journalists are routinely accused of fatalism about politics and a dismissive, often scornful view of the audiences they ostensibly serve (Mellor, 2007; Pintak, 2011). In Egypt the two combined pungently, with journalists criticized for not taking seriously the way that younger generations in particular were engaging in new forms of mediated politics, assuming them to be either hopelessly optimistic or else led by political forces they did not understand (Sakr, 2013; Saleh, 2013). This characterization of Egyptian journalists in particular is a little broad and is not by and large borne out in the fieldwork. It is true that there was a fair degree of scepticism about the scope for change and the ability of young people to lead it, but nothing that suggested an outright dismissal of protestors. Even for interviewees more cynical than sceptical, this apparently did not significantly impair their ability to report protests more or less fairly. In fact most were broadly sympathetic, if unconvinced by their likelihood of success. The same could be said of political journalists in the United Kingdom or the United States: many are plainly scathing of politicians as a group (Brants et al., 2010), finding them venal or self-serving or simply ineffectual; this might cause imbalance in political reporting, but it does not rule out quality journalism altogether. The Egyptian news and political reporters interviewed would cover a protest or a political press conference as something naturally meaningful – which is not to say something they felt they had to believe in personally but something unproblematically newsworthy. To suggest that journalists needed to be more sympathetic to the protestors to understand what was developing politically, that they would have grasped it had they really been listening, is misguided: they were listening, at least to a degree, and reporting what they witnessed as they saw fit. Likewise, the idea that a journalist should have to be personally neutral in order to produce neutral journalism conflates the individual and their work: it is possible for professionals, required even, to write and broadcast even-handedly about groups they find unconvincing or abhorrent. Most significantly, while it has been established that most journalists in the Arab world are driven by political reform than anything else (Pintak & Ginges, 2008), they do not see their role as one of cheerleading, still less positioning themselves at the vanguard of political change. This is unpacked further in the chapters that follow.

JOURNALISM IN A CHANGING WORLD

Being a journalist in times when the industry is undergoing rapid change and politically everything seems to be kicking off everywhere suggests that the experience of flux has become a defining characteristic of the journalistic field. Inevitably much continuity underlies any experienced change, though the literature is rich in research into specific conditions such as the precariousness of the labour market in the cultural and creative industries as well as more systemic, structural conditions such as liquid modernity or mobile privatization that are said to define the contemporary era in Western societies and increasingly around the world. But this sense of things being inherently unstable also has less acknowledged consequences. One is the positing of a past in which one's sense of being in the world was not fixed, exactly, but firmly entrenched in a more predictable temporality. This need not point to simple nostalgia for a less complicated age: against Bauman (2000) and Virilio (2000), the experience of flux by contemporary journalists and audiences alike can be stimulating as well as unsettling, exciting as well as angst-ridden. Flux, liquidity, precarity: all of these sound like conditions to be endured and survived, if at all, but they can also be experienced as less than critical – and the absence of crisis does not suggest inauthentic experience, or at least not necessarily problematically inauthentic. The language of thrownness and liquid modernity invokes a subjectivity always on the cusp of being overwhelmed or destroyed by chaotic forces, but habituation happens in interesting as well as dull times, and the ordinary work of subjectification goes on.

If flux characterizes one aspect of the lived experience of journalism in crisis, then the other is the sense of an accelerating change – simply put, hurtling away from the present towards unknowable futures. This too is palpably felt by interviewees to be variously frightening, sobering, poignant, exhilarating as well as with less heightened affect: grudging, curious, indifferent. Accelerating change also makes possible certain acts of positioning which go some way towards explaining the various experiences set out in Curran's keynote. The first of these posits something about the present or recent past that stands to be lost; it is precisely through feeling one's way through possible orientations to the future that what is precious about the now becomes manifest. For the researcher, this allows us to tease out distinctions between presents as refracted through possible futures, between imagined grieving for an individual's particular experience, or for a way of life for a professional community, or for the loss that society will suffer as a result. Ungenerously, one could paint the first of these as indulgent or maudlin, the second as nothing more principled than gatekeeping and the third as pompous and grandstanding. There are other options, though. Drawing on Butler's (2004) notion of grievability the first can be seen not as mawkish but a felt sense of that which will not have been, a kind of loss which has the potential for solidarity and politicization.

The projected decline of imagined professional community is harder to validate on its own terms: such groups are by nature exclusive, and the rules of inclusion and exclusion are often obscure. They further tend to be structured hierarchically, not a problem in itself, but such a professional distribution of power is commonly shown through sociological examination to be tied to other power relations regarded as unjust and insidious. Finally, the self-selecting nature of such groups, as well as being potentially unfair to those excluded, suffers from the curse of all intentive groups (Sennett, 1977): they eliminate the kinds of assimilation of radically diverse knowledge and experience, as well as the management of conflict, that would make them more useful to society as a whole. Seen from the outside, then, the demise of professional journalism would be no great loss. But there are robust defences of inward-looking professional and cultural lifeworlds, too, with Bourdieu's (1993) going furthest towards balancing scrutiny of their fundamentally undemocratic character with as neutral an assessment as possible of what kind of things – cultural products, ways of thinking – could only have been achieved under those conditions. In our case it is straightforward to proffer that there is a kind of shared journalistic orientation to the world; this is not to say that journalists agree on most things, only that there is a roughly common epistemological relation to lived reality. This is fleshed out further in chapters 3 through 5, but by way of précis it is broadly speaking processual, with encounters experienced as discrete rather than always-already enveloping and sized up according to voiced and unspoken rules enacted in a work-like manner – which is to say instrumental, methodical and with something less than total subjective investment. What is more difficult to establish is the extent to which a shared orientation is defensive, existing primarily to preserve membership as such rather than the principles operating therein, and whether those principles contribute something valuable more broadly.

There is no shortage of commentary averring that whatever society stands to lose from the demise of traditional professional journalism – that is, hierarchical, institutional, with standards maintained through peer review – the net effect will be substantively positive. Hermida (2012) encapsulates these views well, diagnosing without prevarication the 'top–down ideology of traditional journalism', now thankfully being usurped by the 'collective intelligence' of social media. There is much to be said about the latter, and this follows in chapter 8. The first half of the phrase, however, points to an instrumentalist view of the media industries as designed and run so as to achieve specific ends on behalf of societal and global elites. It is also representative of the kind of functionalism seen in much of the literature which holds that the principal teleology of journalism, like all cultural spheres of action, is structural reproduction – whatever the intentions of particular actors and organizations (Mihai, 2016). There are various arguments against media instrumentalism and functionalism, some of which are addressed in chapter 6. Notwithstanding this, however, Hermida goes beyond simply positing assumptions about the systemic functioning of the media industries to identify specific aspects of the journalistic habitus which warrant closer attention.

For Hermida, the top–down ideology of traditional journalism is enforced through a combination of overconfidence and presumption. Over-reliance on journalistic gut instinct is by this view an ingrained tendency to unthinkingly reproduce hegemonic discourses and coercive relations of power. The advent of social media has introduced a degree of tentativeness in journalists that represents a significant improvement to the way they work, a hesitancy that is entirely appropriate when it comes to something as important as the production of public knowledge. Social media have also forced on journalists recursive practice: related to tentativeness, this refers to a shift in journalistic practice in which methods are not wielded but constantly adapted through engaging with other knowledge producers and news sources. This last point connects with the recent literature on the representation of distant victims of natural disasters and war (Ong, 2014) but also goes further, suggesting not only that journalists should do a better job of listening to the experience of those who constitute the objects of their work, but they should also be receptive to different ideas about how that work should be done. The projected end point for this shift is that journalism will have been taken off its pedestal by the social media revolution, with journalists no longer acting as sources of knowledge but rather its champions, not presuming to speak for sources but aiming to facilitate their publicization and engagement with each other. While this amounts to the wholesale retreat of journalistic expertise, the argument runs that since expertise has historically been used to impose dominant ideology, society would benefit from its being displaced by something more like grounded theory – standing back and observing phenomena as they emerge, discovering rather than applying narrative coherence.

This takes on a particular piquancy when it comes to journalists' role in covering political upheaval. On the one hand it stands as good advice not to fall into the lazy compartmentalization of protest movements, as has been widespread since the turn of the century with the reduction of a dozen or so pro-democracy uprisings to branded revolutions: orange, cedar, tulip, rose, all drawing on the romanticized journalistic collective memory of the velvet revolution in Czechoslovakia. It also means acting as political curators rather than producers of political knowledge, and this appears conspicuously contentious given the high symbolic value ascribed to politics within professional journalism (Kuhn & Neveu, 2013) and the fiercely guarded role journalists have historically played as arbiters of what constitutes public knowledge and political meaning in the wider sense. There is a case to be made for the curatorial mode of journalism insofar as it promotes open-mindedness to where politics happens and how it is expressed. But there are also aspects to this commitment to politics 2.0 that suggest that a degree of journalistic expertise would not go amiss. For example, while it will be seen in chapter 7 that there is typically an emphasis in the literature on the ways that mainstream journalism misrepresents, selectively frames or dismisses protest movements, there may also be times when such movements need translating (Negus, 2002; Nixon & du Gay, 2002; Mellor, 2008; Maguire & Matthews, 2010) when their own voices and their own words would otherwise be misrecognized by audiences. Further, making historical and contemporary connections to other uprisings is sometimes more than the suffocating grip of established story templates: journalistic experience, while subsisting alongside other products of field immersion like the internalization of its power relations, can sometimes be useful.

Hermida is also representative of the kind of get-with-the-times critique of mainstream journalism that asks it to acknowledge the anti-political spirit of the age discussed in chapter 6. This is not meant as a concession to public apathy writ large but rather the need to register that political parties and parliaments are not the locus of many people's attention these days. It goes beyond an appeal to take seriously the alternative public spheres of Occupy or the Arab street, as ultimately it calls for a recognition that publics, including those engaged in protest aimed at toppling national regimes, are increasingly focused on the stuff of everyday life. The national and the local are interconnected in any model of the public sphere, but here the idea is that the texture of politics is *intimate*. This tallies with campaigns that prioritize respect, dignity and civility above democracy as overarching strategy, and there is plenty of scope for journalistic explorations of this kind of politics, albeit aligned with attachment journalism rather than reportage traditionally conceived. But there are cultural limits to the adaptability of journalism to what is presented as the new politics, and it is difficult to imagine journalists acting with the deference Hermida recommends when it comes to politics expressed through consumption or performance. As with the point about translation made above, it is likely that protest movements would benefit from professional experience of how different kinds of political activism play in mainstream media and elsewhere.

It was suggested earlier that for journalists to claim to represent anti-establishment interests is disingenuous. Here we can give this rather broad claim more substance. While it is plausible for mainstream journalists to register public disdain not only for the political centre but most forms of institutionalized power, they cannot do so from nowhere. The curatorial model of journalism rests on a disinterest in status at odds with the way that journalists see themselves, and with the conflicted yet recognized public and cultural authority that adhered to the profession historically. It is difficult to respond to the contention that it does not matter what journalists think of their role, or how it was regarded previously; the profession is not widely respected now, and the debates that really matter about the future of societies play out elsewhere. And yet the sheer diffusion of political communication suggests that there remains a necessary role of intermediary, and this is one that goes beyond curation. Journalists' historical self-identification as cultural intermediaries (in the Arab context, see especially Mellor, 2008), the crucial node between the rulers and the ruled, was always misleading, an exaggeration of their neutrality with regard to power and an understatement of their implicatedness in political and cultural reproduction. Journalism's status as a profession may be substantially reduced, but given that the case for existential crisis is at most partial, and that there is continued need for the gathering, contextualizing and communication of information – notwithstanding that a growing proportion of this is being carried out by algorithm (Anderson, 2013) and, less convincingly, through the organic ebb and flow of social media – then it is difficult to see why journalists would perform such functions tentatively, and without one eye on their individual and collective status.

JOURNALISM IN THE ARAB WORLD

Chapters 3 through 5 present empirical analyses of what makes the lives of Middle Eastern journalists meaningful, one on the basis of social media outputs and the other through deliberately unstructured interviews with media professionals in the region. One of the recurring themes of this book is that 'meaningfulness' is not used to indicate the heroism of the journalistic trade and, just as important, nor is it meant to suggest a kind of noble indefatigability in the face of the constraints of authoritarian states and the supposed threat presented by non-professional media production. Instead, the approach taken here is strictly phenomenological, beginning with what makes the routines of journalists' everyday lives relatively stable even amid contexts of futility and flux and only then starting to build an explanatory model to account for the way that historical change is experienced through practices of media production and consumption. However, given that the earlier parts of this chapter have established that we cannot take as given assumptions about crisis or revolution in media technologies, industries and polities, it is important to assess what has changed – and what hasn't – for journalists during the recent upheavals in the Arab world.

Research conducted before (see especially Pintak & Ginges, 2008; Mellor, 2011; Pintak, 2011) and after the Arab uprisings began (see especially Sakr, 2013; Gunter & Dickinson, 2013) shows the kind of nuance and variance you would expect of a region this complex and conflicted. But one finding borne out consistently is a sense of realism about the obstacles faced by journalists and the possibilities media work presents the professional, whether personally or politically. This is variously expressed through healthy scepticism, world-weariness and sometimes desperation, but more frequently in the interviews conducted for this book through humour: an Egyptian editor-in-chief captured perfectly the absurd reality of well-meaning but ill-conceived management policies that led to his newsroom being equipped with rows of state-of-the-art Apple Mac desktop computers – computers that were used exclusively 'as typewriters' because of a lack of connectivity, software and IT support. The lack of resources is felt at the individual level, too: while it is well established that journalists in the Arab world, especially those working for print publications, are badly paid, what is striking in the interviews are the repeated local anxieties caused by the irregularity of payment for work, impenetrable tax regulations and baffling procedures for claiming expenses. This kind of detail is important to register for anyone interested in the lives of journalists around the world and their ability to do their job. But it need not lead to pity, or indeed collective praise for carrying on in spite of everything. As ever, such experiences of work are collective as much as individual, and what they reveal are the micropolitics of the journalistic field – there is a world of difference in terms of self-positioning between recounting such professional indignities with anger or sardonic acceptance, for instance – as much as the collective position of journalists relative to politics or the corporate world. There are also insights here comparable with the experience of many entry-level media professionals in the West, with family support a key factor in establishing a career, as well as a willingness to improvise one's living arrangements and to invest in professional opportunities with a wilful blindness to their probable returns.

As for finance, so too for professionalism, with journalists harbouring few illusions about the constraints under which they operate, while exhibiting an embodied sense nonetheless that a decent enough career remains more or less possible if one makes the right choices along the way. For many newspapers, whether state or private, it remains fairly common for political or business elites to pay for a story to be written and published, and likewise it is widely accepted that editors will be prescriptive and interfering in the way they run their newsrooms. That is not the end of the story, however. Arab participants in Pintak & Ginges's (2008) study, for instance, are vocally critical about the lack of autonomy in the U.S. news media, while several journalists interviewed for this volume explained that autonomy was a matter of personal responsibility: if you want to be free of editorial interference, you have to work on your relationship with your editor, and you have to be good enough to work at a publication where standards matter. Perhaps more significantly, there is a common suggestion in the current research that success as a journalist manifests as the right to be editorial oneself, rather than to aspire to work unimpeded to standards of objectivity and neutrality. This mirrors historical assessments of commentary in the Western press (Schudson, 2003) and encapsulates well Bourdieu's depiction of two distinct levels of symbolic power – one which concerns being recognized as indistinguishable from the position of power one inhabits, the other about the ability to determine to one's advantage what counts as field capital in the first place.

For us, the pertinent question is what this tells us about the state and role of journalism in the Middle East, what opportunities are presented and what stands to be lost as a result of recent historical shifts which, while undoubtedly diverting the gaze from underlying structural continuities, are real enough. If journalism before 2010 was sclerotic, participants are clear that this is only in part due to the interventionist ways of authoritarian regimes – in this they diverge quite sharply from the perspectives of many academic researchers who elevate the totalitarian capacities of the state in Arab countries and often, as will be seen in chapter 8, ascribe it attributes as much psychological as political. The view among journalists in the region is that systemic corruption is a far more profound influence than authoritarianism as such, with political parties, corporations and religious groups able to commandeer media outlets and spread propaganda at will. Media control, then, goes well beyond punitive legal frameworks and extrajudicial punishment. Moreover, broad sections of the public are themselves criticized by journalists for their lack of media literacy, unable to discern the interests represented by the publications they consume and easily incited to orchestrated behaviour. While such scorn for the masses, often cheerfully expressed, was common among Arab participants, it is worth noting that the same is undoubtedly true among journalists in the United Kingdom and the United States (Markham, 2011b). Such statements should be put into proper perspective: general practitioners are known similarly to mock the ignorance and hypochondria of their patients, which is perhaps more easily accepted as a normal consequence of professional habituation than would be the case for, say, politicians. In any of these cases, habituated relations to the objects of their work is not incompatible with professional ethics or compassion.

The more germane point is that with endemic structural flaws and a suggestible, ill-informed public, it makes little sense to speak of this as a moment in which everything is at stake for journalists in the Middle East. Even revolutionary democratic reform, unlikely as that now seems, would not have made possible a radically different world for journalists, and similarly the idea that social media now threaten the very existence of professional journalism in the Arab world is wide of the mark, given that it was hardly in rude health previously. And yet the interviews bear out strongly that despite deep-seated scepticism about how much could actually change, there is an undeniable sense that everything is to play for – that this is indeed a critical junction in the region's history. However, this is not expressed in terms of the stakes involved in revolutions succeeding or petering out; it is, almost uniformly, about the relative position of the different elites and centres of power in the societies journalists inhabit. They tend to include themselves in this power play, with the requisite qualifications of personal agency and rueful reflections on the enervated state of their trade, but not with the sense that change is impossible. While journalism in the Arab world may be facing neither a crisis nor a new dawn, change will happen and is happening, and for those interviewed it matters where they position themselves in relation to it.

Corruption, a lack of transparency, editorial interference, poor resourcing and overt politicization are features of the Arab journalistic field in recent history comparable to many others around the world (Pasti et al., 2012; Elahi, 2013; Mungiu, 2013; Waisbord, 2013), and it is clear that journalists in the region know this well. But there are other perspectives that are more geographically or culturally specific, as well as established academic narratives that warrant an overview. First, the fact that print and satellite television journalism are usually published and broadcast in Modern Standard Arabic (MSA) rather than local vernaculars and dialects means that journalism in the region is at least notionally tied to the broader historical project of pan-Arab nationalism, which has ebbed and flowed since the end of the Second World War (we return to this theme in the next chapter). This is easily overstated, however, as the overwhelming majority of newspapers in this part of the world are national (and many others are local), and pan-Arab broadcaster Al-Jazeera is considerably less popular in the countries of the Maghreb than it is in the Levant, widely seen, as it is, as having a pro-Sunni bias. Al-Arabiya and BBC Arabic have similarly patchy reach, explicable not only by local competitiveness but instinctive institutional trust tied to perceived political and religious affiliation and cultural origin. On its arrival in 1994 Al-Jazeera was widely welcomed as an authentically regional voice (Lynch, 2006) and one which appeared to turn the tide both against the dominance of global broadcasters such as CNN as well as contemporary academic understandings of cultural globalization as representing inexorable homogenization and imperialism. That it is funded chiefly by the emir of Qatar and managed mainly by Saudi executives has led to accusations ranging from a half-hearted commitment to democracy to full-blown 'corporate feudalism' (Pintak, 2008), neither of which quite capture the ambitions of the broadcaster's editors and journalists or indeed the constraints they operate within. Al-Jazeera is also widely accused of knee-jerk anti-Americanism and, almost as frequently, legitimizing U.S. commercial and political policy in the region; it has also been criticized for a sophomoric, sometimes sentimental style of reporting, which is perhaps closer to the mark. We return to allegations that Arab satellite television has coarsened political discourse through its pursuit of ratings in the next chapter.

Few would agree that Al-Jazeera is currently succeeding in meeting its objectives of presenting a viable alternative to CNN and the BBC, one which gives an effective voice to non-Western interests in the region and around the world. But the advent of satellite television in the Middle East has changed the game in significant ways, as comparisons with laughably stale and on-message state broadcasters make abundantly clear. At the political level the broadcaster has a stated aim to give airtime to secular Arab nationalist, Islamist and liberal perspectives, and in its Arab language offering it certainly prioritizes debate. It also presents distinct career opportunities to aspiring Arab journalists than existed previously, though it has been accused of relying disproportionately on middle-class Lebanese staff. Its ownership structure and the Saudi-dominated advertising market in which it subsists undoubtedly raise concerns about editorial independence, but recent parallels of Berlusconi's dominance of the Italian media or that of Thaksin Shinawatra in Thailand are probably no better. It is also simultaneously self-evident and not a little controversial to point out that a free media is not entirely synonymous with democracy, or at least the kind of democracy that pervades contemporary Western political theory – whether social democratic or neoconservative, that tends to mean socially liberal, pro-tolerance and conflict averse. The past decade in Iraq and five years in Libya have seen the proliferation of polarized, divisive and often inflammatory media landscapes that have become battlefields for the wealthy and otherwise powerful (El Issawi, 2013; Saikal, 2013). There is a case to be made for the democratic legitimacy of such free-for-alls, but there are also legitimate concerns about the viability of national public spheres and the protection of minority rights in such contexts. It bears emphasizing here that one can defend the benefits that a less than democratically pure organization such as Al-Jazeera has brought to the region in the same way that a state-owned newspaper such as *Al-Ahram* was and is clearly capable of producing good journalism and holding power to account, within limits, without suggesting that this is all the Middle East deserves or is ready for. The most common line on this that one encounters in the literature is that the lack of an effective civil society in most countries in the region accounts for the failure of democratic institutions – media included – upon the fall of authoritarian regimes. Fawaz Turki puts it more strongly when he asks, 'How responsive can a country be to such [a democratic] ethos when its people have, for generations, existed within an ethic of fear – fear of originality, fear of innovation, fear of spontaneity, fear of life itself – and have instilled in them the need to accept orthodoxy, dependence and submission?' (in Pintak, 2011: 48). But it is possible to make a positive case for media regulation against incitement and corruption that does not resort to fatalism or patronization.

With the notable exception of Tunisia as well as some partial gains by pro-democracy movements, most Middle Eastern countries that saw protests erupt in late 2010 and 2011 have since reverted to an uneasy equilibrium that is not exactly the status quo ante but recognizably authoritarian. Likewise, the media landscapes in Egypt, Libya and elsewhere remain highly partisan, corrupt and exploitative of their workers. That said, however, journalists continue to have an active stake in where things go from here. Even if they are neither agents nor conduits of systemic change, it is clear that journalists will continue to be active in public life as political reality develops and congeals, and they will vie for status within and influence over these futures within the constraints under which they operate. Couldry (2003) has long argued that it is wrong to presume that media form a natural focus for society's attention, let alone a natural home for its politics. And yet to the extent to which journalism sustains some kind of public space in which politics is communicated, debated and maybe articulated with other spheres of action, it is an open question whether social media have effectively displaced journalism as the place people look to for a window on society as it changes, as well as a locus for mobilization and agitation. In chapter 6 it will become evident that such a shift is not attributable solely to the failure of journalism to provide the kind of coverage and scrutiny its audiences expect but to the perceived dislocation of all institutions seen to be part of the establishment – political and cultural as well as journalistic – from the experience of everyday life as well. The final chapter considers the potential for journalism to reclaim its role as guardian of public understanding of social change, by embracing an ethos of worrying away at the conditions of intelligibility of public and private life as it is experienced at the level of the everyday. Laying the groundwork for this, the next three chapters look at how journalists in the Arab world themselves manage – or fail – to maintain an instinctive grasp of what is going on in the world around them while ensconced in apparently trivial, mechanical and affective work and media routines – starting with what appears on the face of it to be the most banal practices of all: their social media posts.

Chapter Three

Empirical Perspectives

Arab Journalists Debate the Upheavals

The next three chapters investigate empirically how Arab journalists and activists – it will be seen that the distinction is rarely a clear one – have lived through the tumultuous events of the past decade. This is about much more than simply asking reporters what they made of the uprisings, instead aiming to capture the everyday experience of being in the world at this time, an experience that is bound to be banal as much as extraordinary. The point is not to demonstrate that what looked dramatic from afar was actually fairly mundane on the ground – there is plenty of testimony to counter that – but that *any* conscious experience, even in the most turbulent of times, is predicated on habituation and givenness at the level of the quotidian. This in part explains a point raised at the start of the book: that the journalistic orientation to the world, primed as it is to look for day-to-day changes within established narratives, can be blind to longer-term, slower, systemic change. Journalists are not alone in this quandary – we are all in various ways inclined to focus most of our attention on day-to-day vicissitudes as it is these that demand apprehension and response – but they make for a revealing case study of how people live through change.

It will be seen that this is not really about criticizing journalists for being short-sighted. Living authentically consists in a reflexive temporal orientation towards the pasts and futures of the presents into which we continually find ourselves thrown, but this is not just a matter of knowing a lot of history and being really adept at predicting the future. Temporal authenticity is more about being conscious of the contingencies that led to the experience of the present as normal, and what is at stake in how things play out from here. Living in even the most interesting of times ultimately reduces to daily routines and decisions about how to spend one's time and energy, and that resolution of the tension between the profound and the mundane is at the heart of our sense of being in the world and being in time. No one can hope to live with eyes fully focused on the big picture, able to somehow shunt to one side the habits that make life coherent and navigable in everyday contexts, but there is something inauthentic, something lacking, about consciousness fully consumed by the stimuli of the present.

Journalists as professional witnesses (Frosh & Pinchevski, 2009) provide revealing evidence about how this balance is struck – how change appears to consciousness, the roles played by skill, expertise and imagination, the daily grind of rationalization and routinization. And social media raise the possibility of a radically different, dispersed and delegated kind of attention that just might underpin a way of being in the world uniquely able to apprehend, respond to, generate and shape systemic change – precisely through the way social media platforms combine, remix and circulate the profound and the prosaic. It is not simply a matter of weighing in on whether old or new media are better at understanding social transformation and giving citizens the tools they need to engage in it. It means pulling apart what makes these distinct orientations to unfolding events possible and usually unproblematically liveable, and with what implications. A caveat was inserted at the beginning of this book that it is important not to take whatever we see on social media as the embodiment of a new politics, but in epistemological terms platforms such as Twitter give a good entry point for how journalists and others understand and respond to dramatic developments in real time, tweeting from their offices, cars and kitchens.

One of the reasons for analysing journalists' tweets here is to avoid the assumption that journalists and social media users are opposites of each other. Convergence culture (Jenkins, 2006) means that practices of media production cannot be neatly separated by medium, and the *cultural* distinction between professional and amateur is similarly problematic in an age when the status attached to each is blurred or inverted. The particular power of amateur social media is a product not only of its endless responsiveness, in contrast to the temporal deadweight of the news cycle, but its freedom from news values and journalistic narratives that seem ever more alien to media audiences, a mainstream mediated world distant from the ordinary lives of individuals. Few maintain that the emergence of a trending topic on Twitter is unadulterated, but, the argument goes (Newman, 2009; Stassen, 2010), it is less sullied by professional gatekeeping and the warped logics of commercial news – notwithstanding the commercial impetus of social media platforms themselves. And while penetration remains limited, social media in the Arab world is especially precious, given how circumscribed professional journalism is there – compromised by not just the usual constraints of simplistic narratives and financial imperatives (Mellor, 2005) but also a journalistic culture of editorial interventionism, newsroom deference and blatant corruption (Pintak, 2011).

Although this paints a picture of Arab journalism right out of the orientalist handbook, affirming all manner of venal and servile stereotypes, it is one familiar to reporters in the region. Arab journalists are under no illusions about their industry's endemic problems and the difficulty of producing good work in such an environment, and research (Pintak & Ginges, 2008) shows that they are also aware that they themselves are obstacles to a free media insofar as partisanship is rife, serving not the freewheeling debate of different opinions and ideologies but the competing interests of corporate, political and military elites. This sounds like a professional culture of resignation and fatalism, and there is certainly a pervasive sense of low expectations when it comes to the trade's capacity to do a better job in the future. But individually the story is a little different, with the interviews conducted for this research confirming the pre-uprising evidence that journalists feel they can personally do good work that has an impact if they play their career cards right. That might mean buttering up one oligarch or another, or picking the right side in a nascent power struggle, but if it gives them an effective platform where the constraints are known and tolerable, then compromise can be lived with.

Now, this could easily feed into a narrative that journalists in the Arab world have low standards not because they are realistic but because they are innately supine in the face of authoritarian power. This fits Said's (1978) critique (see also Guaabess, 2008), taking aim as he did at the Western assumption that Arabs lack aspirations of self-autonomy and secretly love their dictators. The reality for Arab journalists is somewhat different. It is not that they are craven and quietly like being submissive before editors and proprietors, but rather that in comparison to journalists in Europe, for instance, they are much more likely to be explicitly politically motivated than ascribing to the values of public service as such (Pies, 2008). Three times as many respondents in Pintak and Ginges's study claimed that political change is the primary goal of journalism as those who believed that their job was simply to report. At around half of the cohort, the largest group by affiliation were self-identified 'democrats'. The members of this group were younger than average and tended to describe themselves as secular, though they identified government interference as the biggest obstacle to professionalism rather than pressure from religious or corporate interests.

Next, when asked which issues facing the region were the most important, the three named most often were political reform, human rights and poverty – all significantly ahead of Palestine and the war in Iraq, which to Western eyes might have been expected to dominate. Precarity of employment is considered a fact of life, and even journalists with a powerful sponsor cannot rely on their long-term favour or influence. Pay is generally lousy, meaning that, as in many other countries, entry-level positions are often taken by those with other means of support. But combining all of this with the low esteem in which journalists are held in the Middle East, an obvious question arises: Why would someone choose journalism as a career? Despite all the political reversals witnessed in recent years, the current research shows that enough had happened in the years 2010–13 for there to be some hope in future democratization and a clear sense of journalistic investment in the ongoing political tectonic shifts in the Arab world. But what about before 2010, when there appeared to be no grounds for optimism for anyone with the sort of political motivations identified by Pintak and Ginges?

To answer this question effectively, it is imperative to sidestep the glib response of depicting Arab journalists as a tireless, noble tribe. And this means refocusing on meaningfulness in everyday life – not in the sense of a driving mission to change the world, but what makes doing journalistic work meaningful amid the routines of daily work. Mission may well play a role here (see especially Pintak, 2011), but embedded in habituated practice it is likely to look less than obviously virtuous; other factors might include less reflective, affective gratifications, or the collective affirmation of particular practices as meaningful by peer groups. Taken too literally, this line of thought – encapsulated by Bourdieu's *illusio* (2000: 11) – leads inexorably to a view of meaningfulness constituted *only* through participants convincing each other that it is so, without any recourse to external valorization, though the briefest of encounters with actors in the journalistic fields of Egypt and Lebanon or the United States and the United Kingdom, for that matter, make clear that the value of their work is never accorded entirely endogenously – the recognition by other fields and your social circle too feed into the unproblematic knowledge that your work is meaningful. But Bourdieu is a useful lens for thinking about meaningfulness rooted in everyday routines, in one's naturalized orientation to the world. Habitus, those durable and adaptable anticipatory structures that guide behaviour at the level of instinct, even of the corporeal, is what sustains meaningfulness (Bourdieu, 1990: 52–79). It is collective, but not uniform, and it is as much about competition for power and status as it is the stuff that binds a professional community. If you ask a bunch of journalists what motivates them, they will likely respond with references to abstract principles, and these may well be sincere. But meaningfulness is constituted through practice, specifically shared cultures of practice, and these are quotidian things barely registered by those who enact them. The analysis of journalists' tweets presented in this chapter shows that there is such a journalistic disposition, and it has less to do with lofty notions of journalism's role in society and holding power to account, as an instinctive, embodied orientation that finds meaning in responding to any event or stimulus, however predictable or unprecedented, overwhelming or trivial, through practices of filtering, ordering and disseminating. Whatever the scorn or adulation with which journalists are viewed by their fellow citizens at home and abroad, it is this epistemological orientation to the world that makes it naturally meaningful to get up and go to work day after day.

Received opinion (see, for instance, Khondker, 2011; cf. Howard & Hussain, 2011) has it that Arab journalists were swiftly and unceremoniously sidelined when the popular uprisings started to gain momentum in late 2010, rendered patently irrelevant in the face of the coming tide of citizen journalism and the collective intelligence of social media. Such a definitive defenestration is an easy read-off in a region in which journalists were regarded as ineffectual at best and complicit at worst in the endurance of authoritarian rule, but it is best seen as part of a global transition characterized by Boczkowski (2005) as a shift from journalist-centred to audience-centred media. Russell (2011) notes that journalists in the Arab world quickly found themselves all at sea, their instincts for knowing where a story is headed and how to locate sources having deserted them. Instead they were reduced to meta-reporting, simply relaying a conversation going on elsewhere, on social media. Audiences in Arab countries have long been accustomed to television news that looks nothing like what they know to be going on in the streets, and that journalists seemed not to be able to keep up with or make sense of events being tweeted and posted about can only have reinforced that public awareness of the arbitrariness of mainstream, official news.

But hasty announcements of the demise of professional journalism are also partly explicable by the eagerness of media commentators and academics to identify the endpoint of shifts whose beginnings they have detected, to be able to claim definitively where things are headed, where politics is happening now. A much-discussed case is Hermida et al.'s (2014) analysis of the tweets of National Public Radio's Andy Carvin, held up as proof that Western journalists simply bypassed accredited professionals in Egypt in 2010–12 and cultivated an army of citizen sources instead, their authenticity and trustworthiness underwritten by the law of self-correcting social media. By this principle, it is not as though social media are held up as faultless and innocent, but errors, bias and bad faith will be reliably outed as such as the network tends towards deliberative equilibrium. Hermida et al. show that while Carvin did rely predominantly on amateur sources, he validated them by traditional means – by asking known colleagues to vouch for their reliability. Carvin had become iconic of a way of doing things that was not as new or as widespread as many were quick to assume. Another compelling illustration of the gap between the theorized arrival of a radically new culture of media production and facts on the ground is Hänska-Ahy and Shapour's (2013) investigation of amateur video production in the uprisings in Iran in 2009 and the Arab world in 2011: instead of citizen journalists bypassing the techniques and gatekeeping structures of mainstream media, they routinely sent their work to the BBC's Persian and Arabic desks and quickly learned how to ensure that it conformed to the BBC's requirements for validation and broadcastability.

Evidence of social media use breaking through some kind of threshold in the Arab uprisings remains inconclusive. That Twitter users were statistically more likely than non-users to have attended the main Tahrir demonstrations leading up to the resignation of President Hosni Mubarak is a demonstration of correlation rather than causality – any number of external factors could predict for both the presence of social media users and the absence of non-users (see Tufekci & Wilson, 2012). Visualizations of hashtag frequency over time can be persuasive about momentum and tipping points, but the tweets they lump together need to be disaggregated to be fully understood. Lotan et al. (2011), for instance, break down tweets and retweets across the Arab protests by type of user account. Those they identify as bloggers are the most numerous, followed by journalists, activists, bots and finally mainstream media organizations. What, though, is the difference between a blogger and an activist? Mainstream accounts, presumably properly resourced and staffed, were found to have produced the largest proportion of tweets, but these had a different lifespan to others – appearing with a flurry of retweets but quickly becoming inert. Individual professional journalists, on the other hand, were more likely to see their less frequent tweets spread over time, perhaps pointing to an enduring status linked to reputation and communication skills. This may also be emblematic of the valorization of individual over institutional authority discussed in chapter 8. But Lotan et al. also find that journalistic activity on social media is not indicative of a keen embrace of citizen journalists. It is true that they will sometimes rely on 'crowdsourced elites' – non-journalists who have been validated and elevated as authoritative and trustworthy by large numbers of followers including, crucially, journalists. But as Singer (2005) demonstrated a decade ago, journalists appeared keen to maintain a distance between professionals and amateurs. This is not the same as pulling up the drawbridge – any journalist worth her salt spends as much time with 'ordinary' sources as elite ones – but nor is it the dissolution of the expert/lay divide thought to be one of the defining features of convergence culture.

In other words, the evidence is complicated. It is clear from mapping retweets that journalists have not been rendered voiceless or peripheral on social media, overlooked in favour of the authentically unprofessional. And this is before even considering qualitative data, which this chapter does by way of a microcosmic discourse analysis and other research using sentiment analysis is increasingly able to do at large scales. Further, of course, all of this says nothing about all the other interactive loci in which journalists may or may not be present or cited – in cafés, seminars and legislatures. Another way to look at this is to ask whether journalists *felt* sidelined during the uprisings and amid the rise of social media more broadly. The two subsequent chapters put this question directly to respondents, though other research has also touched on the journalist's experience of new amateur media cultures. Papacharissi and Oliveira (2012: 267) surmise that professionals have gone through something of an identity crisis, torn between their roles as reporters, editors, commentators and individuals. This, they argue, is about much more than multitasking: it requires a wholesale shift in orientation towards work from a relation of mutual exteriority of subjects and objects of journalistic discourse to 'finding one's own place in the story'. The notion of journalists writing themselves out of their stories can sound antiquated, evoking a particularly modernist account of journalistic epistemology. But a felt anxiety over the expectation to constantly and personally position oneself in relation to developing events is real enough, and Papacharissi and Oliveira put it in perspective by highlighting how the dispersed nature of agency in social media is not just about fluid, liberated subjectivities but a subjective experience that overwhelms individual motivations and concerns. To misquote them slightly, hashtags do not feel the same anxiety as they happily mingle fact and opinion, the respectful and irrelevant, the prosaic and profound.

While it is tempting to think in terms of an opposition between individual agency and that of an endlessly plastic and adaptable network, looking at something as mechanical as a tweet's lifespan shows agency to be neither simply owned nor ownerless. Starbird and Palen (2012) flag up the difficulty of disentangling agency and intention: it is easy to point to the postmodernist severance of author and text, but the motivation of journalists to tweet remains meaningful, as well as that of their retweeters, and this is often impossible to discern. Conventions have developed for mapping the spread of a tweet across different networks (see Lotan et al., 2011), but it is important to refrain from making a quick inferential leap from this to claims about agency transformed. We can say with confidence that the meaning of a tweet does not remain as its poster intended as it is distributed, but we cannot be so sure that what we witness as we track retweets is the transition from individual to collective agency. And yet this conception of agency in social media as radically pluralized and collectivized is prevalent in the literature (see, for instance, Mustafa Tagma, 2011; Newsom, 2011; Soguk, 2011) and is used as a basis for various claims about the political status of social media platforms. Papacharissi and Oliveira, for instance, posit that the netizens of the Arab Spring, having thrown off the shackles of mainstream media and pooled their subjective agency, qualify as subaltern counter cultures in line with Fraser's (1990) delineation. This is consistent with the theme identified in chapter 8 of radically alternative political cultures imagined to spring up in the absence of establishment structures, but what is especially telling is how that subaltern is painted here. Its main demand is the right to be heard – seemingly natural enough, but seen in context this is predicated on a fairly narrow construction of politics in terms of rights, and of rights conceived in terms of voice. Fraser's model of recognition is palpably alive to the conflicted realities of contemporary public engagement, but it has also been criticized for overstating the agency that we as individuals and groups actually possess over how we are recognized (McNay, 2008). What if misrecognition of socially mediated subalterns is the norm? And not only misrecognition by hegemonic institutions but by advocates of democratic transformation? The voice that comes out of the perceived collective agency of social media networks is, in the literature, overwhelmingly progressive and liberal. It is, in short, a voice that we find familiar, that we are comfortable talking to and find easy to urge on. None of this is to downplay the role of social media in protest movements and the possibilities they afford for mobilization, but it does ask that we think carefully about what kind of phenomenal object we are responding to when we think we recognize a political culture that is at the same time new and a natural fit with our own principles. The corollary that matters here is that we cannot assume either that social media engagement by professionals will reveal them to be left for dead as agents that matter or indeed doggedly wedded to propping up the political status quo ante. The next section presents a step-by-step analysis of what we *can* infer from journalists' tweets during times of upheaval.

ARAB JOURNALISTS TWEET THE UPRISINGS

Professional journalists working for state and private media organizations have been largely overlooked in research on social media protest cultures, impatient as a lot of us have been to locate the new politics elsewhere, in the hands of the people unconstrained by official discourse, outmoded professional values, stale media narratives and the strictures of authoritarian states and corporate agendas alike. But the way they have navigated tumultuous times has much to tell us about the experience of change more generally, caught up as it is in the routines of work and family, social interactions and mobilities. The fieldwork presented in chapters 4 and 5 fleshes this out in more vivid detail, but here the idea is to work from tweets posted in real time as specific events unfolded to establish what, precisely, can be discerned in the way of being in the world: in particular, naturalized orientations, modes of self-presentation and interaction and, potentially, agency. It has been argued up to this point that the latter is hard to pin down; it does not have to consist in the ability to shape events but rather the experience of being fully invested in them, understanding (if not consciously reflecting on) the implications of responding this way or that. We know also that agency is collective, not something clinched in isolated moments of struggle or revelation. But, finally, it is methodologically elusive, and as well as shedding light on how real events played out in the eyes of Arab journalists, the aim is also to establish what can ever reasonably be inferred about agency, professional or political, from their tweets – assuming neither to reconstruct authentic personal experience nor to infer radically depersonalized agency in the context of networked media.

Two relatively short time frames were selected, from early to mid-2012, around very specific political events in the Middle East: the lead-up to and aftermath of the appointment of Mohammad Morsi as president of Egypt and a visit to Syria by UN special envoy Kofi Annan. Twitter accounts were selected through a straightforward search for users who include the Arabic word for 'journalist' (صحافي) in their profile text and had tweeted using the Arabic hashtags for Egypt (#مصر) or Syria (#سوريا). So as to allow for consideration of the context of daily work routines, it was decided to omit those who turned out to have described themselves as former journalists, though given the precarity of labour in the media industries of the Middle East those who described themselves as freelance were included as there was evidence also that their work had been published in recognized titles or used by known broadcasters. This produced a small sample of thirteen Twitter profiles: seven journalists employed by private print publications, one broadcast journalist, also private, and five freelancers. Their tweets – 370 in all across two periods of one week each – were then categorized according to mode of communication (one-way dissemination, interaction and retweet/quoted tweet), referents and tone of language. This last category did not expand to full mapping out of Faircloughian (1992) subcategories – word order, inclusions and exclusions, decontestations, resignifications and so on – but focused specifically on whether tweets were substantively reportorial, rhetorical, deliberative or conversational. Inevitably, there were tweets that sat at the boundaries of these categories, as well as thirty-two that could not be meaningfully classified at all, but most fit reasonably well. The first category was straightforward, with reportorial posts relaying apparently factual information with little editorializing or evidence of an intention to persuade: 'Now announced that Annan will arrive at 12.45', for instance. Rhetorical tweets cover a variety of communicative modes, including rhetorical questions, hyperbole and metaphor, as well as statements of self-positioning: 'I believe that dignity is the best foreign policy'. Deciding what counts as deliberative has proved contentious in previous research, but here the bar was set deliberately low: so long as an exchange was identifiably about an event or issue or person it was coded as deliberative, even if it fell far short of Habermasian criteria and looked more like personal abuse: 'Your support for the Brotherhood makes me sick in the heart'.

An analysis of mainly American journalists' tweets by Lasorsa et al. (2012) found that journalists on Twitter tended by and large to be fairly restrained and professionally focused, speaking more freely than in news copy or editorial writing but with an eye on reputation management. There was a degree of strategic candour, with partial revelations of their work routines and personal lives, but also much held back about how they do what they do. This is a classic manifestation of professional mythologizing, cultivating cultural authority by obscuring what it takes to perform a professional role competently and thus distinguishing themselves from non-professional social media participants. As Hermida et al. (2014: 11) put it, 'In a networked media environment, the journalist emerges as a central node to authenticate, interpret and contextualize communication flows on social awareness streams, drawing on a distributed and networked newsroom where knowledge and expertise are fluid, dynamic and hybrid'. This is not as easy as it sounds to accomplish and certainly does not happen naturally in social media communicative cultures; it hinges on journalists individually and collectively managing to perform their professional identity in such a way that it will be recognized as such by multifarious others – and we know from the sociology of professions (Johnson, 1972) that this involves much more than just doing a job well. Lasorsa et al. demonstrate that performative professional identity is as much about tone as anything, specifically emanating a sense of effortless authoritativeness and enjoyment of their work.

Other research has found that individual journalists make more use of social media in order to break loose from the more stifling strictures of their trade. Harlow & Johnson (2011), for instance, find that reporters on Twitter were much more likely to eschew the classic framing devices that Gitlin identified in his classic work on media coverage of the Vietnam War: trivializing, polarizing, pathologizing and so on but in effect reducible to legitimizing and delegitimizing frames. Harlow and Johnson detect alternate frames in journalistic tweets that emphasize justice, accountability and sympathy – that is, not just reducing to personal support or opposition to whatever they are tweeting about but finding recourse to ethical frames of reference that are usually seen as beyond the reporter's remit. This helps to put in perspective research into Arab journalists' tweets: whatever else is concluded, as an opening gambit we can rule out the possibility that observed deviation from classic media frames is explicable by their Arabness. So, when Hamdy and Gomaa (2012) highlight that Arab reporters tweeting about the uprisings were reaching for words like 'pure', 'noble' and 'selfless' to describe the protestors, it does not necessarily indicate a lack of professionalism – nor for that matter a more authentically Arab kind of journalistic expression. And as with Harlow, such loaded terms may well sit alongside other language strategically oriented towards maintaining an aura of professional authority. Seemingly subjective, strongly normative language was certainly present in the present sample, but was by no means ubiquitous – used by a little fewer than half of the journalists. But it does raise a serious methodological question, and one that has political implications: How to interpret rhetoric that appears so culturally inflected, what Hamdy and Gomaa (2012: 202) describe as 'rhetorical can visual imagery ranging from interfaith prayers to dreams of a successful revolution'?

ANALYSING FLORID LANGUAGE

A good deal of rhetorical and platitudinous content is to be expected in tweets from any part of the world, and in that sense it is not surprising that the present sample included a lot of statements of straightforward support for democracy, freedom and peace, as well as expressions of emotional reactions to events. But looked at in the cold light of translation into English, many tweets are conspicuously florid, full of references to hearts ('My heart aches for the soul of Egypt', 'Egypt's heart is filled'); crying ('The city cries', 'Syria cries for its children'); eyes, love, smiling and death (of abstract nouns such as hope); emotive metaphors ('When dignity committed suicide') and value statements about honour, respect and shame. First, it is important to note that much of this is explicable by the architecture of the Arabic language and cannot be simply read as expressions of Arab culture or cultures. The translations given here are literal rather than contextual, and Arabic syntax is highly referential, metaphorical and often circuitous in its construction. References to the heart, eyes and head are legion and cannot be interpreted as demonstrating excitability and passion among Arab journalists or to support essentialist preconceptions of Arab culture as fiery, volatile or simply exotic. Trombetta (2012) notes the tendency of Western academics to overlook the nuances of Arabic expression, with elaborate allusion and repetition encoding rules for signalling deference, respect and trust. Humour, too, is notoriously evasive: even straightforward exclamations of 'شكرا مصر!' ('Thank you, Egypt!') can be sincere and sarcastic; what is meant by posts like 'the department of love in my heart is closed for maintenance' resists easy dissection. But this is by no means a dead end, and the lesson here is not that we cannot extrapolate anything from these tweets – just that a little cautiousness is in order. It will be seen in what follows, for instance, that it is possible tentatively to set out the implications of a journalistic discourse in which reaching for universal declarations is the norm. Also discussed below is the very live debate going on among Arab media scholars about whether there is something particularly dysfunctional about journalism in the Middle East. That remains on the table; it cannot, however, be inferred from the apparent tone of tweets in translation.

Next, it is perhaps understandable that much Western scholarly work exhibits a distinct wariness in writing about the role of Islam in the public lives and institutions of Middle Eastern societies. This is appropriate considering the confessional and demographic complexity of the region, but methodological decisions have to be made, regardless, about how to interpret references to Allah, the Qur'an, Islamic sects and religious principles – all of which abound in the sample here. Rinke and Röder (2011: 1275) offer a useful way in, starting with a more holistic sketch of the distinct 'communication culture' of the Arab world. That final 'of' is problematic, suggesting as it does that there is a single essential Arab culture endemic to a region defined geographically or linguistically, but with that caveat duly inserted it is safe to proceed. First, they draw our attention to the primacy of one-to-one communication in Arab culture, firmly rooted in oral history but also demonstrable on social media: there is more one-to-one communication in Arabic on Twitter than in other languages. This is an interesting observation in itself and might dovetail with the arguments already set out about the durability of individual authority in journalism and culture more broadly in relation to institutional authority seen in other parts of the world. But it is also distinct from many-to-many communication – everybody piling into conversations with unknown and often undifferentiated others, the communicative mode reckoned to be integral to the leaderless, fluid cultures of social media political movements. The one-to-one exchanges Rinke and Röder detail are mainly, though not exclusively, between known others and, significantly, they retain a clear awareness of hierarchy putatively absent in other social media contexts.

The second feature alighted on by Rinke and Röder is the broad intelligibility across the region of Modern Standard Arabic (MSA). While some national and local dialects are mutually incomprehensible, MSA raises at least the possibility of a regional communicative space and, perhaps, a pan-Arab public sphere (Mellor, 2005: 109–22). This is easily overstated, especially when regional communication amounts to little more than bland statements of support from Arab speakers in neighbouring countries or in diasporas around the world. But the possibility of something more substantive and enduring has been mooted since the rise of national independence movements in the mid-twentieth century and again with the arrival of pan-Arab broadcasters Al-Jazeera and Al-Arabiya. In the 1950s and 1960s, the then Egyptian president Gamal Abdel Nasser's articulation of a pan-Arab nation based on shared language and culture was widely criticized as a fantasy that overlooked local discontinuities and swept deeply held tensions under a utopian carpet, but banal routines of listening to and reading MSA in the home, car, workplace and teahouse has made pan-Arab deliberation an ordinary fact of life. By extension, while it cannot be assumed that Arabic-language social media cultures are consistently deliberative in that same Habermasian sense of being organized around shared values and rules for resolving issues of shared concern, the possibility of such a space taking shape cannot be discounted.

Rinke and Röder then turn their attention to the intricate interweaving of Islamic tenets and customs into all kinds of Arabic language, from the formal to the vernacular. In particular they underline the centrality of نسب (nasab), or family solidarity, and الأمة (al-umma), the international brotherhood of Islam – both concepts usually operate implicitly and are widely misunderstood outside the Islamic world. In the case of the Egyptian uprisings, the pivotal role played by the Muslim Brotherhood from the outset was largely misinterpreted by Western commentators as the hijacking by Islamists of a purely democratic, and secular, protest movement. The conflation of Islamism and Islam muddied the water, with mainstream media treating as suspect any religious overtones voiced by news sources and academic scholars – sometimes (Hollis, 2012) – overcorrecting by casting Islam as the redemptive other of secular authoritarianism. Between this polarity lie the very ordinary references to religion that pervade public discourse in the Arab world: as Soguk (2011) puts it, how 'unembarrassed' journalists and social media participants alike are about Islam's centrality as a frame of reference in everyday life. This is not at all the same thing as singularly praising Arabs for their piety but rather to establish the quotidian meaningfulness of religion in order to make sense of references to the Almighty and the holy book. Some ubiquitous invocations such as 'إن شاء الله' ('God willing') and 'الحمد لله' ('Praise be to God') are often added instinctively or as placeholders in a sentence – little different in function to 'for God's sake' in non-religious English idiom. Then there are phrases that speak to the centrality of religion as an authoritative framework but which appear all the same to be largely rhetorical: 'With God's help Egypt will survive', 'May God protect the children of Egypt' and so on. Finally, there is ample evidence of journalists' opinions on religious matters and the role that Islam should play in anticipated post-revolutionary Arab nations. Most frequently, these took the form of straightforward avowals of Islamic principle, though there were also widespread calls for tolerance of other faiths ('Egypt will not forget her Muslim and Coptic children') and one journalist who regularly blogged in support of rights for atheists in the region.

Having made these categorizations, we are now in a position to start drawing inferences on the basis of the habitually embedded discourses that such tweets have emerged from in everyday contexts. Epistemologically this is a balancing act: after Foucault, discourses are invoked in their entirety in local actions and speech acts; the whole web of knowledge and power of which they are partial effects is activated – partial because observed behaviour is simultaneously the effect of multiple discourses. But this is not the same as claiming that individual acts and words are definitive evidence of said discourses. They are particular manifestations of what discourse makes it intelligible to say and do, but the fundamental nature of that discourse is neither clinched nor revealed in the saying and doing. In practice this means resisting the pull of deep meaning, the temptation to generalize about what speech acts expose about the culture in which they emerge – this can only be done methodically, and especially through research that cuts across different lived contexts, mediated and otherwise. This, though, is a methodological imperative and not a political one. When Hofheinz (2011) cautions against reaching too quickly for the conclusion that Islamic influence on forms of communication in the Arab world underpins discourses of conservatism, moralizing and divisiveness, then, it is because this is good sociological practice – rather than because of a hesitancy to criticize other cultures from a Western perspective. The same logic applies to very visible forms of religious and political communication such as Friday prayers at mosques; we should avoid interpreting these as the ultimate expression of Islamic or Arabic culture not only because this is politically reductive but epistemologically so. Friday prayers can thus be located on a communicative continuum with social media participation and all other kinds of interaction, which for Hofheinz means that what is going on in social media can be seen as a continuation of long-term trends, not the arrival of something radically unprecedented.

Hofheinz points back to the early nineteenth century, when rising literacy rates meant that many Muslims in the Arab world began to read scripture for themselves. Intertwined with the linguistic shift was a cultural one, with 'ordinary' citizens feeling increasingly empowered to challenge their imam's readings of scripture. This in turn is connected to broader changes in the Arab world, especially in North Africa, in which individuals – not all, but certainly extending beyond the propertied elites – started to demand greater autonomy in what they read and thought and platforms on which to voice their own views. Tempting as it may be to detect in this signs of an inexorable evolution towards Western-style, individualistic democratization, Hofheinz is carefully ambivalent about the causes and consequences of a growing cultural disregard for 'the long chain of authority' – all the religious, political, social and familial hierarchies that traditionally structured decision-making in Arab culture. So, alongside the slow demise of the ulama, or Muslim legal scholar, came the rise of inexpert and unqualified, though still influential, religious scholars – that is, not simply the dissolution of religious authority as such. There is much to criticize about that new religious discourse, and the criticisms echo those made of self-appointed social media experts – that they are selective and subjective. Like the gradual disappearance of punctuation and the slow normalization of syntax previously held to be incorrect, however,

Hofheinz sees little point in lamenting one authoritative discursive system being elbowed out by another. This makes a Foucauldian kind of sense, in that history is a succession of discursive regimes and not progress towards a less regimented, more autonomous world.

DELIBERATION AND WRESTLING

Next up are the tweets classified as deliberative. Some of these are self-evidently exchanges of opinion and analysis about shared objects of concern, but many take the form of statements of disagreement with absent others. These are very common kinds of speech acts on social media platforms and in discussion forums, though to class them as deliberative requires a little justification (Larsson & Moe, 2012). If someone tweets that liberals are deluded, or that conservatives are corrupt, there is something less than a dialogue between citizens who have agreed to the same deliberative rules as well as the ultimate goal of debate. But, first, such a tweet could spark deliberation at any time, as others pick up on it, distribute it or respond to it. Further, it could be argued that even the equivalent of the proverbial tree falling in the forest, the tweet that goes out utterly unnoticed, is deliberative. This is not because the space in which the message is enunciated is an inherently deliberative one but because deliberation is at heart about the externalization and internalization of ideas. So, even if there is no actual dialogue, putting an opinion out there is never a unidirectional act; it always proceeds in relation to an exterior object – this is its intentiveness – and in anticipation of what that object would make of it, whether that object is an individual, an amorphously conceived group or just the world out there. It is easy to call arbitrary flaming narcissistic, but it always comes with an external orientation, and even where the object of that orientation is denied an actual voice it is nonetheless not docile. Saying you hate Christians sounds like a straight exterioralization, but it positions the speaker in relation to others in the world, and she is thus rendered as object to them, however nominally. Subjectification is never a one-way street, even if it feels like it, and so one-way conversations with real and imagined others count as deliberative.

The examples used here are a little loose-tongued, and that is indicative of the fairly robust tone that a lot of the tweets in this category took. Those deemed to be on the wrong side of an argument were not simply mistaken but described as everything from 'morons' and 'mentally ill' to 'shameful' and 'sick in the heart'. Beyond bouts of personal abuse, however, there was a preponderance of statements of categorical, insuperable disagreement: polarization is an at-hand instinct, locating another at an irredeemably diametric opposite an effortless accomplishment. Godwin's (1995) law is one way to characterize this, with participants across social media spaces all too eager to play the Hitler card rather than engage in temperate, evidence-based reasoning. But to point to the generalized incivility seen on social media feeds does not mean that it is all the same, and there remains the possibility that there is something about the Arab-language Twittersphere, or at least that bit of it inhabited by journalists, that is particularly declamatory and abusive. It is a question that can be asked without insinuating anything about Arab cultures and how they appear to a Western spectator – indeed it is a question that Arab media scholars have been asking with growing urgency over the past decade or so as regional broadcasters have aggressively sought to expand their audiences and attract advertisers. As elsewhere, on screen this has meant more sensationalized news coverage as well as a prevalence of debate formats that are deliberately confrontational and shrill (Rugh, 2004: 229–48). Social media, the argument goes, both validate and exacerbate broadcast media culture by mimicking and endlessly amplifying combative broadcast cultures, which in turn are desperate to ventriloquize their perceived audiences in order to hold on to them – and we are all debased as a result (see also McRobbie & Thornton, 1995).

Arab commentators refer to this kind of immoderate, name-calling deliberation 'wrestling', and the term is applied beyond television to characterize political discourse more generally. At the 2012 Arab Media Forum, there were a few speakers who blamed this degradation on the corrupting influence of Western cultural and economic values: indulging indiscriminate freedom of speech and the unfettered pursuit of profits can only end this way. They were outnumbered, however, by those genuinely worried at the prospect that there is something about the way political deliberation is done in Arab culture generally that was stunting political development. Two forms of deliberative short-circuiting were highlighted in particular: a quickness to take offence where none may have been intended and the morphing of disagreement about a mutually external object into personal pronouncements on the moral character of interlocutors. For one Lebanese speaker this was emblematic of Arab deliberative inferiority, a lack of political maturity compared to the West, but in reality there are no clear lines of inference that point to either something deficient in Arab culture or a lucid historical explanation of how things got to be the way they are. Now, there are clearly problems with national and regional public spheres across the Middle East, and their specific mediatizations warrant closer scrutiny. For our purposes, the key question is what makes it unremarkably meaningful to resort to umbrage and moralization on debate programmes and social media. There is perhaps an affective payoff, a learned satisfaction in shutting an opponent down and securing oneself by closing down the debate. For Arab journalists, then, there is a self-preservation strategy encoded in rhetorical defensiveness, warding off scrutiny and preventing a discussion from going anywhere ambiguous or genuinely contentious. This is of a piece with the pre-emptive walling-off and self-censorship that characterize news cultures where editorial interference is the norm; it is, then, indicative of a lack of journalistic autonomy rather than a lack of self-restraint. And again, such a culture of practices is not the product of Arab culture but of the economic instability, clientalism, patronage and corruption that pervade the media industries of the Arab world (Springborg, 2011).

But it is not enough to account for a deliberative culture only with reference to economic structures and logics, as there is no simple correspondence between the two; again, observed cultures of practice are a particular case of the possible, not something that can be mechanically predicted from institutionalized corruption and precarity. Economic structures by this view are not extrinsic forces of domination but the things around which professional subjectivity takes shape: they are constraints in everyday life, but also productive of ways of experiencing work. This is not to defend them as benign or even encouraging, but insofar as they are embedded in pre-reflexive cautiousness and defensiveness they are a formative part of the professional's identity, not that which stops it from being what it truly aspires to be. Journalists in other ways actively resist industrial and political constraints, but where they are embodied as instinct there is not relationship of interior journalist and exterior industry. The two are coeval, and the upshot is that this becomes just the way things are, the alternatives unthinkable. The final chapter returns to the question of what role journalists might play in contesting conditions of intelligibility in everyday life, but here the issue is the unintelligibility for journalists of the possibility of professional change, of things done differently. We have seen that there is no shortage of commentary telling Arab journalists what they are doing wrong and what they should be doing instead, as is the case in the West. The point, though, is that cultures of practice congeal not around conscious calculations of costs and benefits associated with acting this way or that but something felt, something affective.

The examples of Fox News in the United States (Cisneros, 2008; Aday, 2010) and the *Daily Mail* in the United Kingdom (Williams et al., 2003; Bowskill et al., 2007) demonstrate that polarization and demonization are about more than straight authority claims or power grabs, though those are certainly at play. Pontificating, denouncing, categorically refusing to agree even on the premises of a debate are more than rhetorical devices; they produce a kind of comfort that comes with in-group membership and an absence of ambiguity. As with Arab cultures of political wrestling, it also forecloses the possibility of exposure of inadequacy or ignorance, an experience which is never just about winning or losing an argument but also about embarrassing and humiliating. Affective defence mechanisms are as important as argumentative ones in understanding how professionals react to encounters in everyday life, instinctively making decisions based on anticipated outcome. This is Freud's narcissism of small differences, also seen in organizational psychology in the tendency of colleagues collectively to conduct heated deliberation about matters of little consequence, a displacement activity that saves all concerned from the risk of exposure of incompetency in relation to the big issues that really count. The utility of this perspective is that it allows simultaneously for a refusal simply to judge Arab journalism as a whole, since the same learned instincts are a feature of professionalism writ large, as well as a rejection of holding our hands up and conceding that however Arab journalists, managers and proprietors want to run their industry is fine. Things go wrong for a reason, and focusing on embodied instinct in everyday contexts is a good way of showing how ways of thinking and acting solidify over time and with what consequences.

BREAKING NEWS

Aside from the rhetoric and wrestling, the final main category of tweets are those in which journalists were, apparently, doing nothing more than breaking news. In among this, there is plenty of editorializing, especially expressions of hope – hope that the Egyptian and Syrian militaries will alternately show self-restraint or act decisively to prevent a descent into chaos. These can be seen as intentive in the reflective, strategic sense, laying out clearly what the tweeter would like to see happen. The phenomenological sense of intention is different, however, capturing the experiential fact that all encounters, even those that appear entirely reactive or passive, are intentive – that is, the result of paying attention to or being oriented towards one kind of phenomenal object rather than another. Here, that includes tweets that are nothing more than the reporting of things that have become known: expected times of arrivals and announcements, contents of statements and reactions to them, as well as some analysis of implications and what will likely happen next. There may be nothing more to this than instrumentality, just journalists making good use of the communicative tools at their disposal to convey information about events as they develop. Or alternatively, these tweets could be interpreted as journalists taking to a new medium for reasons that have more to do with power, holding the powerful to account and ensuring that their audiences are as well informed as possible.

As it goes, there is little evidence of journalists self-consciously acting as public servants when they tweet the news, but this is to be expected; metareflection is not the norm in embedded professional routines, though they may still be motivated by principles that are embodied comprehensively enough to go without saying. However, this dovetails with the temptation to read too much into the mundane stuff of work – a kind of valiant ordinariness, a laudable commitment to getting the facts out there, whatever the surrounding chaos and constraints. And this would be of a piece with the wishful projection diagnosed in much of the commentary around social media protest cultures criticized in chapter 8, a determination to uncover resilience and steadfastness that necessitates its observation. We have seen that commitments to political reform and freedom of speech are known to motivate most Arab journalists, but this does not mean that their every tweet counts as evidence of such motivations. Nor are those tweets meaningless. If we hang on to that distinction between the two inflections of intention, it becomes possible to parse these reportorial tweets using two distinct senses of meaningfulness. Specifically, it means separating any notion of professional mission from what makes it meaningful to get up and go to work everyday: the difference between what makes one's professional life a meaningful one to have lived and why it makes unproblematic sense to pick up a smartphone to check one's emails, or to buy petrol and set off in the direction of the office.

What, then, motivates the regular and incremental dissemination of news on social media, news that is mainly about processes unfolding and timetables elapsing? Even if a journalist possesses an unshakeable sense of professional mission, it is unlikely to play much of a role in the lived experience of tweeting that Annan's statement has been pushed back by twenty minutes. That dedication is rolled into the journalistic routines acquired across the duration of a career, inextricable from the tics and tips that make work ordinarily doable with the time and resources available. Being on Twitter offers up more opportunities for the affective hit of seeing your work being read and spread and responded to, and in the empirical chapters to come there is much more evidence of the palpable pleasures of audience interaction – pleasures that far outweigh the pains of trolling and surveillance. In the present sample, though, there is little in the way of interaction between journalists and followers, in which case affectively felt meaningfulness is more likely akin to the pleasure of seeing one's words on the printed page. As with print journalism, the experience is predicated not only on the physical objectification of those words but also the recognition it makes real; the experience of your tweets going out is rendered meaningful not just by seeing them appear on a screen but having learned through past experience that their broadcasting will be validated as constituting professional practice. Validated by whom is a fair question, and a fair answer is that while it need not amount to actual others – people responding in ways that explicitly enact professional recognition – it cannot be simply posited by the tweeter. Social media users' imagined audiences are just that, works of imagination, but that is different from fabrications, and from Litt's (2012) work in this area we know that even in the absence of actual feedback audiences are not projected fantasies but thought-through assemblages of ideal-type readers, colleagues and, especially, bosses. To put this more concretely, the meaningfulness to journalists of engaging with social media might not be predicated on actual interaction, but nor is it just about faith in the power of journalism or these platforms; it is also the felt awareness of how many people follow them and who those people are. But whatever form validation takes, the point is that in order to sustain tweeting routines it needs to render them just doable; this is not about reporters mopping sweating brows and valiantly posting updates in the face of overwhelming obstacles and inhibitors. While form and content vary and sometimes contradict, this is what comes across most clearly in the breaking-news tweets: an unambiguous sense that for professional journalists this is a culture of practices they are at home in, a culture in which it is worthwhile being invested.

Whether proceeding into the world on the basis of an acquired sense of professional validation is *realistic* or not is another matter: the principle of hysteresis tells us that habituated dispositions have a tendency to outlast the particular conditions in which they were forged. But the disposition is experienced as a natural meaningfulness in persisting in disseminating information despite the countless others now doing likewise. What the tweets considered here show is that such perseverance is worn lightly, and by extension we can say that this is necessarily the case: claims to meaningfulness made desperately, or at great cost, are insufficient to sustain the daily routines instinctively thought of as worth doing. Perseverance need not be experienced as something noble, or something that expresses a commitment to the journalistic mission. It is instead about *work*, the ritualized enactment of journalistic practices. Through a Bourdieusian prism this can be seen as a kind of no-nonsense, uncomplaining, imperturbable professional identity easily recognized as distinct from others active in producing media content. For Bourdieu (1993) this has to be about status more than anything else, the recognition by others of a specific type of authority won through struggle subsequently forgotten as the role came to be accepted as a natural one. This particular professional identity conceived as a serious but phlegmatic vocation is a way of defending journalistic status on its own terms as opposed to the competing criteria against which it is increasingly found wanting: timeliness, adaptability and, arguably, relevance.

It is possible to take the Bourdieusian framing of professional identity too far, to read strategy into every stereotype and accepted in-group marker of tribal membership, and it bears emphasizing that this line of inference comes out of one mode of tweeting. The categories developed here apply to types of tweet and not types of tweeter, because it was readily apparent that rather than tending to go with one kind to the exclusion of the others, news-breaking tweeters were just as comfortable in the worlds of rhetoric and deliberation. There is nothing schizophrenic about this, as all the modes detailed here are underpinned by the same basic orientation to the world. Whether waxing lyrical, sparring with colleagues or passing on information deemed useful, there is a disposition at work that instinctively finds meaning in methodically and repeatedly documenting, categorizing, witnessing and assessing, an industriousness seen as much on Twitter as in more established professional arenas. It is a disposition that does not have to be declaratively asserted, or disingenuously denied, for that matter: against the tendency to see strategizing everywhere when professional practices and the identities associated with them become naturalized, neither pompous proclamations about the nature of democracy nor heads-down industriousness need be regarded as status grabs. Nor does either demand to be romanticized by scholars. Each can be seen as two sides of the same coin, a naturalized inclination to approach whatever is encountered – whether it is momentous, threatening or banal – and to break it down and treat it as work to be done. Personal principle, solidarity and ambition all matter, but it is the workliness of the experience of journalistic practice that makes perseverance worthwhile in everyday contexts.

Inasmuch as the Bourdieusian approach risks reducing all professional motivation to calculation, the everyday meaningfulness line of inquiry can sound merely psychological – ways of coping in a world that is arbitrary and essentially meaningless. Both perspectives have something to tell us, and each seems less overreaching when they are rendered phenomenologically, as things that just happen – albeit with conditions and implications – in all walks of life. The epistemological disposition that journalists enact in this sample as elsewhere does not equate to dourness, relentless professionalism or self-mystification. It has been observed here that journalists, like anyone else, are prone to ostentatious and flamboyant language as well as bitchiness and defensiveness, and this might have real consequences in terms of the health of deliberation in the Arab world. The journalistic disposition is not the opposite of non-journalistic ones, and the tweeters here were happy enough diving into the entertaining and trivial as well as reporting the latest words from political sources and engaging in heated debate: references to sport and links to Michael Jackson videos on YouTube pepper their feeds. It was seen above that for Papacharissi and Oliveira this kind of felicity with switching between the substantial and trivial is something journalists have signally failed to master as yet, but the evidence here shows that there is a recognition among journalists that social media platforms are not newsrooms or gleaming showcases for their unadulterated professionalism, that a different kind of being at home applies here. Comfort in this world is not always obvious from the tweets they left during these events, but it seems compatible enough with a disposition that sees the world as comprising things to identify, interpret and communicate. Among the hyperbole and silliness sits a commitment to sizing things up, responding without hesitation to absolutely any emergent phenomenal object by weighing it, giving it a name, drawing connections to other objects, thinking about what implications it has for how things play out from here and talking about it authoritatively.

At the structural level there is nothing innocent about the epistemological orientation to the world. Journalists with an embodied instinct for turning phenomena into knowledge are disciplinarians, their knowledge imposing and inciting selves and not just enlightening them. The final chapter asks whether it is possible for journalists to play this role differently, making social change intelligible in ways that are usually unthinkable within professional discourses and the local repetitions of daily life. For now, though, the point is that discourse is not some metasystem that has people and their thoughts and actions as effects. We are all in the business of making knowledge when invited to think about and comment on the changing world around us. To argue that we do so as unthinking automata is a normative claim that ascribes primary, always-already agency to discourse itself, and this can only be an act of faith. What is emerging here is the importance of understanding the experience of change not just as something we are required to respond to or have passively done to us but something we actively make knowledge about. This will not always be a reflexive process, and it may or not amount to any kind of agency, but how it is experienced as a mode of practice is central, not peripheral. And that means looking more closely at the lived contexts in which discursive production about change happens, in work routines or social ones, full of affective motivations and payoffs as well as individual and collective strategizing. Only by breaking our analysis down to the basic building blocks of meaningfulness in all their banality and repetitiveness is it possible to understand how people experience even the most tumultuous of times. And this opens up a tantalizing possibility for journalists around the world as well as for publics at large: that maybe it is through, and not in spite of, the merely felt rhythms of everyday life, rather than through revelatory ruptures in that quotidian experience, that we apprehend the scale and meaning of social change.

Chapter Four

Change and Hysteresis in Cairo

We now come to the fieldwork-based section of the book, based on interviews with journalists and workplace observations in Cairo and Beirut. Phenomenological research comes with particular methodological challenges, most of which are concerned with the epistemological status of everyday experience. The objective is not to focus on the banal for the sake of it, but to understand how embedded routines and normalized ways of responding to stimuli instinctively underpin the experience and understanding of political and social change. But this can easily lead to a certain awkwardness in setting up and conducting interviews with journalists and other professionals who, already wary of excitable Western academics and their preconceptions of what is unfolding in the Arab world, are nonplussed by being asked at what time they get up and how they travel to work. This is easy enough to rationalize by way of a little self-deprecation about the tendency of scholars to wade into unknown territories with rigid analytical models and the subsequent need to put human beings back at the centre of the narrative of what we really should not refer to as the Arab Spring. But it is also somewhat disingenuous, in that the ultimate aim of this kind of research is to access aspects of everyday experience which are not usually present to the consciousness of individuals (Bourdieu, 1977: 3). There are exceptions to this, such as those with an already existing tendency towards self-reflexivity, or those who have studied philosophy at some point, or moments in an interview where a participant makes an epistemological break with their habituated being in the world to see themselves as objects for an academic other. As a rule of thumb, however, to get beyond a straightforward description of experience to something more ambitious – explaining why change is experienced the way it is – means reading into participants' words things that are not explicated.

This means walking something of a tightrope, attempting to do justice to their accounts without falling back on the notion that the best way to give voice is simply to relay what someone says. It means pulling back from regarding a participant as disingenuous, merely enacting practices of impression management, or else deluded or in denial about the reality of their circumstances, while affirming the validity of reading between the lines. The only way to do this well is transparently, as will be seen in the following sections that pull apart reflections on three main themes: working life, professionalism and change. Further, it should be emphasized that no claims are made about the representativeness of the samples: almost all of the Egyptian interviewees, for instance, share a view of the Muslim Brotherhood that is not just critical but broadly cynical, but it cannot be inferred from this that all media professionals in Cairo would agree. Likewise, it will be seen in the next chapter that several of the Lebanese journalists who participated had a proclivity for philosophical and academic theoretical frames of reference. There may be a case to be made that the Lebanese journalistic field is distinctly intellectual in its leanings, in the manner of Brazil or, historically, Italy, but this is not the place for such a thesis.

When asked to characterize their working lives, Egyptian respondents unanimously reached for one word: busy. By this they meant busier than before the overthrow of Mubarak, but also busier because of the demands and affordances of new technologies. Several who had worked as political reporters described the Mubarak era as dull, where they were reduced to regurgitating deathless press releases about the activities of the president: opening libraries, receiving forest dignitaries and so on. For others working at *Al-Ahram*, the distinction between pre- and post-2011 was not as distinct, with criticism of the government perfectly possible, though often with a degree of flak and well-established red lines around Mubarak and his family, the military and the police. But for all, the proliferation of strikes, demonstrations and street fighting was manifest in terms of workload: Omar, emphasized that 'now there are demonstrations *every day*' in a way that suggested more than anything a real imposition on his schedule, and Mariam, the editor of a political newspaper and website, spoke about having to make editorial decisions about which demonstrations to cover when they outnumbered the staff available to her. There was also a recognition that Egypt lacked a journalistic tradition of covering oppositional politics (see also Sakr, 2013) and that they were in many cases still finding their feet with regard to reporting political news – it will be seen below that the same is not true for political commentary and analysis, where no such doubts are aired. The same editor admitted candidly that in their rush to get a story out on an attack on Christians, her team erred by referring to them specifically as Copts – against their editorial policy of avoiding sectarian framing wherever possible, a mistake that would not have been made had there been more time. Others variously referred to not having the time to think, to breathe, to make decisions and to catch up.

Busyness is a relative concept, as well as a phenomenologically interesting one (Pontari & Schlenker, 2000). When Ahmed exclaimed with exasperation that he received a hundred emails a day, what was clearly unacceptable to him is par for the course elsewhere. Sara recounted the start of her working day as being overloaded with reading demands – 'I have so much to read! The *New York Times*, the *Guardian*, the *Independent*, and then there's the Egyptian papers, the Arab ones, all this before the morning [editorial] meeting' – which again is open to different interpretations. *Al-Ahram*'s newsroom seemed less than frenetic at the time this research was conducted, though this could have been a matter of timing, and it bears reflecting that newsrooms in London and Washington DC today generally have an atmosphere of quiet industriousness rather than the barely controlled mayhem of cultural mythology (Hemmingway, 2007). Individually, the Cairo journalists certainly had to manage their time and juggle tasks and responsibilities, though no more than encountered in other parts of the world. The particular experience of busyness, however, was one of coping: phrases like 'just keeping on top' of things, 'just managing to do everything' and 'just holding on' pepper the interviews.

Now, popular psychologists (see, for instance, Burkeman, 2013) have observed that for someone to report that they are always busy and barely managing to keep on top of things is both an efficient way to justify the meaningfulness of their work and a means to avoid asking more searching questions about what they do and why. If this were all there were to it, then a group of interviewees claiming to be constantly on the verge of being too busy to get everything done would tell us little about the state of their particular professional environment. And yet the distinct way that busyness is experienced suggests something more complex. Phrases such as those quoted above could well be indicative of Heideggerian inauthenticity: being trapped in the present, constantly thrown from one encounter to the next and forced to react rather than to act with conscious orientation to time, past and future. This could potentially be linked to the political claim that being constantly at the edge of one's ability to cope with workload is not conducive to awareness of the implicatedness of one's position in relation to wider forces of power, instead producing a kind of tunnel vision overwhelmed by the demands of the present. It is also not distant from the argument found in the literature (Neilson & Rossiter, 2005; Hesmondhalgh & Baker, 2008) as well as expressed by two interviewees that precariousness tends to promote a conservative, risk-averse approach to work.

However, what is striking about this cohort is that a clear majority of them reported an unequivocal sense of job security and, usually, satisfaction. Salma was emphatic that her work was making her increasingly depressed because she felt she was doomed to report an ever-deteriorating political situation, but the rest spoke with passion and excitement about their employment and, more to the point here, a feeling of stability and continuity. In some cases this was explicable simply by length of service – twenty-seven years for Ahmed, twenty-six for Mariam and more than ten years for three further interviewees – though it is the texture of this experience that is germane, specifically the reported experience of the self remaining constant while surrounded by flux, or as Ahmed put it, 'like the train running on the same track'. But for less experienced journalists, too, security of employment was fairly unproblematic: for Reem, this meant the guaranteed backing of Qatari funders; for another it was less concrete: Mohamed did not intend to stay in any job for more than five years, so as to retain his 'edge', but there was no doubting the ready availability of work opportunities or his ability to secure them.

Underpinning all of these is something distinct from the realities of the media labour market in Egypt (Mellor, 2005; Sakr, 2013) and also different from falling back on there always being something needing to be done as a means of rationalizing the meaningfulness of work. It is, in short, a relatively stable and enduring investment in journalism as a culture of professional practice. The interviews suggest that this goes further than tribal loyalty or, worse, clinging to a sinking ship. Rather, it is manifest specifically in the epistemological orientation to the world identified in the previous chapter, one which, however chaotic the context, responds to encounters methodically – a learned adaptation to a state of continual thrownness that is iterative rather than immersive. This is at odds with conventional accounts of the Arab uprisings (Berger, 2013) in which journalists were swept aside by the sheer pace of events and technological innovations beyond their ken. Instead, the Cairo journalists locate themselves at the centre of long-term change – not as its agents, but clearly occupying a valorized role in terms of how societies encounter it, and not just how they encounter a never-ending succession of discrete events. Now, it remains a possibility that such faith in journalism's role in society as it undergoes change is misplaced, and it is true that there is little explicit evidence in the interviews of this mooted methodical orientation towards historical change being applied in practice – as will be seen below, futures are conjured up more or less instinctively rather than developed incrementally. But still, it is evident that the idea of journalism as a profession not just existing to document the events of the past twenty-four hours but to take up a permanent position oriented towards the changes coming from within and without society, very much including systemic change, continues to be experienced as stable, and meaningful.

While we will come to statements of journalistic principle momentarily, first it is worth looking at a couple of more concrete manifestations of this idea of journalism having a central position in relation to historic change, if not usually an active one, and not of journalists reduced to the mere cataloguing of facts. Most explicitly, three of the interviewees (Sara, Salma, Reem) were chiefly employed as commentators, and all saw their role as precisely to pull their readers back from the urgency of events as they unfold and to take a broader view. These three made a point of reiterating the continuity of pre- and post-2011 Egypt ('it's the same regime, but with a beard', according to Reem), and Mohamed connected recent events to the rise of pan-Arab nationalism under Nasser, as well as to the arrival of the French in the early nineteenth century. But there is more to this felt experience of journalism's longer-term role than the words of opinion writers, which could, after all, be seen as little more than a land grab of cultural capital. First, there is the obvious satisfaction derived from journalists' standing with their audiences – obvious in tone of voice and body language (Sara, Salma) as much as the words used to convey this esteem. Several (Sara, Omar, Salma, Reem) expressed this in terms of their influence over audiences or the fact that they were trusted to keep abreast of current events (Ahmed, Mariam), but it is also evident in the gleefulness with which several journalists – old and young alike – talked about the quantity and quality of feedback they receive from readers, whether in the form of letters to the editor or posts on social media. Importantly, this is couched as public authority that is achieved only through sustained hard work, and which once attained needs to be carefully nurtured. It is perhaps interesting that in the context of a press as fragmented and heavily editorial as Egypt's, it is felt that individual journalists rather than organizations are regarded as objects of trust and that this applies as much to news reporters as to commentators.

In terms of accounting for the experience of job satisfaction, there is no reason why a degree of egoism should be incompatible with an orientation to the world that has a more durable significance. If this sounds cynical, it is often noted in relation to expressions of esteem in interviews either that the participant is engaging in a strategic presentation of self (Krumpal, 2013) or, more pointedly, that public acclaim is nothing more than popularity, which has little to say about the actual cultural value of the role being performed (Marlière, 2001). The first is easy enough to address: while it is true that all interviewers and interviewees perform their roles according to spoken and more commonly unspoken rules, this does not negate the meaning of that which they marshal as evidence. The second presents a larger hurdle: How can we infer from statements about positive public feedback that a journalist is by some objective measure good at their job, rather than simply adept at telling an audience what it wants to hear, and that this is representative of something rather grandly referred to here as a relatively stable professional orientation? The interviews suggest three factors at play, none of which is unimpeachable. First, it clearly matters where the feedback comes from, and this applies to both the imagined audience (Litt, 2012) – all were asked whom they had in mind when writing their content – and actual interlocutors: variously, colleagues and former colleagues, bosses, other journalists, college professors and friends, as well as respected members of the public. This last category is problematic, as it could refer simply to those who agree with the journalist, but it was common for interviewees to stress that they positively invited criticism but made clear distinctions between feedback that was respectful and 'so rude, so impolite!' (Omar). Second, there is a temporal dimension to esteem: rather than the buzz of receiving some approving feedback, which methodologically could probably only be grasped in real time, the talk was of reputation gained over time and through considerable effort. Finally, and least tangibly, was the manner in which a felt sense of authoritativeness expressed job satisfaction: with hand on heart, or leaning forward to punctuate frankness, or in a hushed tone indicating, imperfectly, genuineness.

Next, several interviewees expressed job satisfaction by way of the authority they possessed in the workplace. Three (Sara, Salma, Reem) spoke positively about 'speaking for' or 'being the voice of' a newspaper or website, though not in a sense that seemed inflated. For Ahmed it was a matter of 'On Tuesdays, I run things', for another it was being the voice of a newspaper in relation to a specialization, social affairs, and a third was frank about how she felt when she was first assigned international politics ('I was, argh! What will I write!? But after three months I was okay, I knew what I was doing' – Sara). While in some of the Beirut interviews journalists spoke of a fierce competitiveness between colleagues, here the tone was not so much collaborative as indicating a collective endeavour which was greater than personal differences ('If my boss wants me to do x, y, z, that's fine, but I also use my own ideas for stories' – Sara). Salma, a female journalist in her early thirties, referred to the difficulties she faced and satisfaction derived from dealing with chairing meetings and line-managing more senior and male colleagues; Reem also talked about the challenges, superable with patience and sensitivity, of working with a team of opinionated individuals ('You can't ask a journalist not to be himself, but if we disagree about something we can work through it'). Others invoked that classic Hegelian mode of professional recognition: being trusted to work autonomously (see also Angella, 2016). Sara, an international politics reporter, had recently acquired a new line manager who was less interventionist and more open-minded about story generation than his predecessor (interestingly, she attributed this to his gender), while Reem, the editor of *Al-Ahram*'s English-language website, noted a distinct lack of government interference, an accommodation suggesting that she was trusted not to cross any red lines but also that she could be trusted to run this government-sponsored publication with a high degree of competence.

Attitudes towards government intervention were revealing. There was a consensus that both journalists and the public enjoyed considerably greater freedom of speech than before 2011, but real professional constraints remained in place – and this is true as much at a privately owned publication such as *Al-Masry Al-Youm* as at the state-owned *Al-Ahram*. However, across the sample there was neither a conceptualization of the state as an obsessive, malignant agent in its own right, still less an embodied sense of professional heroism in the face of official obstruction. Aya spoke of the weekly ritual of sending her copy to the censor before publication as a fairly banal routine. Now, this could indicate the internalization of constraining power, the development of an instinct to self-censor, but beyond the familiar red lines this did not appear to be the case. Instead, she described this process as a hassle, not only for her but for the censor, and one which had become substantively meaningless. It certainly did not have the character of a game of cat and mouse or mutual scheming and subterfuge. Perhaps more evocative still was Aya's depiction of a government censor as someone embarrassed to be doing the work she was doing. This was an individual known professionally by the interviewee, but rather than claim professional betrayal the picture drawn was one of falling on hard times, resorting to demeaning work. While it is impossible to be certain, this did not come across as devalorization dressed up in false sympathy. Interestingly, when Reem talked about the online militias deployed by both the Mubarak and Morsi regimes to police debate and discredit opponents, this was perceived not as the actions of a faceless state but as civil servants being paid – and being required – to do jobs that are less nefarious than odd.

A final specific example illustrates this work-centred orientation to the state and its practices. A growing concern at the time the fieldwork was conducted was government interference in bodies that had historically retained a higher, if still qualified, degree of autonomy, chief among them universities. On the day of the interview with Mariam there was a developing story about a college professor who had, apparently accidentally, killed a student by knocking her down in her car. The word at the time was that the crime scene had been tampered with – cleaned up, essentially – before the police arrived, and it was unclear who was responsible for this act. Government officials in conjunction with the university decided to prevent journalists from entering the campus and issued a press release that was evasive and, more to the point, useless as a news source. What was striking about the way these events were relayed is that while there was clear evidence of a cover-up in play, there was no suggestion of a broader conspiracy. Aya was not surprised at the obstructiveness, but nor was she wholly cynical about it – annoyed would be more accurate. What it meant for her primarily was that on a day that was already very busy, she would have to get involved herself in a story she had hoped to delegate to staffers. Hardly an act of valour or sacrifice, it was simply that she had the contacts who could confirm or deny aspects of a story that would, unquestionably though with more labour than was ideal, see the light of day.

In addition to public esteem and authority among peers, the embodied meaningfulness of everyday work is manifest in another habituated experience which came across in the interviews as felt or affective rather than rationalized. It is also, like popularity, one which is difficult to isolate from egoistic satisfaction and which could easily be branded as superficial: seeing one's words in print (Mohamed, Omar) or hearing one's voice on a recording (Salma). There is ample evidence that, at least for particular media audiences, there is something distinct about the experience of reading words on paper that is held and navigated manually. Here, though, it is the experience of professional selfhood that attains a specifically valorized meaning through the material form it takes. There are a few options for interpreting this. The first is that it represents, in a fairly obvious way, an externalization of the self. In the phenomenological tradition, identity, be it professional, social or cultural, does not emanate from within some idealized self but is developed iteratively, through repeated externalization of posited or imagined identity and internalization of the structures and norms of its environment and fellow actors. While this can be oversimplified as positing that professional identity is a melange of what you think of yourself and what others think of you, the balance between the two depending on individual or collective tendencies to narcissism, solipsism and so on, the nub is not so much *what* others think of you but recognizing the fact *that* you exist as an object for other subjects ('being at home with oneself in another', in Hegel's words), and the world in general. A frisson is produced by seeing one's article in print (Ytre-Arne, 2011), on the one hand recognizing it as an article like any other, an object for audiences to apprehend, while at the same time being conscious that it is also externalized subjectivity.

It should be acknowledged that the emergence of this theme in the interviews is partly explained by methodology. It came up unprompted in three of the first four interviews and subsequently was suggested to interviewees as a potential response to questions that left them lost for words. Specifically, interviewees were told that the research was looking into professional motivation, but it was quickly added that this did not necessarily mean motivation in the change-the-world sense but rather what makes work meaningful (or if this seemed too abstract, what gives professional satisfaction) on a day-to-day basis. Seeing one's own words in print was for many an instinctive response to this line of inquiry, but it is possible that this just made sense as a reasonable answer that would meet the expectations of the interviewer.

However, the affective nature of the responses suggests otherwise. Sara spoke with obvious delight in relating that 'even after eleven years I still keep all of them. I like to have them with me' and 'it never stops being exciting seeing, seeing my name on the front page', while Reem talked about 'pushing the button to make the website go live, knowing that I'm responsible for all that'. Omar used similar wording ('there's nothing like it, even now I think, I can show this to my parents') as well as a similar tone – heightened, confiding but also admitting failure in expressing exactly what it is about this act that elicits such a response. As with public esteem, the key here seems to be the temporal dimension. There is certainly no sense of print newspapers being tomorrow's rubbish, and as such the pleasure derived from seeing a self-authored text in material form could be interpreted as a fantasy of solidity and a denial of ephemerality. But the interviews reveal a conception of journalistic production not as valorized as an act in itself but as something collective and cumulative. Rather than the individual article being turned into an object of (self-)love, then, it is the feeling of being part of an ongoing endeavour whose significance is not in doubt. In some cases that endeavour takes the form of something like a public sphere where the overriding concern is continuing debate, if not the resolution of issues of shared concern. For others it is closer to the clichéd notion of journalism as first draft of history: it is clear that all those interviewed in Cairo regard their past work as a living archive, not labour whose fruits have been consigned to the dustbin. The ultimate return on a day's labour might not reach fruition for years, or indeed not at all, but there is something in seeing one's work objectified that attaches it to a more or less stable, long-term project whose meaningfulness at the level of the everyday is unproblematic.

This feeling of collective endeavour was put eloquently by Ahmed, who characterized himself as the most vocal critic of the government at *Al-Ahram*: 'I write for the readers. The government? They'll do what they want. They won't change because of me. But it's an accumulation: the revolution came because of what we collectively wrote.' This captures well the notion of journalists not only as authorized witnesses but active agents of social change (Pies, 2008), but whose role in such change is not and cannot be apparent in everyday life. While in his case such a perspective is the result of many years' experience, statements about journalists' collective mission can appear more than anything as articles of faith, or even platitudes. This is not to suggest that any statements of journalistic principle by interviewees were disingenuous, but epistemologically they operate in particular ways. In short, if a participant is asked about their motivations and the responses are generically moral, for instance, then this should be seen not as the expression of quotidian meaningfulness but the spontaneous invocation of a collective set of values and norms whose internalization is necessitated by immersion in a particular symbolic world. This is a statement neither of conspiracy nor condescension: it means that the more or less seamless conscious experience of the world that we all share is predicated on much – most – of it taking the form of encounters experienced as given, not emerging to consciousness at all. When asked, or when it feels like one has been asked, to express one's professional values, it is normal enough instinctively and unreflexively to enact a shared moral code whose recognition is itself a condition of mutual recognition of subjects in a particular professional – or political, or cultural – context. With that in mind let us turn to in vivo expressions of principle in the Cairo interviews.

First, statements about speaking for or representing the interests of the Egyptian public are liberally scattered throughout the interviews. Sara, whose work involves refracting international affairs through an Egyptian lens, states straightforwardly that she sees her role as 'speaking for Egypt.... I have to write about Egypt, because we're *Egyptian*'. Others talk of writing for generically identified 'readers', or being responsible to and for said readers. There are a couple of related claims around this theme that ring less than true, however. The first is that there is blanket acknowledgement of the partisan, fragmented nature of all Egyptian media, whether press, television or online, as well as a sense that this is getting worse in the post-2011 era ('people are starting to live in bubbles' – Reem). With the exception of Omar, who talks of the importance of 'representing your perspective', though, they all claim to speak for all Egyptians – 'I'm always neutral', 'I never put my views in', 'it's important to be objective' – while working for organizations that have a clear house political line. In some cases this came across as questionable but reasonable, such as Reem, who claimed that she's always neutral *because* her perspective is humanitarian (see also Seib, 2002). For others, there is palpable equivocation between claims of neutrality, being employed to write on specific issues for particular publications and clear satisfaction derived from having influence over their audiences. The second claim is one of humility: two journalists (Mariam, Salma) use the word 'humble' explicitly, Omar refers to seeing himself as a public servant, while others claim an affinity: 'I'm used to communicating with ordinary people. I have my own channel' (Ahmed); 'I use simple words to talk to people on the street' (Mariam); 'Interacting with my readers – *this* is what makes my work different from everyone else' (Sara). If phrases like 'ordinary people' and 'people on the street' are ambiguous in the relationship they posit between subject and object, there are many more occasions where audiences are openly criticized for being credulous, naïve or apathetic.

Public credulity is expressed in ways familiar to journalism studies elsewhere: 'People believe what they want' (Omar); 'I know that he [a journalist at *Al-Shorouk*] is writing from an anti-government position, but do they [the readers]? No' (Ahmed); 'The followers of Ikhwein [the Muslim Brotherhood] would commit suicide if they were told to' (Sara). Naïvety is sometimes indicated in fairly disparaging terms – 'Readers think it's easy to know stuff. Just go and *read*, I want to tell them' (Reem); 'But what are they *really* angry about? What do they want, *really*?' (Omar) – but also in ways that are perhaps a little patronizing but sympathetic: 'Now we have an open political environment, the clash of ideas. People are nervous, they're not used to it' (Omar). Apathy is indicated in broad terms: 'People want to stay at home and do nothing' (Ahmed); 'Egyptians are not interested in politics. They're interested in things running smoothly' (Mohamed). Empirically, all of these statements can be read as straightforward authority claims: that is, aside from the claims made about the character of publics or audiences, and the varying ways in which they are made, they all have a secondary function that is to position the speaking subject in a privileged position relative to the spoken object. There is nothing remarkable or uniquely Egyptian about this: sociologies of Western journalists (Tumber & Webster, 2006; Markham, 2011b) have previously found similarly that both contempt for audiences and avowals of public service alike encode claims to cultural authority. It does, though, add a further dimension to the finding that Egyptian journalists, advisedly or not, have not found themselves sidelined or felt their status endangered by recent developments, political or technological. Empty pieties about professional values have limited efficacy in sustaining meaningfulness at the everyday level; explicit or imagined self-positionings in relation to audiences or 'ordinary people', however, offer multiple, routinizable practices that could very feasibly underpin an orientation experienced as meaningful.

All things considered, there was very little outright scorn displayed towards Egyptian news audiences. Ahmed expressed the views of several interviewees when he said that 'People need to change before we have democracy', but responses varied as to the likelihood of that transformation. It is striking that only one interviewee – Mariam – articulated a perspective heard in so much of the academic literature on the Arab Spring: that it has been led by ordinary people, and that conventional politics and mainstream media have been left floundering in its wake: 'People on the street are moving faster than we are. We have to keep up'. She does not exaggerate the effectiveness of new social movements but is optimistic about the implications: 'Are they organized? No. But whatever happens is something good. If it's crushed, we'll get up again. Parties will have to change, and institutions, too. Ultimately it's about social justice, human rights'. This makes sense given her long career as a political advocate and activist, and also the nature of the organization she runs. For the rest, however, there was a clear sense of a populace that has to be led towards political change: Egyptians are used to being led, too ready to follow the word of Mubarak or the Brotherhood, and if things have to change then new leadership is required. It is tempting to read this as a sign of out-of-touch elitism, but this is not how it came across, at least not in general. Rather, there was a sense of a cohort that did not sit aloof from its public, which felt a conflicted solidarity with it rooted in everyday practice, and which felt a responsibility for it that simultaneously lent solidity to its own confidence.

Integrity can likewise sound hollow if expressed in vivo in an interview, but if looked at relationally – through distinctions made between particular practices and individuals – the work it does becomes clearer. This is not to suggest that any of the interviewees lack integrity, simply that for us to make sense of professional principle it is necessary to unpack how it is collectively recognized – and as ever, there is much more to this than following a code of conduct or winning awards. One mode of integrity that came up a number of times was speaking the truth to audiences. We are used to journalists viewing their role as speaking truth to power, and it will be seen immediately below that while this is certainly pervasive among the Cairo cohort, it is a principle that is simultaneously bluntly stated and fudged. But in light of the fact that audiences often appear to the journalists as infantile, there is integrity in telling them what they do not want to hear – as distinct from those commentators, referred to as 'lazy' and 'big-headed' (Omar), who routinely spoon-feed their readers content designed to confirm their existing prejudices. Sara, for instance, was working on a story on child abuse: its prevalence in Egypt, but also the injustice of a legal ruling that prevents women from removing children from the familial home where the father has been convicted of abuse. Sara was clearly passionate about breaking her story, and when asked if she thought it would be a hard sell to her readers, the response was unequivocal: 'We have to save these children, because we're all Egyptians'. What is striking about this is the marked absence of a distinction between personal values and news values, nothing about likely editorial resistance or the need to develop an angle to engage readers – perhaps by personalizing it ('This could happen to you') or linking it to a high-profile case. Integrity is absolute and deontological, not something ineffable and exuded through obtuse markers of authority as existing sociologies of professionalism would predict (Waisbord, 2013). But what becomes apparent is that this in no way means that professional integrity in an Egyptian journalistic context is a simple matter of heart-on-sleeve morality.

Perhaps because of more years spent at the coalface, or maybe because of the subject matter, Ahmed was less emotive in explaining why he was working on a story on mismanagement of the water of the river Nile. He was, though, similarly deontological: he knew full well that readers find this topic dull, but it was so self-evidently important that the question of working to make it newsworthy did not arise. Looked at comparatively, this is arguably admirable: in a British newspaper, whether tabloid or broadsheet, such a story would tap into broader grievances about state ineptitude or home in on what it means for a reader's family. Whereas Sara had been explicit about the need to foster public engagement ('We have to tell them what's important, to say here, look at this'), for Ahmed the integrity consists in the writing itself – it is up to audiences whether they bother to keep up with the issues he reports on; the importance of the work is a given. This did not come across as arrogant; this was one of the participants who spoke about the humility with which he approached his work, though to speak of humility and acting in a way recognizable as humble in a particular context are two different things. Likewise, to laugh self-deprecatingly as he did at 'whether it pays to be good' in reference to his own refusal to accept bribes can be interpreted as charming, or strategic, or both (see also Vobič & Milojević, 2014). In any case, Ahmed spoke eloquently about the two questions he said all Egyptian journalists will be asked at some point: 'Are you with us?' and 'What do you want?' – the former a thinly veiled threat, the latter meaning anything from 'a small piece of land, or a villa in the north' to a college place for your child. Integrity, then, is something more equivocal in this case and seemingly tied to day-to-day job satisfaction: taking work seriously, but oneself less so. If we wanted to, we could pick apart the strategic effectiveness of this kind of performance of integrity, but what is more relevant is what it says about a professional orientation that is self-assured and derives personal satisfaction, knowingly reflexive, from the forgoing of glamour and riches (Matheson 2003).

Ahmed, like nearly all of the participants from *Al-Ahram*, clearly enjoyed working there, and central to this was the ability to work with a fair degree of autonomy and not having to compromise one's values beyond what is editorially necessary and politically pragmatic. There is a glaring dissonance between this more or less happy situation and the picture painted of the rest of the journalistic field in Egypt (Sakr, 2013). For Aya the factor that distinguished her ability to work with self-respect was that she was employed by an English-language publication: 'Anyone working for Arab papers is always under lots of pressure to be on-message, and just to make stuff up. And journalists need work, they need to survive, so they go along with it'. From her point of view this has got worse since the fall of Mubarak, with a proliferation of politicized titles owned by 'people trying to buy a piece of the message pie'. Several others spoke of the fragmentation of the Egyptian press as being obvious to anyone working in the industry but little understood by the public at large. Reem sums this up well, talking of the crystallization of a partisan media landscape from around 2007 onwards: '*Al-Watan* is National Security; *Al-Shorouk* is basically a wing of the Muslim Brotherhood; *Al-Masry Al-Youm* is its owners, kind of the neo-liberals not close to Mubarak, plus the Army; *Al-Akhbar* is on the left, well sort of. And young reporters need to be schooled, because they don't know. You hear what you want to hear' (see also

Khamis, 2009). For Aya, though, in the post-2010 period ownership increasingly lacks transparency, and this means that despite a growing number of titles, work is increasingly precarious for journalists. Larger newspapers – she cites the *Daily News* and the *Egypt Independent* – are 'cutting wages, firing people, doing whatever they can to raise funds and cut costs', while if you find yourself at a start-up website or print publication it can be difficult to know where the money is coming from and what you might be asked to do in its service. Working within the red lines of the Mubarak era was tolerable on a quotidian level because 'at least you know where you are'; Aya's obvious discomfort working under new but unidentified owners stemmed in large part from not being told where the lines were.

Reem spoke for many when she said, memorably, that 'I don't want to be a flower in anyone's jacket'. Autonomy and not having to compromise one's professional standards clearly represent something more than values instinctively invoked when prompted and are embedded in the basic meaningfulness of working life. This, though, raises some questions. It is not the case that this group of journalists wax poetic about the necessity of professional values in the abstract while inhabiting working environments where routinely enacting such principles is impossible. Three interviewees openly defended the idea that there were times when rules should be broken in the pursuit of other, specifically political goals. Reem, for instance, worked at Al-Jazeera up until Mubarak's fall and then left to work at *Al-Ahram Online*. She explained that during the revolution she broke her own rules of objectivity – not, she emphasized, broadcasting lies, but sending messages intended to help the revolution on its way. Her departure, however, demonstrates the limits of professional flexibility and the durability of self-perceived integrity: she felt that Al-Jazeera was morphing too quickly into a mouthpiece for the Muslim Brotherhood, and that 'later you'll be asked to break objectivity rules for something you *don't* believe in'. In short, principle matters. And yet the manner in which principles were often articulated suggest a significant disconnect with daily professional life, and the empirical status of such statements warrants a closer look.

Most generically, a majority of interviewees used imperatives to explain their motivations: 'I have to do it', 'Whatever happens, we must tell people about it', 'But I just have to continue', 'We must live together and love each other and we can contribute to that', 'We're new to this [democratic politics] but we must speak it'. For most this is a matter of embodied personal conviction beyond any broader claims about the importance of the role journalism plays in society: 'I work really hard to get the truth', 'I will never give up', 'I'll write my opinion and I'll leave it to God', 'I'll keep trying as long as I'm alive'. We saw in the previous chapter that there are methodological options for responding to what might be regarded as fairly typical use of heightened rhetoric by Arab speakers: put simply, it is possible to pull back from an essentialist generalization and look at what such phrases do, particularly in the context of a research interview. And what they do primarily is decontest: they put beyond the realms of discussion the idea that perhaps embodied, habituated practices of virtue are degraded to the point of futility in such professionally compromised circumstances. In one sense, such phrases appear to fall into the rhetorical category of 'even if it's impossible, we will continue to strive, no matter what'. Now, such expressions certainly have the effect of closing off a line of questioning, and they also play into romanticized notions of valiant journalists persevering in the face of unimaginable obstacles. For this reason it makes sense to regard them as decidedly less meaningful in everyday contexts. These are precisely the kind of phrases elicited instinctively when speakers are pulled out of everyday context, but they are most certainly not what these journalists tell themselves on a day-to-day basis to give their working lives meaning. That which underpins quotidian meaningfulness are not inspirational bromides, and it has been seen here that even if it were not the case that participants happened to find themselves in some of the few workplaces in Egypt where it is possible to work with autonomy and principle, integrity can subsist as a locus of meaning also in contexts where its outward application is compromised or degraded.

We are now in a position to assess the ways in which the journalists interviewed experience systemic change on a day-to-day basis. However, it is important to table a couple of caveats. First, anyone's conception of the future at any given point in time is of course determined in large part by the present and past, and the aim is not to belittle any such conceptions as naïve or quaint. The second is that no one is in the course of everyday existence able to grasp shifts in the preconditions of one's own consciousness: if the way we think is, broadly speaking, a determination of social and material context, then every incremental twist and turn of history will not be experienced as such. And yet, to the extent to which respondents all keenly sense change going on around them – for better or worse, or simply an experience of things being in flux – such experiences cannot be simply dismissed, though, nor should they be taken as given. It is likely that some reported experiences of change are just unreflective projections of an inhabited present, that which you spontaneously invoke when someone unexpectedly asks you to relate how your world is changing. But others appear to suggest something else: if not an idealized Heideggerian authenticity, fully conscious of past determination and oriented towards all possible futures and their implications, then an embodied sense of stakes and orientation towards and investment in how things may turn out in the long term.

Let us be clear about what would constitute evidence of such an experience of change. First, it is not the same thing as the positing of agency: just because someone tells you they have a part to play in determining the future of their society, this does not in itself demonstrate an experience of everyday presents oriented by an embodied awareness of longer-term change. Likewise, it should not be assumed that the positing of futures, as represented by dispositions of optimism, pessimism or fatalism, proves an absence of longer-term temporal orientation. The interviews are suffused with such statements, and what they amount to empirically are either perfectly reasonable responses to questions posed in an artificial, discursive setting or instinctive enactments of naturalized disposition, or both. But there is also plenty of evidence that these are not individuals perennially trapped in presents, 'just coping' to respond to each encounter into which they find themselves thrown, unable to do more than throw out an imagined future like a bodily reflex. It is by no means consistent, but there are ample indications of a temporal orientation that is iterative – not in the sense of one damned thing after another, but as encounters even amid chaos and instability as sequential and coterminous with broader change, the stakes of which are felt, again haphazardly, in everyday professional experience.

Most viscerally, several interviewees relayed experiences of changes in personal security (Sakr, 2013). It is now well documented (Rice, 2013; El-Din et al., 2015; Kurtz, 2015; Tadros, 2015) that sexual assaults against women have increased significantly in Egypt since 2010, and two participants (Sara, Rana) talked about feeling unsafe on the streets of the capital, about not going out either alone during the day or at all at night, and about worrying about their children as they make their way to and from school. For both, this was a new development. Ahmed talked specifically about the dangers facing journalists in the post-Mubarak era, albeit in a fairly offhand fashion ('It's easier to get killed now'), while Omar elaborated in more general terms on the growing sectarian violence directed at media professionals. In all of these cases, the corporeal nature of the threats might suggest an orientation to the future based on self-preservation: faced with the prospect of being killed or raped, daily encounters are experienced at least in part through anticipation aiming at survival rather than gaining advantage or maintaining equilibrium; posited future stability or anarchy then reveals little more than the projection of a desire to continue living. But the manner in which these sentiments were expressed points to something more complicated. For Sara, the felt sense of being personally at risk was very much tied to political and technological change: soon after depicting the streets as unsafe she said 'you can't trust the police, the government, no one' and later added Facebook to this list. Ungenerously, one could attribute this to a paranoid outlook – she reported placing a sticking plaster over her laptop's webcam so as to prevent them, the government, from spying on her – but naming particular institutions suggests an orientation which goes beyond blanket fear and also the attitude of generalized decline one often encounters in interviews, not to mention world views typical of many news organizations.

More to the point, all four journalists were unambiguous about their love for their work. And importantly, this love was manifest not just as deeply felt pride about their sense of mission but also quotidian enjoyment. It is perfectly feasible for both Sara and Salma to speak of personal, bodily risk while deriving pleasure from what they do; this is by no means a matter of grimly persevering in the face of personal sacrifice. It is similarly possible to refer to journalists being the targets of sectarian violence while simultaneously being gleeful about the opportunities that freedom of speech and access to networked media have brought. The perceived parlous state of institutions does not, quite, have the ring of Western malaise theory: it is true that mistrust of authority is rife, but this is more commonly attributed to a collective failure – 'all Egyptians are responsible', said Ahmed, for a present characterized by political conspiracy and bureaucratic incompetence – that may or may not be corrected. None of this is to impart a noble refusal of fatalism, and many of those interviewed were strongly pessimistic about Egypt's political future. But it is striking that both a perspective which views the current state of Egypt's state institutions as essentially rotten (a failed state, according to Reem) and one which holds out little optimism for their reform nonetheless coexist fairly seamlessly with future orientations – personal, professional, societal – that are, whether dispositionally positive or negative, open, experienced as up for grabs.

As for the events of 2011 themselves, there were mixed accounts of what exactly had changed and with what implications for the future. The phrase 'Arab Spring' was still widely used in 2013, though either with a qualification inserted early on in the interview that they did not personally view recent regional history with anything like the connotations of political awakening this carries or simply a tone of voice or facial expression indicating complicity between interviewer and interviewee, indicating that the vacuity of the term is taken as understood. The term clearly remains useful as shorthand for a complex set of developments. A small majority were comfortable referring to Mubarak's overthrow as a 'revolution' unqualified, though Omar makes it clear that he never uses this word ('uprising, maybe'), while Reem calls the Tahrir Square protest movement a 'rehearsal'. Three explicitly stated that 'nothing has changed', with Ahmed adding that 'it's all the same, just with Islamic slogans on top' and Mohamed explaining that 'the uprising was only against the regime, not the system'. Two other misconceptions were also addressed. The first was that the protest movement was peaceful: while many protestors were of course non-violent and principled in being so, for others agitation and provocation were central strategies. The second is that the uprising in Egypt was popular in origin and only subsequently hijacked by the Muslim Brotherhood. On the contrary, this cohort identified the Ikhwan as key players from the start, corroborating research (see also Frisch, 2013; de Smet, 2014) documenting their role in setting fire to police stations in the build-up to 25 January 2011.

It says something of the lack of representativity in the sample that all but one of the interviewees (Reem) were committed opponents of the Muslim Brotherhood. Be that as it may, what comments about them reveal is not so much the role they played in the overthrow of Mubarak but what is at stake in recent events. Mariam notes that burgeoning freedom of speech has not changed the country's politics substantively, but it is 'bringing to the surface deep divisions' that were always there. Similarly, Omar says that sectarianism was always there 'beneath the surface', but only now is it emerging into the open, as political groups vie for power and, crucially, a partisan media exists to amplify differences and incite 'uneducated' masses to action and, in some cases, violence. It is noticeable that for no one were recent power struggles about principle as such, namely about whether Egypt should be run according to democratic or Islamic doctrine. Mohamed notes that 'historically, Egypt has been just a bunch of gangs', and five others emphasize the view that the Muslim Brotherhood are only interested in power, not religion, which is used only as a means to recruit and control their followers. Hypocrisy is widely alleged.

But it is again the way such claims are expressed that is of primary interest to us. Sara seemed to relish characterizing the Brotherhood's desire for power as a hunger, an obsession: 'They *dreamed* of this. They have power in their *hands*. They want to control *everything*, including *people*.' Thus is the connection between the rise of the Brotherhood and the decline of women's rights made clear: this is about power over individuals, over bodies, rather than parliaments and councils. Omar, meanwhile, resorts to a conspiratorial whisper to explain the Brotherhood's appetite for destruction. 'Relish' is again the best word to convey the tone with which he details how they are intent on bringing about not just violent confrontation but a total national collapse, as this would enable them to seize absolute power. Consistent with Mariam and Mohamed above, this conception of historical context sits easily enough alongside a satisfying working life. When asked where he thought things were heading, Omar agreed that Egyptian politics was becoming increasingly polarized, with moderate and minority groups rapidly being squeezed out until only the Brotherhood and the Salafists remain. Reem and two others derisively compared Egypt's future to Lebanon's, with a straight-down-the-middle fissure patched together by cynical politicking and sectarian media, all in the interests of a self-serving elite distant from the interests of 'ordinary people'. But, as with Mariam above, Reem holds those ordinary people as responsible as the elites carrying out the conspiracy: 'things are changing, but people don't notice, they don't want to know'.

Others imagine a more positive future, with Sara going so far as to suggest that while the Brotherhood 'will never leave, never give up power', 'something more genuine will come', and it will take the form of a regional force of democratization – comparisons with Lebanon aside, this was one of the few concessions made to regional politics, the frame invoked in the interviews being otherwise resolutely national. In any case, neither Sara's nor Mariam's predictions are the point here. What is important is that each has voiced something other than a present-filled future, a future whose arrival has been worked through and anticipated in markedly different ways, but each suggesting a temporal orientation that goes beyond now and then. This is above all professional and not simply indicative of an inability to imagine a future in which one's work is impossible or irrelevant. For Omar, expression of opposition to the government (if not the head of state) has always been possible, and it is reasonable to presume that given what has not changed as well as what has, this will continue to be the case. Not straightforwardly, perhaps, but not extending professional adaptability to breaking point. For Mariam, her 'better tomorrow' is qualified by the fact that 'some people will work with any regime and resist change' and that these will include people she works with. Again, whatever the validity of her prediction, there is more than wishful thinking in what she says: an acknowledgement of the broader political stakes, as well as a not unreasonable assumption about a degree of continuity in the way that workplaces operate. In both cases there is no denial of history being made, nor simple affirmation that they will not be bystanders to it. Rather, there is a consciousness of the naked struggle for power that lies at the base of all historical change, for better or worse and however it is understood in narrative terms, as well as a consciousness of that which does not change in the midst of political upheaval. Presumed contextual continuity as an adaptive mechanism in the face of turmoil seems reasonable rather than fantastic.

Among all of this were scattered remarks about Cairo's notorious traffic, colleagues not pulling their weight, husbands not doing their share of the housework, the opening of a new café or a new film, holidays and school choices. These were encouraged rather than indulged as marginalia, and when interviewees began to wax, grandiloquent care was taken to prod them back towards the everyday. This is less artificial than it sounds: both generalized pessimism and optimism about the future is easy enough to translate into the prospects of the next generation, as well as the likelihood of mobile telephone and transport infrastructures improving in the next few years. Social rituals prove more impervious to experienced and anticipated change, with birthdays marked and networks maintained whatever the political weather. More such details will be drawn out in the next chapter, and then in chapter 9 the prosaics are embedded more firmly in the principal analytical framework of the book overall. The point is this: These journalists are not noble martyrs to freedom of speech and democracy, but nor does focusing on their quotidian routines reduce them to unthinking machines whose behaviour is explicable only by conditioning. They are self-evidently serious about their work and the others it brings them into contact with, but this seriousness is not usually clinched in critical moments, still less in metareflections on the nature of their vocation. It is a seriousness which sits among all manner of banal realities, worked on day to day, sometimes unevenly but always oriented towards possible futures – and future selves – that remain undetermined. It is finally that sense of stakes, of the future of society as well as who they are and will become being up for grabs, that sustains an experience of change that is not entirely overwhelmed by the demands of the present, nostalgia for the past or wilful future projection.

Chapter Five

Flux and Atrophy in Beirut

The Beirut fieldwork was conducted in April 2014, by which time the initial wave of international optimism about the potential for an Arab Spring had given way to disillusionment, if not despair. This was before the Israeli summer offensive against Hamas in Gaza, as well as the declaration of a caliphate by the Islamic State in Iraq and Syria (ISIS, later rebranded Islamic State) after substantial territorial gains made in the two countries. While the election victory of El-Sisi in Egypt and the escalation of conflict in Libya dominated headlines in the Maghreb, in the Levant the civil war in Syria, which by this time had claimed an estimated two hundred thousand lives and left around two million displaced, generated more column inches and airtime in the region than any other development, and also featured heavily on the international news agenda. The conflict had already spilled over into Lebanon, with Hezbollah actively engaged in combat in Syria in support of the Assad regime, and with sporadic violence in south Lebanon as well as the south of Beirut itself.

However, the Syrian war did not figure as prominently in the interviews as often as or in the form expected – not, apparently, out of any reticence to discuss divisive political issues, but rather because of the particular ways conflict emerges to consciousness in lived, in this case professional, contexts. Others have observed (Tumber & Webster, 2006; Rodgers, 2012) that one encounters a surprising degree of normality when travelling through most war zones, and it is not unreasonable that conflict taking place just over the border thirty miles away, or indeed violence unfolding in different parts of the same city, will be experienced as distant, or even largely absent. Here, this is explained by the fact that Syrian conflict is seen not as something unprecedented and threatening to erupt into daily life. Instead, it is perceived as a continuation of a regional conflict with deep roots, a manifestation of the same forces that led to Lebanon's own civil war that officially ended in 1990 but is viewed by most as unresolved. Certain aspects of the Syrian war, then, are taken as given and as such do not necessarily register in the conscious experience of everyday exchanges – or, it seems, in interviews focusing on the daily routines of professionals whose work inevitably intersects with that conflict and its victims.

Most of the interviews took place in Hamra, historically the Muslim quarter of multi-confessional Beirut but in recent decades home to a thriving café and bar culture noticeably Western in its aesthetics, music and cuisine – a nascent hipster scene was observable at the time the fieldwork was conducted. This area is also home to the headquarters of the newspaper *As-Safir*, and it is a good cultural fit for its staff: several younger employees preferred to meet in their favourite haunts, usually chic cafés with a fashionable clientele. Other interviews were conducted in Gemmayze, traditionally the Christian sector with historical architectural attractions – Greek Orthodox churches and *fin-se-siècle* Parisian style streets – as well as some higher-end restaurants. This is not intended as tourist advice but to give a sense of the atmosphere in which the fieldwork took place: less tense than in Cairo, and rooted in a public culture more pervaded by particular kinds of cultural signification and discourse. Briefly, it is worth noting that between Hamra and Gemmayze lies the rebuilt downtown area known to all as Solidère, after the business consortium associated with assassinated president Rafic Hariri that led, and profited hugely from, a scheme involving construction on a massive scale of high-rise office towers and luxury shopping precincts, as well as the removal of the sector's former, poorer residents. Solidère is also a byword for the consumer culture which was observed by several interviewees (and sociologists such as Khalaf, 2012) to have entranced Lebanon's middle classes, and in particular its youth, evident in the ubiquitous iPhones and Mac PowerBooks in Hamra's coffee shops. The reason for making this point is that some make a direct link between the new consumerism and a collective amnesia about the Lebanese civil war, a kind of denial. If true, this would suggest that the general absence of conflict past or present in the interviews might be a manifestation of something other than its givenness. What became apparent, however, was that all interviewees were in their distinct ways politically engaged and invested, and most motivated by a commitment to humanitarian principles and a desire for national and regional conflict resolution. Such engagement is sustained amid the ordinary and often apolitical rhythms of everyday life, but one is not antithetical to the other. This, then, feeds directly into one of this book's main arguments: that the banalities of quotidian experience are not a barrier to political subjectivity capable of grasping systemic change but the very conditions of its emergence. The final chapter refracts this claim onto audience engagement with distant conflict and suffering, positing that the critique of cosseted western audiences blithely ignorant about the realities of war and revolution is, mostly, misplaced. It is possible for subjective recognition and even solidarity, or something close to it, to subsist even in the context of habituated media experiences that seem on the face of it superficial and fickle.

As in Cairo, when asked about their daily routines, the predominant theme raised by the Beirut cohort was busyness. This again often took the form of just managing to stay on top of things: 'If I just work, work, work all day I can cope with it all' (Dina). There was also the same sense, though, that being at the limit of one's capacity can nonetheless be enjoyable. Louis, for instance, talked of leaving a better paying position at *Al-Hayat* newspaper, describing it as 'a Saudi-backed retirement home' where life is easy so long as you do not rock the boat, because 'I want excitement in my life'. Moving to *As-Safir* meant working harder for less money, but there was no question that it was the right thing to do: in contrast to a professional environment characterized as 'nepotistic, exploitative, dull', he was freer to work on stories he developed himself ('whatever provokes me'), though within reason – he was also happy to take direction from his boss since she shares 'the same mentality, the same spirit'. This is part of a wider discourse of 'being the kind of journalist I want to be' that distinguishes the two cohorts; while it is true that many of the Egyptian journalists emphasized the importance of professional autonomy, here it is more about individual expressiveness and creativity, and that in turn is associated closely with who one *is* and not simply the work one does.

It is true that this might be explained in part by age – Louis was twenty-five, after all – but other evidence points in the same direction. Zaina, for instance, talked about the importance of 'having your say and doing what you love'; Dina said that while in general she enjoys her work tremendously, there are 'robotic days' that have to be endured. Amir juggled three jobs – press, television and teaching, as well as working on a PhD – and while describing himself as having 'workaholic tendencies' took great satisfaction in being able to 'switch mindsets', itself a classic marker of a journalistic skill that is innate rather than learned, the ability to move between different cultural milieus and feel at home in each. As with Louis and Leyla, variety was central to Amir's job satisfaction, as well as a sense of responsibility: while Leyla echoed several Cairo journalists' pride at 'speaking for' her publication, Amir's optimism for his own future lay in part with his being made page editor for comment and analysis at *As-Safir*. Here, then, we find the same combination of esteem within an organization and public profile, being recognized (Angella, 2016) by peers or managers as competent to fulfil the duties of a role seen as strategically important to a newspaper's brand and/or circulation figures, and in doing so to use this platform to engage with and to influence readers: 'I get to decide what to talk about, and what I say about it changes how people think'.

Louis put this clearly in terms of career motivation – 'I got into journalism to be *known*. That's what keeps you going' – while making it clear that he did not mean fame for its own sake. There were fairly lengthy discussions of profile on social media in the interviews with Khalil, Amir and Louis, and it emerged that all of them had several thousand friends or followers (on Facebook one can have up to five thousand friends; beyond that a page is turned into that of a public figure who can be followed). A distinction was consistently made, however, between journalists and commentators who are merely popular and those who are followed by people properly engaged in debates over public issues. Louis dismissed the former category as 'cocktail party' journalists, citing Robert Fisk as an example of someone who has a wide following whose adoration he thrives on, but who no longer has his ear to the ground and writes without fully understanding what is going on. (It is worth noting that Fisk accused *As-Safir* of being effectively run and resourced by the Syrian government in the 1990s.) Technology reporter Khalil had a parallel conception of being known in the right 'kind' of community of writers and readers; he described this as a hacking culture in which all members are collaborative rather than domineering or passive. And, consistent with Louis and Amal, while his was a relatively conventional role at a newspaper, he saw his role as 'not an occupation, it's a way of life'.

Out of context this looks platitudinous, but what he is referring to is something quite particular about the way that symbolic capital works in the journalistic field. Like other fields, this consists in collective valorization, but instead of that collectivity being endogenous here it is as much about links with specialists outside of journalism. For Khalil that means all of the programmers, pirates, activists and geeks as well as journalists interested in technology and sharing a certain world view: there was much talk of Gramsci, for instance, and a forthright belief that journalists are, or should be, public intellectuals who bear a responsibility to lead society towards change. We return to the political dimension of the journalistic field as experienced by interviewees below; for now, what is important is that professional esteem among this cohort is contingent on recognition in other quasi-autonomous fields in a manner that was not at all evident in Cairo. Without denigrating one or the other, the palpable sense of self-confidence evident in the interviews with Egyptian journalists appears to derive from a combination of self-belief, popular feedback and the mutual affirmation of fellow media professionals; in Beirut, however, while peer review is not insignificant, it appears that the day-to-day meaningfulness of work is predicated on factors exogenous to the journalistic field, on engaging with and being recognized by other communities that have their own rules, routines and value systems.

The interview with Ghassan bears this out well. Ghassan is a film writer – it was important to the aims of the study to hear perspectives from all corners of the journalistic trade, and not only the political – with thirty-five years' experience. The interview was slightly elegiac in tone, since the vibrant Lebanese film culture he knew early in his career had declined significantly in the intervening period, with the years since the civil war in particular marked by a reluctance among film funders, distributors and audiences to tackle the serious issues facing the country. But despite this decline a dedicated film culture does endure, coalescing around various film festivals and a busy programme of exhibitions, debates and screenings populated by filmmakers, critics, students and interested members of the public. It was clearly this 'community' ('communauté' – the interview was conducted in French), collectively invested if only sporadically interacting, that provided the preconditions of meaning of his daily routines, even though he spent far less time in cinemas and at events than in the newsroom, and far more time with journalists than cineastes. He spoke in detail about the ongoing conversation (Steensen, 2014; Min, 2016) he was involved in with his readers, relying on his own tastes and instincts for an 'event film' when deciding what to write about and how to frame his review but also having a finely tuned sense of their predilections and knowing he could expect a fairly high degree of film literacy on their part. *As-Safir* and his fellow employees barely rated a mention: as with the technology writer, he is accorded autonomy and trusted to fill the page with professional, engaging content whose worth does not depend on the input of colleagues, editors or managers.

Now, this in itself is hardly earth-shattering. Indeed, it is very much in line with what sociological perspectives on journalism would expect to find in journalistic specializations in Western contexts: what is true of technology and film could be said of political (Neveu, 2002) or sports journalism (Boyle, 2006). But what it brings into sharper relief is the absence of such articulations with distinct, autonomous fields in the Egyptian context. Without going so far as to claim that Egyptian journalists are cut adrift from the society that they report on, one can see here a valid response to the twin claims often made about Egyptian journalists at the time of the Arab uprisings: that they were quickly waylaid by events and that the absence of civil society in Egypt meant that they were unable to perform their basic role of providing accountability. Both claims are simplistic, but we are in a position to posit something more substantial. It is not so much that journalists were sidelined – they witnessed the events and reported them to not insubstantial audiences, after all – as that they did so through a culture of practice unarticulated with other more or less autonomous symbolic worlds. The case has been made (El-Nawawy & Khamis, 2013) that Egyptian journalists were not properly cognizant of activist communities and protest movements, but more broadly, it can be argued that the Egyptian journalistic field lacks external linkages tout court, relying on what it tells itself as well as its pact with its audiences for professional valorization. There may be democratic merit in status unmediated by potentially obscure fields and imagined communities, but the examples here show that such immersion in non-journalistic cultures at least affords distinct perspectives and perhaps gives journalists a degree of autonomy from the structures of their own field.

However it is sustained, the previous chapter makes clear that for the Cairo cohort journalistic orientation to a tumultuous world around them is stable and durable. While on one level things are changing rapidly, there is an awareness that there are many underlying continuities; either way, journalism will continue to be a culturally and politically meaningful practice, and individuals feel able to adapt to any changes in the field without either their competence being undermined or the basic day-to-day meaningfulness of their work being disrupted. There is a considerable amount of overlap between the two groups on this point, but also some striking differences. Most notably, while the Beirut interviews are similarly peppered with statements of principle about 'doing what I believe in' (Lena), 'I'm motivated by the Lebanese people' (Dina) and so on, there is overall less of a sense of ongoing professional and individual relevance being a matter of working hard and according to principle. Now, it was seen that in terms of quotidian motivation there was little grandstanding or self-importance among the Egyptian journalists: whatever was said about the importance of their trade, at the individual level meaningfulness consisted in a more straightforward seriousness, a sense of methodical application to events experienced as temporally consistent amid surrounding flux.

These media professionals, however, manifest a greater degree of precariousness as well as a keen awareness that their job security depended on things other than journalistic principle. Nepotism was widely reported, for one. This was also observable in Cairo, but as criticisms of other parts of the journalistic field; here, three spoke of getting their current positions through family or social networks – 'It's just how it is here', as Leyla put it. Louis, meanwhile, talked candidly about the competitiveness of the labour market, making it clear that one can never rest on one's earned reputation or assume the ongoing relevance of one's skills: 'There's always someone to replace you'. For him this meant a '24/7 campaign' to maintain his public profile (or profiles – this largely took the form of interacting with followers on social media), making sure that he was constantly visible, though again not merely in terms of presence but as a valorized authority figure. He also came closer than any other to expressing the disjuncture between the impossibility of this as a long-term career strategy and his motivation to proceed day after day as though it were not: 'You just have to keep doing it. If you stop to think about it you'll only get depressed'. However, existential futility was not a matter of journalism having no future in Lebanon or anywhere else but a generational concern: he was keenly aware that just as he was pushing aside the 'retirement home' model of *Al-Hayat*'s old guard, a new wave of hungrier, savvier journalists was always waiting in the wings to take his place.

It would be wrong to generalize overly from this very particular rationalization of day-to-day motivation in the face of the inevitable irrelevance of one's – anyone's – contribution seen in the greater scheme of things. But there are two broader characteristics of the Beirut cohort that can be fleshed out. The first is a keener sensibility of the extent to which the country is subject to regional forces and conflicts, and that these are perceived as continuous with historic struggles going back at least four decades. The upshot of this is a resistance to seeing contemporary events as signalling a new phase in Lebanese history: beyond the idea that nothing in Egypt has 'really' changed despite the overthrow of Mubarak or later Morsi, this is closer to the belief that Lebanon was headed towards an eventual, inevitable rupture between Islamist and Salafist interests. This reveals a subtle distinction against the tendency of journalists in other contexts to adopt an attitude of continuity to history as a marker of professional wisdom. In Lebanon, in particular, the consensus is that sectarian conflict is inevitable, not because of a sensed building momentum of factionalism or extremism, but because of the fact of a deeply fractured country unable to steer its own historical course.

This places journalists in a distinct temporal orientation: instead of experiencing flux in the present and either projecting or working methodically towards possible futures, here slower historical change is assumed, sitting alongside a political present that in 2014 at least appeared to be experienced as history on hold. There is more to this than a reluctance to discuss the Syrian civil war, the role of Hezbollah in that conflict as well as its displacement of the Lebanese army as guarantors of security in large parts of Lebanon – though all of these were discussed. More pervasively, it is the system of consociationalism that underpins the feeling of stasis among journalists. Designed to prevent another descent into civil war within Lebanon, it has simultaneously entrenched rather than resolved factional differences by operating according to principles of balance and counterbalance rather than negotiation in political policy, and fencing off certain areas of debate (Salamey, 2009). It is then aimed at the suspension of conflict and the postponement of resolution, a depoliticization of politics that makes the life of a political reporter difficult, and of any journalist that works in the absence of anything like a national public sphere. For the political reporters interviewed, this meant negotiating fairly transparent red lines: the legacy of Hariri is largely a no-go area, and there are rules against stating the sectarian affiliation of corporations and public figures out of context. Beyond that, however, it is precisely the sectarian nature of the press and broadcasting industries that constrain professional practice, and not only in the sense of imposed editorial lines. The proliferation of titles and stations in recent years (Salamey & Hussain, 2013) means that work is inherently unstable – new publications tend to have short lives and quixotic identities due to rapid turnover of proprietors and editors. It is against this backdrop that the meaningfulness of day-to-day work in the media industries has to play out, and it will be seen in what follows that how this is rationalized exhibits both similarities to and differences from the Egyptian case study.

First, a fair few of the interviewees invoked specialized journalistic traits familiar globally to explain their unique cultural value: the hazily defined instinct for a story, the ability 'to use all your senses' (Dina) in finding out and explaining what is going on, being trusted to have readily at hand all of the relevant backstory and context ('to have access always, up here [points to head] to all the information' – Amir) needed to prioritize and make sense of contemporary events. A couple spoke simply of timeliness: 'Journalists know what's going on before anyone else, so we have to tell them what they should pay attention to' (Dina). And even when pressed about the opposite being the case, of journalists being the last to know about things developing on social media, the responses were instinctive and not markedly defensive: 'Journalists bring something extra to social media – their experience, that they know how about deliberation, their education maybe … their responsibility as professionals' (Amir). This brings us to two aspects where interviewees apparently rationalize aspects of their work that are in tension, if not contradictory. Louis and Dina explicitly mentioned the problem of the filter bubble, especially in a media landscape where partisanship is so pronounced, but also spoke of the need for filters – meaning themselves: 'The problem is people just saying what's on their mind without thinking – we need filters', as Leyla put it. Lena and Dina stated that filtering was not a problem where they worked, *As-Safir* in one case and *Al-Araby Al-Jadeed* the other. This looks disingenuous on paper, given that one title is linked to Hezbollah and the Assad regime in Syria, and the other funded by Qatar, in both cases with expectations of following an editorial line. But the reality of working with 'filters' can be nuanced a little. What Dina meant was twofold: first, there is a difference between selectivity and bias, and it is an increasingly important function of journalism that it separates the wheat from the chaff. Second, filtering operates at different levels. The political and cultural leanings of *As-Safir* are well known, but responsibility to the paper's readers goes beyond telling them what they want to hear, and while some perspectives would be expected by all – owners, employees, audience – to be bracketed out, she would not dream of excluding opinions or evidence simply because she disagreed with them. Dina was very upfront about her editorial constraints – 'There are red lines.

I respect their views' – but also unapologetic about the benefits of stable financial backing: 'Having job security helps! Not being fired helps!' But she was also readily able to illustrate that the situatedness of her own work underpinned rather than undermined its meaningfulness for her. She was fairly vehement about the partisanship of Lebanese Broadcasting Corporation International (LBCi), Al-Jazeera and Al-Arabiya, and especially how each used selective and often graphic depictions of violence to frame news stories in ways that worked to the advantage of their owners. She was opposed to such depictions on political grounds, but also moral ones – straightforward respect for victims and the dead (cf. Maltby, 2014) – and as such her work criticizing the competition was rationalizable on both humanitarian and professional grounds – notwithstanding the implications of *not* broadcasting violence, the interests that this decision may serve. Similarly, at the time of the interview she was working on a story about marital rape – its lack of recognition in Lebanese law and limited redress available to women in cases where convictions are made. Here too she criticized the legal status quo specifically on sectarian grounds, but for her the values underpinning the story are both journalistic – in the sense of reporting injustice – and humanitarian, in that it concerns what she regards as inalienable human rights. In both cases the intention here is not to question the merit of the story but rather to emphasize that representing one's own sectarian or factional interests does not present itself as a motivation for work; that comes from something experienced as universal or deontological.

Given the age of Dina and Lena (they were both in their early to mid-twenties), it is not surprising that they see online media as an opportunity rather than a threat to their careers. Three journalists overall reported that working for the 'online wings' of mainstream publications is 'freer' from the constraints of sponsorship, though their age is also used against them: Khalil says that his editor is always pushing him to target the youth market 'by writing about Beyoncé and Jay-Z'. Amir observed that his older colleagues do not have an instinct for discerning facts and fiction in online media, and this is exemplified vividly by an episode Khalil recounted. He had recently set up his own website – a common thing for the younger journalists to do, beyond their paid work and activity on social media – whose remit was political satire. He published an invented story about a prison riot, the idea being that the prison represented the Lebanese state and the prisoners represented extremists. The way he told the story suggests that the language used was heavily sarcastic (it is no longer accessible to check), and he said that he clearly stated that the images he used were not authentic – they were not even produced in Lebanon. Nonetheless, LBC ran the story more or less unabridged, he was quickly detained by police for seven hours and on his return home he received calls from international broadcasters including CNN about his inside track on this prison riot that the authorities were trying to hush up. It is an entertaining story, and one told not to highlight the paranoid tendencies of the Lebanese state so much as the ineptness of mainstream media – and, of course, his own competence by comparison. Above all, though, what it highlights is the fact that professionalism for these journalists – which consists in seeing through sectarianism and artifice, keeping up with societal and technological change and working with moral integrity – is an individual rather than institutional or tribal-professional motivation.

The vividness of many of the interviewees' accounts can threaten to overwhelm analysis and bears restating that the aim of the methodology used in this research is to establish what underpins the everyday consciousness of the journalist, a consciousness generally experienced as seamlessly meaningful – not literally in the sense of full of meaning, but as instinctively worth doing, not requiring repeated self-justification. Further, seamlessness does not imply a life breezed through unquestioningly but rather a way of being in the world that does not require a great deal of work for it to be experienced as complete and not radically contingent. But while both of these aspects of conscious experience point towards a kind of homeostasis, a being in the world characterized above all by continuities that can be taken for granted, it is also a given that the systemic preconditions of everyday consciousness are not static. As well as living instinctively, through a habitus oriented towards their environment in such a way that it appears journalistically ready to hand, not something that has to be searched for meaningfulness, our journalists also live historically, a temporal condition which may be more or less present to consciousness. From the Egyptian cohort it was seen that this mode of being in the world is obscured both by quotidian continuity and, especially, the fact that instinctively invoking pasts and futures is the easiest thing in the world – everyone has a ready-to-hand future that can be effortlessly given form in an interview, but these are more often than not spontaneous expressions of present orientations. But it was also seen that beyond these lie other indictors of temporal being in the world, manifest especially in motivation and stakes, both of which are simultaneously collective and individual. As such, we are in a position to move beyond in vivo accounts of journalistic principle to assess not only the kinds of embodied investment that sustain the meaningfulness of daily routines of work, but also how these are lived amid historical change both objective and felt.

The feeling expressed by several interviewees that history is on hold at the surface of public life in Lebanon, cracks papered over in the interests of consociationalism, appears to make more acute the awareness of what is at stake for the country and anyone working in a publicly directed profession. Because the highly fragmented Lebanese media are simultaneously heavily partisan and notionally at least disavow sectarianism, journalists and audiences alike experience a constant barrage of heightened disagreement that never quite gets to the point, of half-truths and exaggeration that simultaneously demand attention and defer the kind of engagement with the country's real fault lines. Amir went so far as to express sympathy with those journalists who acquiesce to this 'media saturation', by which he meant ubiquity of rhetoric, who opt out of its theatricality ('they say: no more drama') and keep their heads down. For him, however, 'it is worth spending every minute, it is worth spending every penny' to stay in the game, however maddening and divorced from reality it becomes. Echoing a few others, this means that while he is disparaging about the state of public discourse in Lebanon, it remains important on reflection and meaningful in daily life to immerse himself in it, actively inviting criticism from those who disagree with him while making light of their reasons for doing so (because they are paid to, as online militias of official bodies of power or the astroturfing minions of corporate and political nabobs). In his words, 'You can't stay detached from it, you have to be in the matrix'.

There is more than a little braggadocio in this, and also the way he relays his philosophy of fighting fire with fire: 'You have to be more extreme than everyone else, that's the only way to win'. When pushed on what he meant by 'extreme', he made it clear that he did not mean extremely subjective or intending to incite violence, for instance, rather not flinching from criticism no matter how powerful and connected his targets. But what could easily be read as a fairly hollow expression of professional zeal was underpinned by pragmatism: he went on to explain that it is only by being 'extreme' that one attracts an audience and thus accrues public influence. Likewise, when he claims that 'journalists have to cross the line, otherwise they're mediocre', this could be read as a core belief that risk-taking is essential to the journalistic ethos, or else that it is only by taking risks that one will succeed, and the two are quite distinct propositions. There was nothing cynical in the way that he came across in the interview. Instead, while there was a recognition that the game he was playing was in some respects ridiculous, he was committed to succeeding in it, and not only for its own sake: he was positioning himself as a valorized authority, or at least focus of public attention, in a projected future whose stakes were more real.

If Amir was playful in describing his commitment to the 'game' of political debate, Khalil was more conventionally political about the role that journalists play in reflecting and potentially directing historical change. This could again come across as grandstanding – this is after all the participant who drew on Gramsci to describe his professional philosophy – but it came out of a fairly innocuous discussion of some of the things that annoy him in his day-to-day work. Chief among these was buzzfeedification, the pressure to recycle content from other, often Western, news sources rather than researching and developing original material. Now, this could be seen in terms of

Marxist alienation: the work is not really his creation, and so it could never bring him professional satisfaction. But he went further than this, explaining that this is not about labour as such but journalists' unique position: they are more than curators, because 'they have access to ideological tools'. Pressed to unpack this further, he set out a role that did not involve political leadership as such but a responsibility to ensure that information is directed towards the public interest, something which his profession, as a self-identifying intellectual, had the authority to identify. The something extra that journalists add, then, is not framing, ranking or narrativization but the harnessing of knowledge for the public good: 'at the end of the day, information and morality are related'. Undoubtedly this sounds idealistic, but it was contextualized in a way that echoes recent theses put forward in academic literature and revisited in the following chapter: namely, Deleuze's control society (1994), in which individuals lose agency over their own discourse through digital media which carves it up and presents it back to them as alienated versions of themselves, or Andrejevic's (2011) analysis of the free labour that social media production represents. Khalil sees comments on websites inexorably 'being taken from the public and given to the private, the corporations, everything shiny' – and that his role is to serve as the guardian of public debate against commodification. It is true that this seems more like a personal anti-capitalist conviction than a mission statement for journalism (he connected this to the recent trend in Hamra bars playing Lebanese music from the 1990s – 'selling us back our nostalgia'), but it is significant that beyond sectarian divides, close to half of the interviewees named neo-liberalism, consumerism or capitalism as historic forces fast changing the country. This was often expressed in generational terms: the young were seen as embracing 'ephemeral' or 'superficial' culture, too relaxed about consumer debt and wilfully ignorant about politics ('They're disgusted by politics!'), though such a view was hardly unanimous, with others pointing out that revulsion against politics channelled young people into art and music, or that social media means that they will have to learn to be more self-reliant than their parents, who slavishly followed the editorial line of a single newspaper or broadcaster.

This is only a modest tangent, as it will be seen below that engaging both the poor and the feckless, materialistic middle classes is seen by many as central to journalism's future role. But what of their status in the present? While nearly all participants relayed an affinity with social and other digital media (admittedly, they had an interest in doing so), the picture painted of the journalistic field more broadly was firmly rooted in the past, but perhaps no more so than the country at large. Louis spoke of how *Al-Akhbar*, in many ways a very progressive newspaper, remained nostalgic about print publication, the conventional newsroom and inner-city office space – and perhaps too in thrall to the romanticized memory of Lebanese culture and politics in the pre–civil war period. At the time of the fieldwork *As-Safir* still had a typing department, with more senior correspondents and columnists filing their copy in long hand. It is not that these colleagues do not know how to use computers – they do so on a daily basis – but in terms of journalistic production, writing is what they know and cleave to. Louis is in no doubt that 'journalists have lost their aura', adding that while he is still respected for the job he has when he visits his home village, in the city it counts for little. Journalists are simply not seen as central to public life, not so much because of the arrival of citizen journalism or online social movements, but because they are too implicated in sectarianism: 'War is there, just below the surface, and media can't help because all of their money comes either from parties or from abroad' (Leyla). More specifically, several indicate that no news organization presents balanced coverage of Hezbollah, still less bridging the chasm between pro- and anti-Hezbollah sections of Lebanese society.

As for future predictions, there is considerable disagreement among interviewees, as well as uncertainty. Some are fairly sanguine about the possibility of digital media reducing operating costs to the point that politico-corporate sponsorship is no longer needed, though what this portends about the viability of paid employment in journalism was not broached. Khalil notes that the 6 April movement has used online media effectively, not just to spread propaganda but to reach the people it claims to represent. This is something that journalists can learn from, seeing any digital media platforms not simply as new ways to amplify existing messages but to connect with 'ordinary' or 'the poorest' people. Against this, however, Dina cites the examples of the 8 March and 14 March movements as the ultimate embodiment of the filter bubble, with mutually exclusive online communities convincing themselves of the rightness of their own position and refusing heterogeneous dialogue. (The rivalry between the two movements was also reflected in newspaper affiliation, with *As-Safir* backing the 8 March group and An-Nahar supporting the 14 March alliance.) Others also speak of the 'contagion of lies' encountered on Facebook and Twitter, as well as the spread of 'fictional identities' in discussion forums, giving form to the more generalized feeling that journalists are suffering at the hands of a broader deterioration of the public sphere. Whatever the implications of new platforms for public expressions of opinion and campaigning and politicking by various groups online, however, the consensus is that journalism's reduced status is explained by its corruption by the money and power of factional interests.

And yet there is considerable hope for reclaiming a role for journalists, if not at the organizational level then either individually or collectively. Lena speaks optimistically about journalism offering some kind of alternative to the empty narcissism of contemporary life in Beirut, while Khalil is confident of the ongoing ability of journalists to lead public debate, though not to indoctrinate: 'We intellectuals are quite good at getting people talking about certain things.' Amir mounts a qualified defence of young people, suggesting that they are less apathetic than apprehensive, and understandably so – this is the direct result of consociationalism. Film critic Ghassan observes that the city's universities have started putting on more screenings than previously – so far absent the debates that accompanied such events in the past, but an encouraging sign nonetheless. The approach taken by Lena as editor of a magazine still only twenty-two months old is in some ways a throwback to political journalism of the 1960s, but also forward-looking. Citing Rancière's politics of aesthetics (2010) and Deleuze's (1994) rhizomal theory (she sees her role as 'cultivating the rhizomes across the Lebanese people'), the aim is to deploy political theory and philosophy in an unadorned, straightforward way to discuss everything from unemployment and Palestine to Tahrir Square and women's rights, drawing parallels as she speaks to Balkanization, the Peasants' Revolt and the barricades of the French Revolution. The motivation here clearly goes beyond maintaining the architecture and plumbing of public discourse, to tackling what she calls 'a habituated spirit that doesn't believe in change, or for that matter in politics', by way of 'talking to people *in consecrated positions* about what is going on, on the ground'. The italicized phrase in this last sentence did not indicate a position from which she spoke down to readers but rather a space in which all can grapple with issues in an intelligent, enlightened way – which she defines in opposition to the tendency of the U.K. newspaper the *Guardian* to exoticize violence, to the nonsense of talk of a third intifada or to the childishness of the phrase 'Arab Spring'.

Characteristically for the Beirut cohort, Lena's analysis is explicitly ideological, underpinning the political dimension which unproblematically sits at the centre both of journalism's role in society and the motivation of an individual's work. This is not to suggest ideological unanimity, however, and while others share her commitments regarding human rights, inequality and the dangers posed by what she describes as predatory privatization, hers is perhaps the most classically class-focused account. What made the West's fascination with the Arab uprisings particularly hypocritical was that in the decades leading up to it the bourgeoisie of Egypt, Lebanon and Syria had acquiesced in the continued dominance of the Hosni Mubarak and Hafez and Bashar al-Assad regimes. While the failure of the international media, not to mention academia, to hold these rulers to account has been widely noted elsewhere, Lena perceives a pact between the West and what she derides as 'les beaux quartiers de Cairo' with their supermarkets, cinemas and nightclubs. In Lebanon, too, middle-class self-interest explains the denial of Hezbollah's complicity in the mutation of popular protest in Syria into outright civil war – and of the de facto partitioning of Lebanon and the injustices faced by the Palestinian refugees it houses. In both cases, there is both denial of the ongoing 'impoverishment and indignity' experienced by the majority of citizens, as well as a wilful misrepresentation of politics that Western media and academic researchers have been all too willing to parrot. Lena emphasized that in Egypt, Syria, Lebanon and Tunisia, as well, coalitions between Islamists and those on the left go back at least to 2004. In her view this made it inevitable that where new regimes have come to power they were 'just as repressive, just as exploitative' as what went before – but 'no one wants to talk about this'.

And this brings us closer to an embodiment of journalistic motivation which goes beyond simple truth-telling and which is temporally oriented in a way that exceeds faith in principle or morality in everyday practice. Lena clearly sees her role, as do all of those interviewed, as more than a warden of information, but also as something less than an agent of social change in her own right – something which is conceivable on reflection at the collective and historical level, but not as immediately ready to hand in daily life. Instead, her role concerns making politics intelligible, giving people 'the conditions to think politically'. This needs to transcend both journalistic cynicism and what she sees as the understandable despair that most Lebanese feel at finding the same sclerotic, unedifying factional politics at every turn: 'young people need to believe in the right to think, we need to develop the conditions of democratisation'. It would be possible to read this as a little artful, claiming to hold back from leading audiences, just furnishing them with a space in which they can explore politics independently, while clearly having in mind a certain kind of political alternative to the status quo. And yet she combines an insistence on historical and philosophical rigour with an unequivocal qualification of application: 'My publication can point to the signals of change, it can detect movements, and general convictions are important, too. But, most important of all, I don't accept that there is one right approach.'

Making politics intelligible is a motivation held in common with several other interviewees, and, crucially, it is not conceived as making politics understandable, merely simplifying it. It is instead about making politics thinkable, a theme to which we will return in the final chapter. This, further, explains why the journalists in this cohort do not see their role simply as translators – taking the words of politicians, say, and making them comprehensible to mass audiences. That undoubtedly plays a part – plain-speaking, using ordinary words are phrases often encountered – but there is also an evident motivation to make clear where there is an absence of intelligibility, situations where translation is not a possibility. For Amir this becomes manifest in his writing aiming at a regional audience: he describes his Lebanese and Egyptian readers as 'mutually incomprehensible', meaning that as well as lacking an awareness of the other country's history and politics there is a general ignorance about what life is like for most people in different parts of the Middle East. His aim, though, is not to translate those different experiences of daily life but to make clear the impossibility of doing so and thus to open up the possibility of there being 'other things to talk about'. Rather than representing an abnegation of the journalist's role as cultural intermediary – he provides endless links to external sources in his online writing, for one – he appears to see himself as creating distinct spaces where meaningfulness becomes possible by the act of acknowledging unintelligibility. By no means is this seen in the grand terms of opening up spaces in which new regional subjectivities can emerge – it is not that this is inconceivable, but on current evidence it seems unlikely, and in any case this is not what underpins the meaningfulness of his day-to-day work.

This same principle is abundantly evident in the case of Dina and Lena, who talk openly of the impossibility of overcoming the mutual incomprehensibility of the pro- and anti-Hezbollah online communities. There is a degree to which they see their work as breaking through the silo effect that characterizes all contemporary online media experiences. But there is also a frank acknowledgement that it would be exhausting, and ultimately futile, to devote their energies to helping the two camps understand each other. Again this is not experienced as a chilling concession of an audience's wilful ignorance: it is not a matter of giving up and just getting on with whatever one finds personally interesting. The impossibility of intelligibility is not just accepted; it is identified, methodically, making clear not just what is unknown from a certain perspective – that would only come across as didactic and partisan – but what is mutually unthinkable between multiple perspectives (Ascher, 2011). This rationalizes today's writing task, giving the writer reason to 'get on' with their work, but it is experienced as a collective ethos of resisting Balkanization or sectarianism – not by going to each group and telling what they do not understand, but by refusing the mutual incomprehension of different fields through its acknowledgement and thus the possibility of working towards alternate conditions of intelligibility.

Lena uses the examples of Iraq and Palestine in a way that at first seems rhetorical to express the difficulty of the task: 'Where do you even begin to explain?' The implicit answer is to accept the futility of three distinct journalistic strategies. First is the myth of maximal backstory: simply give readers a comprehensive enough history of Iraq and the region and they will understand its present predicament. Second is the perspectival approach: give a balanced enough account of the different 'sides' with interests at stake in Iraq and readers will grasp the truth of the current situation. Third is the journalist as cultural intermediary, translating the way that Iraq is talked about in different fields – political, legal, humanitarian and so on. All of these involve potentially useful sources of information, but none provides a way in to being able to think about Iraq in such a way that thinkability is open-ended. The job of the journalist, then, is not to reveal the ultimate truth of what is happening in Iraq but to present enough relevant factual information, to consider interpretations from various quarters while making clear their own limitations of intelligibility and thus to allow for discourse about the country to develop in a less prescribed manner. This is not the same as marking out an undetermined space in which freer thinking can happen – none of the interviewees is anything like as optimistic, for starters, and the idea of discursive spaces lacking constraining structures is a fantasy in any case. It is more of an embodied orientation towards unfolding events, one which acknowledges the limitations of what is thinkable about them but regards such limitations like any other encounter to respond and adapt to, iteratively, rather than simply homeostatic. This makes sense of the use of philosophical and historical allegories in Lena's publication: quite the reverse of demonstrating that current events are simply echoes of universal truths or inescapable predetermination, the idea is to decontextualize from competing, self-certain perspectives and to demonstrate that the 'meaning' of what is going on in Iraq is still in play, and as such worth investing in.

In many ways this translates into solid if straightforward advice for journalists: Be aware of the constraints of journalistic cynicism (Cappella & Jamieson, 1997; Brants et al., 2009), and especially the tendency to report all new events as though history were already written, as well as the alienating effect that assiduously relaying claim and counterclaim in the name of balance has. But there is also an insight here into the way that journalists, usually less vocally, situate themselves and their work in relation to ongoing change. Louis was at the time of interview working on a story on the legal status of political activists in Ramallah – essentially, at issue was whether the Israeli indictment of an activist organization as terrorists means that *any* campaigning on the part of past or current members of such an organization constitutes a crime. He clearly had a personal opinion about this – indeed, it was the motivation for covering the story in the first place – but was also very aware that anything he wrote which a reader could respond to with 'Well, you would say that, wouldn't you?' would, in journalistic terms, be useless. Instead, he parried the item into a broader, and apparently fairly open-ended, discussion on the legal status of Palestinian refugees in Lebanon itself, acknowledging that to do so was to wade into a fiercely partisan debate that excites participants and leaves others cold. His aim was to be as 'authoritative' as possible, while also 'holding back'; this amounted to demonstrating his authority not by declaiming his rightness but by making clear how little scope for insight there is between the main 'sides' in the debate over Lebanon's Palestinians. This enabled him to skirt the constraints posed by consociationalism, and to do so in a way that felt instinctively to him like contributing to history still unfolding rather than someone venturing another salvo in a war of attrition.

Self-aware as ever that his motivation was in no small part ego-driven, this meant that he had to be adaptable to changes on the ground, and to refrain from grandstanding. For him there was a sense that change is rapidly accelerating, with the implication that for anyone to claim certainty of perspective reveals them as naïve or lazy: 'People aren't able to cope with change, but you need to be there to see it happening, otherwise you just see what you always see'.

Dina was one of several interviewees who saw the cultural value of her work in bringing to readers' attention knowledge they would not otherwise come across – not dissimilar to the film critic bringing to his work experience of a self-contained field that few outsiders would understand. For her, this meant bringing to bear on current events perspectives from diplomacy and think-tankery, not because they were uniquely insightful, and not because doing so made her journalism better than anyone else's, but mainly because of the serendipity it produced: 'You find that you read things you wouldn't normally read, or things you didn't know you were interested in'. Checking Facebook and Twitter 'every twenty minutes' amounted to the same thing – rather than bouncing from one hackneyed view to another, she found that this jolted her out of her conventional way of thinking about unfolding events. She was pessimistic about the future ('Everything was all over the place, but in a good way, it was a new beginning for the people, but now families are fighting families … and there is a battle on social media, so much hate speech'), but the meaningfulness of her work was not in question. This did not amount to a self-belief that she was right and would ultimately be vindicated, nor that she was in the business of producing hard facts whose cultural value is obvious, but something less readily discernible: that her work pushed a collective discussion forward by making clear the limitations of what we, and she, are or had been able to think about a situation. There was nothing obviously moral about this, and certainly no sense that she sat above the fray writing from nowhere, but rather a normalized orientation to events comfortable with sizing them up as they appear and weighing up responses and implications.

That journalists have a future-oriented role to play in responding to, framing and de- or re-contextualizing political and technological change did not appear as a reflex reaction geared towards validating the speaker's profession in the longer term. Even if it had been, however, this would still have been potentially useful, insofar as it reveals the ready-to-hand practices of valorization that an interviewee spontaneously enacts in a given present. Here, though, there was less certainty about the implications of change, and also about her own fit with a habitus appropriate to respond to it – this was no display of over-confidence. Specifically, amid inflammatory political communication and heightened aggression on social media platforms, she felt that authority figures trusted by all or at least most would become only more important as conflict escalates. Consecration as an embodiment of trust-worthiness, however, is no simple matter: she struggled to define exactly what she thought trust is in her professional context – certainly not something as straightforward as being trusted to be objective or neutral at a given point in time. Rather, trust was seen as work ('really hard work'), as something which had to be built over years and even then constantly, effortfully enacted in pursuit of collective recognition.

This temporal dimension to being recognized as valorized cultural agency is interesting insofar as it differs from traditional theories of consecration, especially Weberian (1978), where it is more absolute in form: once you are recognized as the embodiment of a particular value, you are indistinguishable from it, and may after Bourdieu have some scope to redefine how it is recognized. For Dina as for others, it is something difficult to hold on to, though nonetheless worth struggling to maintain. This, though, is not expressed as an affirmation of professional principle: Always be the best journalist you can, otherwise you will lose your exalted position. Instead, it is something less tangible, arrived at through feedback and engagement with readers and peers, building up a relationship which is as much about familiarity as getting things right – she is clear that for most of her audience, their motivation to read her work is largely a matter of habit. This leaves her more circumspect about her public status, though not about her own ability to do the work, and it has also made her more conservative about her career ambitions – she initially wanted to be 'one of those journalists who move every five years' so as to maximize her exposure and 'make myself known', but she had come to see the benefits of staying put and enjoying the benefits of having a readership who know her and trust her. This goes against comments made by Dina, that readers follow trusted individuals from organization to organization, rather than investing their trust in a particular publication, but both make clear a professional orientation which is not simply rooted in the present, responding to one discrete thing after another, and nor is it oriented towards a future merely posited according to disposition or presumption.

The shared temporal orientation takes on a different inflection for those whose experience of Lebanese politics is one of stasis rather than endless, constant change. Here it might be thought that making clear the limits of intelligibility is explicitly aimed at breaking the deadlock in various debates, but in practice there is not such a straightforward equivalence between seeking to rise above sectarianism in one's work and to supersede it, eventually, in society writ large. For Leyla, for instance, there is an awareness first that her own position cannot be described as neutral, and a more pervasive belief that 'media never trumps politics': political divides are encountered in every corner of daily life, and there is in the medium term no prospect of this changing. Leyla perceives this in strikingly physical terms, emphasizing that the city remains very much divided, in people's minds if not through decree, and while quarters such as Hamra and Gemmayze are certainly more porous and less homogenous than previously, she claims that she still comes across taxi drivers unwilling to ferry her to one sector or another. It is true that her work aims directly to assess and critique the partial coverage of events seen in the region's broadcast media, but her function is more subtle than encouraging different groups to talk to and understand each other or presenting a definitive meta-view, something like Mannheim's general-total conception of ideology (2013 [1929]) – even if that is what some of her phrasing suggests. It makes sense in immediately responding to a question about motivation to reach for the kind of catch-all explanation that sums up the value of her work, but it is when she expanded on what this looks like in practice that its meaning became explicable in the context of the model developed so far in this chapter. In short, her role is not to overcome the sectarian divide – to her it is insuperable – but to produce new knowledge which could, possibly, produce new conditions of intelligibility. She does this methodically, one issue at a time, though in an ordered, not haphazard, fashion, with an unproblematic sense of meaningfulness in daily life but no overstatement of her agency in the broader scheme of things. Primarily she achieves it by producing quasi-legal discourse: journalistic research on cases under consideration by the Constitutional Court, leading to contributions that are themselves subjective, yet potentially productive of ways of thinking about, say, domestic violence that do not currently exist. The distinction is a subtle yet important one: her role is not experienced in grand terms as opening the eyes of sectarian groups to the truth but producing knowledge from different perspectives, different discourses, with the confident yet undramatic expectation that this will, over time and in conjunction with the work of others, open up discussion of the issue. No changing-the-world sense of mission is necessary to make this uncomplicatedly meaningful at the quotidian level: she is adamant that the extent to which Lebanon is implicated in regional political forces means it will never have a 'decent' media.

By contrast, Amir finds that his work focusing on Lebanon invariably has more impact, measured in hits and comments, than anything more regional. But he demonstrates well the way that conditions of intelligibility change, often in ways that cannot be directed or anticipated, in the words and slogans used in political demonstrations and online activism in recent years. While 'you can't reduce politics to a slogan', he saw it as self-evident that the verbatim reproduction of certain phrases from Tunisia in Egypt and Yemen meant something, if not evidence of political contagion as such, then more pragmatically Arabic speakers in different countries taking inspiration from each other. And yet a word like 'thaora' (revolution) has taken on a variety of meanings, encompassing everything from anti-authoritarian fervour to sectarian campaigns, and secularist activism. He claims that the word has even come to mean its literal opposite, in that policies aiming for stability over change – Qatar's moderating of its support for Islamist groups, the intention of some El-Sisi supporters to slow down reform – are themselves sometimes referred to as thaora. This might be nothing more than an example of words reduced to floating signifiers, but it seems to go beyond the instrumental, propagandistic wielding of terms for political ends. The claim heard on numerous occasions that the Lebanese, like the Egyptians, 'don't know what they want' (Louis, Dina, Zaina) is based on the observation that they seem to want different things at different times. This might make them capricious, naïve or reactionary, but it also suggests that the conditions on which change is apprehended are actually quite fluid, and that it is the job of journalists to keep on top of how these conditions morph, and more practically to register not just what claims are made by whom, but on the basis of which assumptions and motivations they are made.

Even for those more outspoken about their desire to 'wake people up', it is apparent that this cannot always be reached for to give meaning to – and indeed can look a little ridiculous in the context of – everyday work. Khalil describes as 'sick' a situation in which 'celebrity and lifestyle advice' are crowding out more serious issues in formerly restrained, politically committed publications – 'and all this while we have illiteracy, unemployment' – and yet he understands well the editorial shift towards search engine optimization and even derives some perverse pleasure at his facility with a kind of journalistic practice he sees not just as flippant but corrosive. He can do so because he still feels in touch with 'the masses' who are 'there in the comment section', but who need 'nurturing' and 'protecting' from the spread of consumerism; for him, it is the rise of neo-liberalism which represents the greatest threat to Lebanese society, precisely because unlike sectarianism it goes unremarked. He comes closest to identifying all-out false consciousness, despairing not so much at the narrow conditions of intelligibility under which most people labour, as the profusion of intelligibility – that is, people's suggestibility. This takes many forms: he lists bots on social media, doctored images and an editor asking him to write a piece on whether Malaysian Airlines flight MH370 may have crashed in the Saudi desert.

As a technology correspondent, Khalil does not see it as his job to correct specific misapprehensions, though he does feel he has a role to play in combating the culture of credulity he diagnoses. The problem, he argues, is that 'people just always want *stuff*', and this covers literal stuff like the smartphones and cars young Lebanese people buy straight out of college, lumbering themselves with considerable debt, as well as the twitchy addiction to new posts, images and angles, and also to politics – when he says that politics has been reduced to 'giving people stuff' he means this both in the sense that politicians have to appeal to people's material self-interest and that they are obliged to offer up an endless array of consumable, usually mediated, experiences. Also among the stuff that people have come to expect is the experience of having a say and getting a reaction, leading to what he sees as a worrying trend of people inventing artificial personalities online, often provoking official responses from people in positions of power in the government and the media. Now, this goes against arguments laid out in chapter 6 that if anything, social media are leading users towards less creative, more boxed-in performances of online identity, and it is also potentially problematic to characterize the chief implication of the spread of interactive and social media as a culture of inauthenticity – without rehashing the arguments here, the idea that there is a counterposed authentic real of communication is at best debatable. But still, it should be possible to assess the statement that 'Then again, perhaps the people posting false opinions on Reddit are looking for a real conversation' as signalling a meaningful contribution that his work could make to an otherwise anchorless user experience characterized by a thoroughgoing absence of trust – as well as playful sophistry.

One thing that is clear is that a constructive corrective on his part would not take the form of unadulterated factual reporting – because audiences and colleagues alike are unable to discern fact from fiction, or in other words that the conditions of intelligibility of what constitutes truthfulness do not exist in today's media environment. Unsurprisingly, then, among his strategies is to dive headlong into a relativist symbolic world and engage with it on its own terms: he often produces digital images satirizing or commenting on current events and notes that these always prove more popular with readers than his textual blogs. He also mentions that he is writing the Arab world's 'first cyberpunk novel'. Beyond that, though, his suggestions echo both the political arguments put forward by Fenton and Barassi (2011) and the architectural ones posited by Bennett and Segerberg (2013). He cannot change things on his own, of course, but no more than a handful – five, he specifies – could make a real difference by developing an alternative public sphere. He contrasts the fissiparous nature of social media with the threads and feeds of web 1.0 – these earlier platforms were better suited to focused attention and debate, and this is where some kind of distinct form of intelligibility could emerge to challenge the consumerist blanket that smothers all other discourse, be it mainstream top–down communication or the many-to-many forums of social media. It is intellectuals who would most appropriately populate this space – 'the internet isn't classless after all' – but, importantly, this is conceived not in abstracted, idealist terms but very much like journalistic work: not prescribing but responding to events, offering perspective, decontextualization and, crucially, a map of possible futures around specific issues, and the stakes encoded therein.

The principal theme that emerges from these rich individual voices is that the key to journalism's future as a viable form of cultural authority is its monopoly on a particular kind of intelligibility. This is not so much about knowing more than everyone else, or even knowing it first, but being perceived on a daily basis to be capable of grasping the contingency of contemporaneous discourse and thus making that crucial distinction between newsworthy events and change on a bigger scale. The journalistic orientation to the world, then, is not just about novelty or sensation but also a rationalized, operationalized weighing-up of the scale of what is going on around us, knowing better than other groups of actors what is at stake in how events play out from here. This could be misinterpreted as an authority claim to be better futurologists than anyone else, but we know from other sociologies of journalism (Schlesinger, 1981) that getting future predictions right is not really a marker of ability or status. Rather, it is about the methodical and usually confident weighing up all and sundry, the big and the trivial, in everyday professional practice – conscious of the limits of thinkability that surround any contemporary phenomena and unabashed about pushing those limits. In the interviews this often comes in the form of statements which sound dramatic or apocalyptic but are really just evidence of a willingness to imagine futures minimally unconstrained by the status quo: 'Why should Lebanon continue to exist indefinitely?' 'There's no reason to think that the worst wars are behind us'. But as with the previous chapter, thinking of this kind is cut through with references to fashion and gadgets, as well as expressions of bitchiness, petulance, impatience, irony, humour and bemusement. And in the final chapter these twin orientations are knitted together – seemingly contradictory facings towards the profound and the banal that are in fact each other's precondition in everyday encounters across time. First, we take a step back and ask: In an age characterized by apparently simultaneous accelerating change and grinding repetitiveness, in the Arab world as much as in the West, what kind of historical moment are we living through?

Chapter Six

Anti-Politics, Populism and Social Media

If we are to stand any chance of teasing out the role that media play in how we experience structural change amid the routines and givens of everyday life, we first need to understand what kind of times we are living in. Postmodernism did away with the fallacy that we are – always – living at the culmination of history, historiography militates against assuming that whatever we are experiencing is unprecedented, while historical materialism foregrounds the deeper continuities – usually political and economic ones – underpinning observed shifts in the way that people interact with each other and organize themselves. What, then, can we say is distinct about the contemporary age? Certainly there is much about our media use that is novel, though there is a risk in elevating the importance of social media or assuming that these platforms are the only or fullest expression of what the 'social' actually means these days (Couldry, 2015). In order to avoid that trap, this book takes the line that while social media afford all manner of significant opportunities as well as less welcome implications, the gamut of values that animate debate and disagreement in the social sciences are not fully at stake within the confines of these platforms. Social media matter, not least in how they become embedded in our everyday rhythms and how we see ourselves individually and collectively. But, crucially, those individual and collective selves that are realized through social media are not all there is. This is not the same as insisting that there is life outside social media: indeed, any invocation of life outside media makes the mistake of thinking of media as exogenous to ourselves – external forces that do things to us, rather than part of the environment in which we emerge as selves. Instead, the key word is 'part': new kinds of media offer up different possibilities for subjectivity, but nothing higher, purer or deeper than what went previously. And a corollary to this, a reassuring one at that, is that the selves enacted through new media contexts are not the fully determined products of those environments. This proposition has all sorts of consequences, and it is one that this volume aims to test theoretically and empirically. It means, for one, that social media platforms designed to maximize profit do not have the capacity to summon up fully formed, obedient, neo-liberal selves – not quite. It also means that social media cultures that are disrespectful, intemperate or even abusive do not wield the power fundamentally to undermine the subjectivity of their users. And it means that radically different, massively networked media configurations do not necessarily contain the possibility of generating radically new subjectivities.

As with media, in politics too it pays to think of the times we are living through neither as the final, inevitable expression of the broad sweep of history nor as the start of something entirely new. This might sound like a statement of the historically obvious, but it has an important consequence that is easily overlooked. Precisely because there is so much at stake in where we are now – the things we value, how we want to organize ourselves collectively and structurally – there is a tendency to think that the present contains the ultimate or fullest expression, whether manifest as challenge or opportunity, of those principles. But what is at stake now does not complete the meaning, in ontological and epistemological terms, of those principles, and we stand to lose something if we forget this. In political terms, the current era in the West is often characterized as post-political (meaning either that we have forgotten or had taken away from us what we used to mean by the political; see, for instance, Wilson & Swyngedouw, 2014), anti-politics (we have rejected or been abandoned by previously agreed fora for public deliberation and contestation; see, for instance, McDowell et al., 2014) or populist (we are demanding or being suckered by new, usually post-institutional ways of doing politics; see, for instance, Mudde & Rovira Kaltwasser, 2012). Tempting as it is to contextualize each of these as the next logical phase of late capitalism or the start of something new (and uniquely transformative or apocalyptic), to do so unnecessarily narrows political ontology and epistemology – what constitutes the political, and what counts as knowledge of it. So refusing to accept that everything is at stake in what we face now is neither fatalistic, nor some kind of world-weariness; it is simply an attempt not to substitute the way the political is experienced now with the sum total of what the political means. And this in turn is not meant to be nostalgic or utopian about what the political meant or could mean, but rather not to lose sight of the work that the concept of the political can do for us when fully realized. That accounts for the phenomenological bent of the book. Defined in opposition to metaphysics, the idea is to investigate in detail how the political is experienced in everyday life, in all its banality as well as its urgency. But crucially, phenomenological inquiry does not stop at flat description (see especially Throop & Murphy, 2002), bracketing out bigger, normative principles. It looks instead for its conditions of possibility, what afforded and constrained the inevitably narrow way politics is lived now.

And as for the political, so too the cultural. The current era in the West has been described as characterized by a demotic turn (Turner, 2010), though other turns – affective, hedonic, phatic – are available. In normative terms, the demotic turn can be interpreted alternately as the overthrow of deference and hierarchy (Fiske, 1989) or the relentless enforcement of conformity (Sparks, 2007). Each argument has its merits, and yet each runs the risk of making the things that people pay attention to now stand in for everything that that slippery term 'culture' has meant and can mean (see also McNair, 2003). To assume that everything is at stake, for better or worse, in what people are currently looking at and listening to is not just being historically short-sighted; it substitutes debates over current cultural phenomena for much more fundamental questions about what culture is and what it is for. And so again, in this book the aim is to look at how culture appears phenomenologically in and around everyday life – not to reify or pathologize whatever forms it currently takes but to look at what made this possible, what made it normal that these observable forms are at present what stands for culture writ ontologically and epistemologically large. Later on in this chapter, trust in social media cultures is examined through such a prism. Rather than supposing that networked media either dupe people into misplaced trust or facilitate new and better kinds of trust than have been possible previously, the idea is to look at what trust is actually *for* in these mediated interactions between often unknown actors, before asking what wider trends have led to this mode of trust becoming socially meaningful – without losing sight of everything else that trust is and everything else that can instantiate it. Trust, or its systemic decline, is also at the heart of a generalized turn away from institutional politics as well as the media that exist to air it, and it is to this that we now turn.

ANTI-POLITICS AND POPULISM

An anti-political attitude is said to link everything from the election of Donald Trump and the British 2016 EU referendum result to the popular uprisings of the Arab Spring (see, for instance, Pace & Cavatorta, 2012). Anti-politics is an evocative term, though one that encapsulates a mood rather than an unequivocal orientation to the world, one which is alternately sceptical, weary and incensed by the normal way that politics is done. Insofar as the anti-political disposition remains interested in relations of power, injustice, inequality and so on, it does not amount to a negation of the political, and in most cases it does not call for a rejection of electoral politics and its core values of representative democracy. In this way it is perhaps less than radical, an expression of discontent that all of the politicians and parties on offer in each given context are inept or corrupt, too disconnected from the lives of 'ordinary' people, too much like each other. It will be argued here that anti-politics is not simply nihilistic, as has been posited in the context of both the Arab Spring and Western democracies (Jeffrey et al., 2015), most often on the basis of the rejection by protest movements of traditional met-anarratives of power and utopianism. But nor is it quite the same thing as a collective turn to populist politics, historical explanations of which abound in the literature (see, for instance, Wodak, 2013). Instead, anti-politics is contingent on the ongoing erosion of institutionalized power of all forms, whether governmental, bureaucratic or corporate – or dissenting, for that matter. Importantly, this goes significantly further than a decline in trust in institutions, a trend well established across the last half-century (Nye et al., 1997; Putnam, 2000; Blyth, 2002). It is about the basic credibility of institutions as units of social organization and, potentially, of the very conceivability of institutions as naturally meaningful heuristics for understanding how power works (Granovetter, 1992).

The implications of this orientation away from institutions, the notion that institutions are not ready to hand the first thing that appears to your consciousness when power is at stake, are considerable. For one, it undermines the claim that academics and other experts failed to understand the reasons for and meaning of recent political phenomena like the Arab Spring and the Occupy movements because they clung to outdated theoretical models that presume long-term stability both of social structures and the concepts conventionally used to interpret them (Fenton & Barassi, 2011; Volpi, 2011; Pickerill & Krinsky, 2012). There has certainly been some soul-searching in the international relations community (Cottle, 2011; Gause, 2011; Bellin, 2012), which largely failed to anticipate the events of 2011, at least in part because of a reliance on a predictive model that assumes the durability of autocratic political systems. Overall, however, the opposite is the case: rather than cleaving to canonical perspectives of politics and historical change, the academic habitus too, in some disciplines at least, has orientated away from those conventional objects of perception and interpretation (Ang, 1991; Wellman & Haythornwaite, 2002; Bird, 2003; Stevenson & Papadopoulos, 2006; Hobson & Seabrooke, 2007). This may be no bad thing if it is simply a matter of being open to new realities, but in some cases it also produces an over-readiness to identify new and radical forms of politics on the basis of an absence of institutional structure, in social media or on 'the street' (Sassen, 2011). Such a keenness can be thought of as a manifestation of the 'habitus of the new' (Papacharissi & Easton, 2013) that some detect in contemporary social media cultures (and that Heidegger identified in relation to much older waves of new media), though as that theme recurs throughout this book it will be seen that this is never just an orientation towards the future as such – it is a turn towards the projection of a particular future rooted very much in the present. The eagerness, gleefulness even, with which some scholars have claimed the arrival of a new Arab politics (Aganthangelou & Soguk, 2011; Allagui & Kuebler, 2011; Axford, 2011; Elseewi, 2011; Newsom et al., 2011; Rinke & Röder, 2011; Soguk, 2011; Wall & Zahed, 2011; Greene & Kuswa, 2012; Lim, 2012; Lewiński & Mohammed, 2012) suggests a degree of anxiety among researchers working in this area, an enthusiasm to identify with the popular or populist rather than the establishment in which academia is traditionally, if problematically, implicated. If anti-politics and the role of the media in making it possible are to be understood, it is necessary to retain a critical distance from the valorization of de-institutional, or elite, conceptions of power and politics.

THE VIEW FROM POLITICAL SCIENCE

This is not the place to rehearse arguments about how mediated representations of official politics influence the kind of political engagement that the public has. By way of encapsulation, current thinking downplays the linear or cumulative effects of sensationalized or superficial political coverage (Neuman, 1991) and emphasizes instead the distortions that result in relations between political elites and the public when the former partially or comprehensively adapt the way cultures of practice are structured in politics to the logics of the media field (Strömbäck, 2008). This is about more than the tendency towards sound bites and evasion in interviews and stump speeches, but the very way that political meaning comes to be recognized instinctively, unproblematically. The nature of broadcast communication means that visual cues play a significant part, but it is not only about the prioritization of one sense over another. In the context of the United States, the relation between television and political authority has been debated and dissected since the presidential debates of 1960 (McLuhan, 1964), with a broad acceptance that the constraints and affordances of television have contributed to the concentration of power in the person of the president, as well as a handful of other recognized players, and away from a faceless Congress with its absence of readily available visual shorthand. That television pushes politics towards presidentialism is uncontroversial, but what is perhaps more relevant is the undercurrent that individuals generally become the public's ready-to-hand phenomenal object of politics – whether that object is valorized or detested. The advent of networked media has not usurped this valorization entirely, since while it facilitates the dispersed production and distribution of political content, it also enables massively concurrent symbolization. All kinds of things can become iconic of the political quickly in social media, from jubilant crowds to acts of violence, speech acts ('I can't breathe') to masks. But actual individuals continue to be instinctively graspable as political objects, too. Much of the analysis of the rise of populist parties in Western Europe has fretted about the authenticity of their leaders (Nilsson, 2014; Wodak, 2015; Aslanidis & Rovira Kaltwasser, 2016; Jennings, 2016), but in many ways this is beside the point: what matters is the longer-term trend in which the charismatic individual is as natural a go-to for a political subjectivity on the lookout for inspiration as a manifesto or demonstration.

Writing about populist politics in Western Europe, de Blasio et al. (2011) posit first that the role of the media is not an illocutionary one. Borrowed from linguistics, the illocution/perlocution distinction is a useful one for thinking about media influence: the media are not illocutionary in that they do not enact political realities through what they broadcast or publish. This shifts our focus away from what media content does, or indeed what audiences do with the political media they consume, interpret and sometimes negotiate, and towards the conditions of intelligibility that media create. Taking the Italian political scene as a case study, de Blasio et al. show how it becomes possible for political objects, including individuals, parties, the judiciary and so on, to appear as embodying particular positive or negative qualities. What does it take, for instance, for an establishment institution or individual to be understood as either inept or grasping? Blanket negative coverage of a politician or party, whether simply reflecting reality, the shape of a concerted smear campaign or a more systemic process of delegitimization for one reason or another, does not straightforwardly effect the recognition of that individual or group as an object of derision or scorn. Recognition is only tenable insofar as it is experienced as instinctive and unlaboured, meaning that our politician or party would have to appear as already, plausibly, inadequate or self-serving. While such stereotypes are legion, and while some scornful recognition is well earned, the upshot is that it is not easy to manufacture a negative (or indeed positive) phenomenal object that feels unforced. Certain preconditions need to be in place to ground a particular experience of objectification as natural.

THEORIZING MEDIA CYNICISM

De Blasio et al. suggest that a generalized conception of the state itself as venal, rather than its constituent elements, can provide such a grounding for instinctive pathologization – as well as for the self-evident credibility of populist alternatives. But how common is a generalized orientation to a state recognized as degraded and immoral? In the case of the Arab uprisings, it is fairly common in the literature to find depictions of the state as monolithic and driven by a nefarious kind of totalized agency (see, for instance, Ismail, 2011; Fuchs, 2015). Indeed, in chapters 7 and 8 it will be seen that this tendency to other a malevolent state can produce a blinkered understanding of dissent and resistance. In ethnographic studies of authoritarian political systems, however (Hammoudi, 1997; Hansen & Stepputat, 2001; Lee & Zhang, 2013), people tend to make distinctions between, say, the police and the army, with disgust at one set against ambivalence or more positive attitudes towards the other. It is well established in opinion polling (Levi & Stoker, 2000; Ermisch et al., 2009) that people's levels of trust in or satisfaction with elements of the state reduced to catch-all abstractions – health, education, politics – tend to be much lower than those registered for specific incarnations of those sectors: individual hospitals, schools or even politicians. But while this can be explained in methodological, identity-management terms (to say you trust the media carries the risk of appearing naïve to your pollster; see, for instance, Naef & Schupp, 2009), it remains possible that this generalized sense of disaffection, existing alongside more variegated and positive-specific objectifications of state or media institutions, is genuine. Philosophers sometimes identify dominant orientations to the world – modernist, risk-averse, narcissistic, future-fixated. But orientations are adaptations, albeit ones that exceed our individual consciousnesses, naturalized ways of anticipating and projecting different kinds of objects across multifarious encounters in the world. We are not limited to one blanket orientation, and it makes sense that orientations can find meaning simultaneously in the generic and the specific, and also that these might not be in alignment. Structured anticipation seeks to maximize predictability as we navigate the world across time, and this applies to specifically mediated spaces as much as any others. But being at home in such a world, living authentically in Heidegger's daunting prescription, does not entail an imperative to be consistent.

This means that we can theorize prevailing political trends, in the Arab world as much as in the United States and Europe, without deriding them as fickle or immature. If anti-politics is more of a mood than a specific stance (Gilroy, 2005; Pasquino, 2007; Fenton, 2008), it appears to fit that more generalized orientation to the world, the background hum against which more overt relations between political subject and various objects intercede. Such a background will certainly help to shape those more specific objectifications and posited subjects, but not definitively. Further, it does not follow that such a generic orientation is unreflexive, or passive, or simply apathetic. Drawing on de Rivera (1991), Baker (2011) has written about the way collective moods appear to consciousness, whether in a city undergoing political turmoil or a social media network at any given point in time. One can usually sense a more or less collective orientation to events or the world at large, and this orientates the recognition of specific objects, but it is important not to conflate the two. If this sounds abstract, consider the example of anti-intellectualism that de Blasio et al. raise in relation to anti-politics and populism in Italy. A generalized anticipatory framework of wariness towards intellectuals in public life has explicit effects, with academic engagement with public issues dismissed as abstract. In broader terms, however, it shapes the apprehension not just of individual pronouncements but politics itself, manifest in exactly the kind of illocutionary modes of language that media by themselves cannot concoct and impose. Anti-intellectualism here provides the conditions of ontological credibility of statements of an 'I think that' form, that is, statements which in their utterance produce realities, not simply referring to an object or commenting on it but creating one. As for anti-politics, the dismissal of all formal political structures as corrupt or bureaucratic has similar implications: namely, the illocutionary production of truths of injustice, victimization and dissent through their utterance (Austin, 1962). There is a short-circuiting of recognition that inoculates it against counterfactuals: individuals are not in denial about specific encounters that go against the grain, but they need not disrupt the seamless experience of a world in which the malevolence of institutional politics and the innocence or nobility of its others is always at-hand.

This line of thinking goes beyond the criticism (Bloom, 2013) of politicians and commentators for whom facts are immaterial so long as their sense of conviction is unshakeable. It is not about selectivity of facts deployed in political argument but the abnegation of facts as things with ontological force. The problem with an experience of the world that starts from its inception with a generalized assumption of venality is not that it is pessimistic or fatalistic; on the contrary, the problem is that it authorizes itself. Now, since recognition is a collective act rather than an individual one (Chant et al., 2014), it does not follow that such authorization is narcissistic. But collective recognition of the illocutionary force of utterances of injustice and so on, whether through social media or in academic or journalistic discourse, closes off the possibility of understanding the *conditions* of the experience of injustice in its infinite variations. In the context of anti-intellectualism, for de Blasio et al. the result is the elevation of rhetoric which aims at and increasingly insists on consent for particular ends, with little regard for deliberation that acknowledges the complicated contingency of lived experience, or the pre-deliberative inconclusiveness of the facticity of that experience. Anti-politics reduces to statements of victimization that authorize their own insistence on particular ends. This phenomenon is increasingly acknowledged in the protest cultures literature, too, with campaigns for particular causes rendered incoherent by chains of equivalence (Husted, 2015). Each linked claim is self-authorized through its utterance, simultaneously unimpeachable yet productive of an increasingly mushy agenda of 'Down with this sort of thing'. This is distinct from but relevant to contemporary arguments around intersectionality (see, for instance, McCall, 2005), or the idea that one cannot presume that all injustice, or oppression, is experienced uniformly. In line with the anti-political stance outlined here, one logical conclusion of intersectionality is that only individuals understand their own suffering and as such are solely authorized to produce the truth of that suffering. The critique developed here inverts this logic, arguing that the facticity of individual suffering is inconclusive, does not produce its own truths and only assumes *political* meaning in deliberative context. What counts as deliberation remains an open question, but the suggestion is that in order to arrive at demands for corrective action properly articulated with principles such as justice, fairness or equality, a necessary condition is the recognition of the sheer contingency – that is, variability and conditionality – of the experience of injustice, unfairness and inequality. In the context of the Arab uprisings, the insistence on the removal from power of particular individuals, for instance, is certainly symbolic and potentially transformative but hardly concomitant with acknowledgement and deliberation of the full range of possibilities for manifesting said principles in political practice.

So the generalized turn away from institutionalized and ideological forms of politics is part of a broader cultural shift away from the instinctive recognition – as a ready-to-hand possibility if not in actuality – of authority in valorized objects including institutions of state, professions and social and cultural elites. In one sense this is nothing more complex or problematic than the decline of deference and the democratic opening up of formerly closed worlds of cultural production such as science, the law and the arts. The consequences of such openings-up have inevitably been partial, variable in their impact and dependent on how informed and armed with relevant skills new entrants have been. Politics can be treated as a special case with regards to this last variable, with it being at least plausible that a democratic imperative might trump deliberative credentials. It is less controversial to argue that debates about science actually benefit from being restricted to specialists (Bourdieu, 1993) than to ask whether non-professional politicians – activists or just interested citizens – have a right to engage in policy-making processes beyond simply having their say. But it is reasonable to ask whether political organization, expression and activism that bypass both institutional and traditionally authoritative forms operate according to a different kinds of logic and are oriented by distinct conceptions of the political. Historically, the public/private distinction or its absence has dominated this debate, with Richard

Sennett (1977) arguing that the relocation of politics to more intimate terrain is essentially a retreat from public life or a contamination of public discourse by private logics, and others (Fraser, 1990) countering that it is precisely the private that Habermasian principles of deliberation neglect and that political discourse needs to accommodate. Papacharissi (2010) pushes us beyond the public/private dualism and in the process mitigates some of the anxiety surrounding the dissolution of the boundary between the two, by making two salient points. First, embracing politics as it is organized or disorganized online does not necessitate a wholesale rejection of conventional electoral politics: the former can be used as a lens on the latter, though the view might be a distinctive one. Second, maybe it is precisely by 'retreating' into private realms that individuals perform the preparatory and experimental work required to participate in public.

As regards populism, then, what we have seen is not a straightforward rejection of politics but a turn away from one model of cultural authority towards another, which in turn leads to an orientation towards a different kind of political object – one which is deinstitutionalized and self-organizing, or national and electoral, or, in the case of populist parties, all of the above. Scholars critical of populist movements frequently start from the observation that they are not all what they seem: while they claim to be horizontally structured and non-hierarchical, they tend to retain top–down decision-making sublimated in the figure of a magnetic leader who exudes ordinariness, enabling the projection on the part of prospective voters of a parasocial relationship with the leader, a kind of intimacy, immediacy and complicity that substitutes for the usual machinations of representative politics. Far from a genuine sprouting of grass-roots politics, the literature is instead peppered with references to astroturfing (see, for instance, Cho et al., 2011). For de Blasio et al., however, the problem is not that Beppe Grillo's Five Star Movement is fraudulent but that its essential character is misrecognized by its followers with the result that political change as a phenomenal object is misconstrued. As with the illocutionary model above, the Five Star Movement is built around a kind of founding myth of direct participation, the experience of which produces consent for particular ends rather than ideological ones. And as a direct result, anything more abstract or noumenal is occluded. Previous accounts of populist politics (see especially Mudde & Rovira Kaltwasser, 2012; Wodak, 2015) infer from this point that the visibility of superficial or token change renders invisible the continuities and inbuilt conservatism of 'deeper' political structures. De Blasio et al.'s conclusion differs in that they identify not surface change and underlying continuity but change above and below, in the experience of the political world and the way that it is structured and reproduced across the longer term, the relation between which is little understood.

POPULISM AND THE POLITICS OF POPULAR CULTURE

De Blasio et al. are keen to avoid being lumped in with the popular culture as a conspiracy camp (Herman & Chomsky, 1988), at pains to point out that while there is something mythical about the participatory nature of a populist movement its followers cannot be characterized as deluded. James Hay (2011), writing about the rise of the Tea Party in the United States, comes closer to claiming that there is something about populism which tends towards, indeed is designed for, dissimulation, allowing elite leaderships and centralizing institutions to project the appearance of grass-roots movements organically brought into being by innocent technology. Hay is wary of the historical tendency to conceive of popular culture as primarily existing to disenfranchise 'ordinary' people and entrench hierarchical relations of power. But while he grounds the discussion in more ambiguous readings of the popular culture, his conclusions, on the whole, confirm the functionalist thesis. As with many others seeking usefully to complexify claims about media effects that otherwise run the risk of appearing presumptuous (Shrøder & Phillips, 2007), Stuart Hall serves as fulcrum for this debate. The Hall that has become familiar to us in recent years has been the one emphasizing that while popular culture is frequently the expression of hegemonic oppression, under certain circumstances it can be the vehicle for radical resistance to that same hegemony. But while it is true that Hall opens the way for thinking about audience empowerment, to revisit a short but dense text such as *Encoding/Decoding* (1973) is to be reminded that, for Hall, the focus remains very much on the political and industrial contexts of media production rather than the agentic possibilities of active consumption. Likewise, although Gramsci, in the context of whose work Hall should be read, identified the essentially unfinished nature of the relationship between the dominated and dominating, it is clear that his own vision of cultural hegemony was more totalizing than the sometimes romanticized accounts of his work that circulate in more recent theorizing about empowerment and disempowerment by and through media (see, for instance, Gerbaudo, 2012; Block, 2013; Briziarelli & Guillem, 2016).

In any case it is this more oppressive conception of the popular that comes to encapsulate Hay's view of populist politics orchestrated through social media. He writes that a combination of media convergence, the new colonization of the territory of the 'popular' by right-wing political interests, the durability of nostalgia for a national culture whose authenticity is at best questionable and the affordances of social networks themselves means that citizens engaging in these kinds of popular political movements are very effectively disciplined by them. There is a strong vein of techno-scepticism in this account – which is not to say that it is misplaced entirely, but it does highlight the continuing dominance of Foucault's model of governmentality (Foucault, 2008) in contemporary thinking about social media. It can be helpful to slow our thinking down when it comes to governmentality, especially when it comes to that eureka-moment experience of understanding power as productive rather than restrictive, something we willingly enact and submit to rather than something imposed from without. As it is, Hay performs a neat inversion from user-generated content to generated users of content, meaning that by encouraging users of networked media to 'customise, individualise and be productive' they reveal much about their investments and pleasures and thereby consenting to regimes of population management. Now, Hay does not use the term 'thereby', and nor does Marc Andrejevic (2008, 2011), whom he cites and who is a leading proponent of the argument that networked media are above all instruments of control and exploitation. But it is worth exploring how engaging with such media, agreeing to its rules and adapting to its architectures actually enact coercive relations of power.

Foucauldian governmentality is in many ways a good fit for the way that the emergence of the conscious self has been framed so far in this book. Whether it is by the priest in a confession box, the therapist or the journalist (see also Dent, 2008), the idea is that individuals are invited to externalize their interior worlds, their desires and fears and anxieties, and these are then reflected back to them as seen by the privileged other – ostensibly neutrally, helpfully even, but invariably encoded in categories, nominalizations, measurements and evaluations. The point is that the individual does not hear 'thou shalt not' at every turn, but willingly, or unreflexively, adjusts her sense of self so that it becomes ever more identical with this categorized self – and along the way internalizes signals from this reflected externalization about what is moral, desirable, normal. The rub is that new forms of populism based on networked media are not really about empowerment or expressivity or creativity, though that is how they are presented to new recruits. Instead, they are about making that expressivity conform to the 'rationality' – we could alternatively say *logic* – of these media so that it can be directed, controlled, disciplined. There is much to be said for this argument as articulated by Andrejevic and Hay, not least that it presents a neat explanation for the way that individuals submit, voluntarily, to the rules, terms and conditions of Facebook and Instagram, including conditions regarding privacy and surveillance that from particular academic or historical perspectives seem suspect. It is also compelling that by being presented not just with externalizations of ourselves as we are but as we could be, our desires can be said to be not so much elicited as constituted through interactions with political and corporate social media. And it is evocative, even romantic, to think of domination of something we offer ourselves up to, something in which we are complicit.

However, there is a gap here between an attractive model of power that accounts for its always-already relation to conscious will and the variegated way that we respond to opportunities or demands to externalize and internalize amid the banalities of everyday life. When introducing Foucault's *The History of Sexuality* (1990) to students, one useful exercise is to ask them to think of sex in women's magazines. While it might at first glance appear liberated to have an increasingly candid discussion of sexual desire and practices in the public realm, what is really offered is comparison, conformity and rationalization: a reader will instinctively externalize their own sexual self as it would be described in the language of the magazine, make adjustments according to what is presented as normal or abnormal and come to understand the ideals underpinning the magazine's discourse as their own desire. This is instructive in what it tells us about broader cultural phenomena: an emphasis on technical proficiency ('10 Tricks to Drive Your Man Wild') points towards the instrumentalization of identity, while a focus on self-expression ('Find Your True Sexual Self') would invoke the valorization of personal authenticity. Directing our gaze inwards, on the other hand, looking at the effectiveness of such regimes in disciplining individuals raises different questions. First, we know not only through Hall but also through Umberto Eco (1994) and others that the dissemination of particular values or categories is not straightforward: there may be competing discourses on offer, a reader's mood, context or predisposition will affect the reading she produces and so on. Put simply, the offering up of the self to evaluation and discipline happens discontinuously, in different directions. There may of course be a dominant discourse that one comes to align oneself with over time, but it remains an open question whether our global, national and local media are characterized more by chaos than control, as McNair (2003) has it, or whether the apparently infinite variability of the digital age occludes an underlying uniformity – whether that is defined aesthetically, psychologically or with reference to capitalist or neo-liberal logics.

For Foucault, at least, the functions of governmentality are prioritized over its uses: the eliciting of expression and confession and its ordering and assimilation will have wider truth effects from which other groups in society might benefit, but there is little in the way of planned orchestration to speak of. And Hay makes a similar point when, like in our teaching exercise, he turns to lifestyle media to put populism in perspective. As with sex advice features or agony aunt columns, makeover programmes do not demand that viewers take notice and conform to whatever ideal is presented but simply invite 'ordinary' people to tell their stories, and viewers to relate to these stories and maybe contemplate their own possible future selves while they are at it (see also Cantó-Milà & Seebach, 2015). Similarly, Liesbet van Zoonen (2013) has observed that makeover programmes specializing in cosmetic surgery are an eloquent expression of the relation between media, power and identity, in that those ordinary people undergoing surgery are not already given selves seeking aesthetic enhancement but individuals becoming their true selves. But although it is self-evidently true that there are people and companies that profit from lifestyle media, and others who could reasonably be argued to be exploited by taking part in this kind of media production, it is not clear that there is a specific relation between exploiter and exploited – certainly not for Foucault, for whom the primary relationship is between each of these groups and discourses of power, not each other. When Hay transposes the trope of lifestyle media to politics, it is then implied that a kind of instrumentalism is possible, that those leading a populist movement can design and orchestrate the way that ordinary people engage with it to ensure their consent and to benefit from their labour. Lifestyle media provide a powerful metaphor for explaining the way that populist leaders operate as floating signifiers, and they work well in the context of the 2008 Obama campaign that appeared to be designed to allow people to see whatever they wanted to in the candidate – and by extension themselves. But it is less convincing to suggest the level of sophistication, deception and simple directness in the orchestration of people's buying-in to the Obama campaign that this account does.

But however masterful the owners and designers of social media platforms, the quandary of false consciousness endures. Simply put, while there is no shortage of theorization of the ways in which individuals willingly submit to coercive relations of power, how do we account for a felt positive experience of that submission? In Andrejevic's account, subjective experience is secondary to the requirement that individuals offer themselves up for exploitation: whatever privation is entailed in providing data or free labour, it will come to be experienced as normal over time, as all states of affairs do. This seems to explain an overall, if uneven, consent for data mining and surveillance: against a more radical model such as Deleuze's control society, research (Best, 2010) indicates that individuals are aware of the various ways in which they are monitored, and also that such surveillance is used for both political and economic ends, but on balance it 'feels' a reasonable trade-off to be 'electronically frisked' at regular intervals in exchange for the convenience and pleasure that media afford. As for outright enjoyment of operating within the confines and demands of Snapchat or Twitter, or of taking part in a populist campaign whose overriding motivation is to control and exploit its members, options are perhaps more limited. It is fair to claim that new media forms – an iPad, a new social network – do not emerge to satisfy innate, if latent, desires, and instead that such desires only come to exist in their elicitation and prospects for satisfaction. This, however, is not the same as holding that the iPad generated those desires – the two are coeval. Similarly, populist political movements do not manufacture their own appeal, though it may be true that the feeling of goodwill many felt towards Obama did not come from his meeting existing deeply held ideals of leadership, but rather that the desire for the leadership he offered emerged only in the context of the campaign. Psychoanalytic perspectives (Stiegler, 1998, 2013a; on the relation between psychoanalytic and Bourdieusian perspectives, see Darmon, 2016) explain this well through the generalized idea of lack (manque) that comes to have meaning only in relation to particular objects. It is feasible too that extant political and economic systems alike are predicated on our existential state of constant becoming, taking advantage of our perpetual orientation towards future selves as well as future worlds. But this is distinct from the argument that if social media users actively take pleasure from using Facebook, or if voters feel inspired by or affection towards Obama, it is because they have been ideologically indoctrinated.

While there is clearly widespread evidence of a willingness to respond to invitations to engage or express or seek advice, there remains finally the question of how to reconcile observed resistance with the governmentality frameworks. All models of hegemony allow for the possibility of resistance, but with divergences appearing over their transformativity or ultimate futility. And as with the populist projection above, it is instructive to look beyond, say, resistance to the seductive messages of a charismatic political performer to cultural debates over the personal and private. Though amplified through media coverage, there was a clear illustration of growing scepticism towards elicitations of self-governing discipline in the widespread derision that met the publication in the United Kingdom in spring 2013 of a guidebook for pregnant women (see https://www.rcog.org.uk/en/guidelines-research-services/guidelines/sip37/) that, among other things, advised readers to avoid non-stick frying pans. Could it be said that this amounts to resistance to paternalistic advice about how best to live one's life? The Foucauldian model is predicated on an embodied receptiveness to valorizations of certain practices over others, whether in the form of curiosity about subject matters previously unknown or, especially, phenomenal objects that invite or demand reflexive positioning: in short, what one's reaction or attitude says about oneself. Underlying this is a normative proposition that governmentality works because the socialization by which all individuals come to experience identity embeds a desire to conform, or else simply the sense that conforming is unthinkingly appropriate. First, it is arguable that this diagnosis of homogenization as a basic feature of social structures rests on the normative proposition that heterogenization – of practices, and by extension of identity – is a worthy goal to pursue. To do so risks reading too much idealism into Foucault's thinking, and even in his late reworkings (1993) of the notion of selfhood worked on in the manner of artistic practice there is no sense of a latent, dormant individual to be liberated in the absence of structure. There is no logically prior individual constrained by homogenizing discourses, only individuals that emerge in the midst of those discourses. But there is a clear and consistent sense in Foucault across his main archaeological and genealogical phases that variety is a good thing, especially when it comes to subjectification: freedom may well be a fantasy, but we are closer to being able to live authentically, in Heidegger's sense of having a reflexive sense of one's simultaneous orientation to future, past and present and of what is at stake in each situation that one finds oneself confronted with as already given, when we are not constrained by a single internalized instinct for thought, action and being.

That idea of making the self as a work of art (Foucault, 1990 [1984]) has been widely discussed and reinterpreted (McLaren, 2002; O'Leary, 2002), and for all the elasticity manifest in Foucault's theoretical framework there is an unmistakable consistency in the argument that individuals do not choose their identities, but that there are nonetheless moral imperatives associated with the way that we become selves. This is important to unpack, as it is precisely morality, or moralization, that functions to discipline behaviour, in media discourses about sexuality and health as much as collective cultures of practice in social media that are quick to police moral infringements as seen from one perspective or another. But while convinced about the disciplinary uses of morality, Foucault is nonetheless interested in what it means to live well: there may be no outside of discourse, but the differences between ways of living in and through discourse do not dissolve into relativism. Associated with this is the status of resistance to power, which is held to be ubiquitous, impossible to own as such, but is to be defended in the alternatives to linear determination it affords. What, then, do we make of the pregnancy guide? On the one hand there are straightforward political critiques of the abnegation of leadership and critical deliberation in public life, the kinds of argument that decry the substitution of political interference in everyday life for the bigger questions about how society should be organized and with what aims. The opposition is simplistic to be sure, as even the most lateral-minded or utopian political outlook still faces the necessity of generating policy on sewers and traffic. But the implication is that resistance to advice on how to have a good pregnancy, along with the moralization that entails, should be welcomed, in the same breath as statistics indicating that while U.K. citizens may smoke less and ingest lower amounts of ecstasy, they drink and get pregnant in flagrant violation of what is discursively appropriate. There is more to this than a celebratory two fingers raised to the nanny state of libertarian nightmares, if there is something about risk-taking that renders life more authentic, in that same Heideggerian sense of consciousness of stakes and care. This is where Foucault is less helpful, and it explains the circuitousness of his later writing on authenticity: if resistance is implied everywhere, then observations of collective practices of resistance are explicable only as non-conscious determinations of discourse whose very transgression is geared at some level towards homogenization or structural reproduction. What if resistance to governmentality in relation to pregnancy, for instance, is no more than the expression of discourse aimed towards the reproduction of hegemonic, internalized norms of class?

The deliberately idiosyncratic examples raised here are cover for a debate over structure and agency that inevitably exceeds the remit of a book like this. But since social change is front and centre in the discussion, it is important to keep in mind the different starting points for analysis open to us. If a change is observed in the behaviour of a particular group or of society at large, is our first instinct to read this as change demanded by shifting structural conditions – say, economic or technological? Or does the impetus for change come from the group itself, manifesting either morphing tastes and interests over time or a collective will to transform things for the better? Or are any observed changes in what is experienced more or less entirely as a symbolic world fundamentally disconnected from, even unrelated to, systemic historical change? These three perspectives are not as mutually exclusive as they look, for instance with the notion of hysteresis (Bourdieu, 1990) capturing the durability of cultures of practice in the face of structural change, less generously conceived as a time lag between 'real' change in the world and change in how that world is experienced. But by and large the social media literature begins either from the proposition that the behavioural changes we observe are coerced adaptations to historical forces involving ever greater exploitation and iniquity (Fuchs, 2014) or that they are signs of resistance to those same forces (Castells, 2009, 2012). This is not to characterize the field as bifurcated between social media evangelists and naysayers, however, and chapter 8 teases out the political status of the individual – that is, the individual as prior to power or vice versa – as a pivotal distinction running through much of the debate. Each begins from a normative proposition about power, and as such it is valid to question the assumed politicality both of inculturation to new social, political or media practices and of resistance to such incitements to submit to regimes of governmentality.

A QUESTION OF TRUST

Is it possible, for instance, that the apparent shift in phenomenal projections of trust from mainstream political and media institutions to less structured or more networked political and media forms is neither a sign of democratization nor of submission to new discourse of power? This section of the chapter contends that the only way to answer such a question is to move away from normative claims towards something more microscopic and methodical. To begin with, it is helpful to pull apart what a relational value like trust, conventionally conceived of in normative terms, is and does in the realm of ordinary social interactions. As a methodological term, trust is slippery, instinctive and amorphous in how it appears to individuals and is distorted by expectations and observations specifically because of its perceived moral quality. Against this, it is possible to think about trust in less loaded terms, though it entails a modification of the influential proposition that all relations of subject and object are, in part, moral in nature because they are inevitably relations of power. This is what underpins Silverstone's (2006) notion of proper distance, which pushes us beyond care in the sense of having an interest in how a situation plays out, towards care as mutual recognition of humanity. This view, and there are many others who share it (Chouliaraki, 2006; Madianou & Miller, 2012; Orgad, 2012), is based on a fundamental yet contingent premise about media. Put simply, it starts with the idea that there are people, individuals and groups, who do things to, with and for other people through their use or experience of media. Those things can of course be normatively positive or negative and may be willed, unintentional or simply unknown. But insofar as media are means by which relations between people are posited, then we should naturally care about whether those relations are respectful, helpful, dehumanizing or oppressive. In the context of this book's main concerns, it is this presumption that makes it meaningful to ask whether distant support for protest movements is instrumental, collectivizing, patronizing or neocolonialist. More fundamental to the book's principal claims, however, it is also possible that this is asking too much of media, social or otherwise, for it is at least conceivable that Twitter is not the kind of space which we can expect to sustain relations of respect, or indeed of harm. This is by no means to downplay the passions that social media spark, in contrast to the banality that is otherwise ascribed to it, but rather to question what manner of interaction occurs in them.

Looked at phenomenologically, to interact with another through social media is to be thrown into an encounter that comes fully formed, immediate and demanding to be comprehended, not as something towards which one can make tentative steps in order to establish familiarity, terms of exchange and common goals. Rather than a relation which lay dormant prior to the interaction, it appears as always-already in the interaction itself. Finding oneself thrown into this immediate relation between subjects and objects, or objects and objects, or subjects and subjects, requires moral consideration specifically because of the future and past encompassed within that present. How things got to where they are now and how they play out from here matter to all concerned. But there are two distinct characteristics of media thrownness that warrant further consideration. One is that while paying attention to media invokes whole worlds to be apprehended in real time, that means instinctively grasping how the media world works, not the worlds it represents. The second is that the selves summoned in media encounters are selves adapted to the logics of that media world – economic, generic, public even, but not necessarily the kind of selves adept at subjective recognition. It is precisely the absence from felt experience of temporal self and other that leads to indifference to or contempt for the distant other on the news or the Twitter user about to be trolled. But a case can be made for seeing less at stake in these interactions: whatever message is sent or received, in most circumstances it cannot amount to full recognition or dismissal of another's subjectivity. The counterexamples of individuals driven to suicide by online bullying, campaigners arguing that lazy or strategic media coverage can mean the difference between life and death or the political contention that stereotypical representations have the effect of dehumanizing great swathes of people mean that it is no simple matter to claim that Twitter is a site in which people do not and cannot expect to have rights conceived in explicitly political terms – the right to recognition or respect, for instance. But it is plausible that what in other contexts we call thin trust (Putnam, 2000) – trusting others not to do you random harm, to pay their taxes and so on – is applicable here too. This, in turn, means thinking about trust in functional rather than moral terms.

Trust is by no means the only social principle to have morphed in the context of networked digital media, but it is emblematic of shifting orientations to the world away from monolithic repositories of authority – known individuals, institutions, organizations, professions – towards something more informal, dispersed and diffuse. One way of thinking about trust as functional is to begin with what is at stake in individual interactions and then to extrapolate outwards. In sociology it is generally held that many-to-many interactions are qualitatively different – that is, not just more complex – than one-to-one interactions, and focusing on trust can cast these into some relief. Thorsen Quandt's (2012) recent research is very much concerned with the moral aspects of social media; indeed, he finds it palpably troubling that while most people by default distrust mainstream media, many are willing to place their trust in the unrepresentative and unknowable others they encounter online. Rather than seeing this through the prism of moral panic or technophobia, however, Quandt shows that it is possible instead to focus on the work that trust does. In one-to-one interactions, trust is essentially about saving time and mitigating risk and uncertainty: since it would be intolerably laborious to determine another's trustworthiness from scratch in each encounter, assumptions are made based on experience, learned cues and the seriousness of possible outcomes. It is in more complex relations within larger groups that thin trust becomes relevant, based again on familiarity and predictability of contexts, potentially alongside more explicit rules learned through familial and educational socialization. Next, at the level of interactions between different groups of people, trust is not associated with particular individuals, or necessarily with an embodied sense of familiarity, but with roles – with the underlying assumption that while little is known about the person performing the role, they would not have been appointed if they were not fit for the purpose. And it is precisely the stabilization and proliferation of recognized roles that provides the preconditions for trust in institutions. This, however, is only viable in contexts where the populace an institution is intended to serve is relatively homogenous – not, presumably, in the demographic sense, but in terms of how institutional roles are perceived. For Quandt, it is the complexity of a media-saturated world that undermines trust in institutions, a fairly straightforward contention that media institutions, especially those with roots in the twentieth century, cannot compete for responsiveness and adaptability with the spontaneous, endlessly malleable networks of social media. This would not be problematic in itself if the quality of trust in this new environment was appropriate to its form – by implication, for Quandt, appropriate trust would be both sceptical and generalized. Instead, however, he finds that the form trust takes in online networks is, inappropriately, one resembling that between individuals – reading selective cues and deciding more or less instinctively on the trustworthiness of individuals and contexts alike.

But it is also possible that what looks like the kind of trust familiar in relationships with known others is precisely appropriate for networked interactions, because it works. It has been seen so far in this chapter that the literature often invites us to interpret the broad cultural shift away from political and media institutions as natural objects of authority, trust and so on as a shift towards ever more embodied, less visible regimes of governmentality. Yet these are normative arguments based, on the one hand, on the assumption that power tends to change over time from the monolithic and explicit to the internalized and insidious and, on the other, that networked media represent an irresistible proliferation of incited subjectification. Such commitments can be rejected without adopting a benign attitude towards either disaffection with party politics and mainstream media or the power implications of networked communications. An alternative perspective is not based on wishful thinking but the observation that individuals experience social networks as less than fully immersive, demanding and critical – the last in the sense of there being vital stakes for them and their interlocutors. On the whole this experience works for them: it is navigable, predictable enough to be intelligible, neither overwhelming nor usually a serious threat to their sense of self and seamless experience of the world around them. It is common parlance to refer to a Twitter stream, and in the academic literature as well as public discourse descriptors such as 'flow' and 'torrent' are legion. There is one sense in which the experience of social media is as an undifferentiated flow, an effect of increased speed and volume of communication (Virilio, 2000, 2006) that means one is always anticipating simply whatever comes relentlessly next rather than anticipating particular encounters through reflexive experience. For phenomenologists *all* orientation involves anticipation, but Berry (2012) demonstrates that this particular future-oriented phenomenal intention is distinct from the anticipatory intentionality in Husserl's model of perception. There is something of Grusin's (2010) conception of premediation in this, deployed by Papacharissi and Easton (2013) to tease out the implications of a dominant orientation towards 'the future' in professional contexts such as journalism. Like Berry, they write about the trance-like experience of paying attention to Twitter, and in the sense that this is clearly parallel to the flow states that characterize the experience of gaming or running, it is logical to think of such flows as undifferentiated into their constituent tweets. Orientation in the flow state is towards the immediate future tout court, to temporality as such rather than temporally constituted contexts of social meaning.

But this is either an impressionistic view of a certain mode of social media consumption or a normative commentary on a cultural fixation on what comes next. Shaun Moores's point (2017) about the practical knowledge needed to operate a laptop only being summoned into existence in the physical act of doing so remains germane here; we return to this in the next chapter. Such knowledge operates precisely in anticipation of what comes next, but this means something different at the phenomenological level: here again anticipation is iterative, oriented towards the next discrete encounter rather than an undifferentiated nextness, and shaped according to past encounters, minutely adjusting orientation so as to maintain as far as possible the seamless experience of at-homeness, where the conditions exist for such a state of comfort. Discreteness and seamlessness have always been compatible: it just means that experiencing the world as continuous is contingent upon sensations, impressions that comprise distinct moments of objectification – this applies to a particular finger swiping a touchscreen (Pink et al., 2016) as much as to value judgement ascribed to someone on Twitter on the basis of a single tweet. Seamlessness is precisely the work of habituation, but in the same way the deluge of visual stimuli we process when navigating a physical environment does not cultivate an orientation to undifferentiated next, there is nothing about the amount or frequency of social media stimuli that futurity itself displaces learned anticipation of particular possible encounters. The upshot is that in phenomenological terms, at least, there is nothing about social media which necessitates a valorization of the new; it is simply how practices of perception are oriented, a condition of experiencing the largest part of our being in the world as given. This view does not fetishize discrete moments of perception, anticipation and reaction, as such practices are linked temporally through habituation and hysteresis, and in any case most encounters leave negligible impressions, if any at all. But it does resist the common conception of convergence culture that too readily reaches the conclusion that media practices have become liquid.

This in turn helps us to explain two things. First, while much research into contemporary media emphasizes their disorienting and chaotic aspects, habituation is still the norm when media practices are observed over even fairly brief periods of time. And second, it allows us to resist being pushed towards thinking that the logical conclusion of being exposed to a deluge of communication on social media is either that users feel confused and at sea or, conversely, as has become more prominent in the literature since the advent of Twitter, that the impossibility and desirability of attending to all communication that presents itself is actually liberating, enhancing the individual's autonomy and propensity to experience communication as water off a duck's back (Neuman, 1991, quoted in Castells, 2009: 128). Discrete moments of perception may produce an effect in the form of eliciting a response or an orientational adjustment or retained knowledge for future moments – but some more than others, and some not at all – and the cumulative result is a kind of positioning by a million nudges. Networked media call forth particular selves in particular moments, inciting certain practices and over time habituating them, including practices of subjectification. Those selves are expected to adapt to the logics of social media, but they are only partially implicated in those logics, and there is more than one way to habituate. This is not to downplay the impact of social media and their role in social change over time but rather to push to one side the idea that there is something about the design or business models of social media that necessitate particular changes in individuals or the world at large. Those impacts and roles are variegated, discontinuous and contradictory; they do not reduce to an effect that social media have on their users.

BEING IN THE WORLD WITH, AND THROUGH, MEDIA

We saw above that for Quandt it is the recognizability of roles and the qualities associated with them – trust, or respect, or fear – that provide the preconditions of professions, qualifications and institutions becoming recognizable as objects. Thinking in terms of efficacy, it is the unreflexive recognition of authority that does the most work for us, though this will range from generic institutional authority in the form of a heterogeneous organization such as the BBC, or particular authoritativeness pertaining to culture, finance, international affairs and so on. As a kind of capital, authority is relational, meaning that with time spent immersed in a given field individuals will develop a sense of how different authorities can be called on collectively to come to a decision about what is at stake in any given moment and how best to confront it. For Quandt, this functionality is stable so long as institutions are perceived to operate in good faith, but thinking specifically about media or consumerism this need not be the case: with each, there is a keen awareness of media organizations and corporations vying for one's attention, of games being played. This goes beyond media or economic literacy: the experience of responding to competing demands for attention can be pleasurable – it can be felt as flattering – and according to de Zengotita (2005) and Sontag (2003) there is even a frisson of power associated with choosing to attend to one message over another. In a context of media abundance, the piling up of such choices may come to be experienced as something *like* surfing a flow of continuous stimuli rather than responding to discrete prompts – but not necessarily. And crucially, a felt user experience of surfing a wave does not compel those in the business of theorizing social media to follow suit: in the same way that biochemists talk about the discrete moments of perception that underpin perceived continuity, ambient or immersive media do not necessitate a reconceptualization of the ontology of media in networked forms. The flow metaphor is loaded, encoding either a liberating sense of fluidity or the insecurity associated with liquid modernity, or simply the visceral thrill of riding a surging wave of information, none of which can be presumed. However, stripping away the more normative elements, it is clear that trust amid saturated or ambient media is distinct in that it is not a matter of accumulating trusted sources of information and interpretation. It is frequently not instrumental, and inseparable from the sometimes pleasurable knowledge that some messages are designed to distract, seduce or cajole you into doing something you would not otherwise have done. Simultaneous and even contradictory orientations can afford a feeling of at-homeness in a particular mediated world, but in phenomenological terms such a feeling simply describes the effortlessness of navigating it, rather than the sense of self it engenders or deeper moral implications about the multifarious relations to others it posits or any sense of shared, imagined community. The flipside of this is that a failure to secure at-homeness means that navigation of a mediated world feels cumbersome, laborious, even pointless – but it does not follow from this that individual and collective subjectivities are at risk.

The dominant normative perspectives on social media boil down to a novel orientation to the world that is characterized by either active curation or helpless thrownness. The first takes a more instrumentalist view, with users increasingly able to attend only to what they choose, with all the freedom that entails, but with a clear downside: self-selecting, like-minded groups of individuals forming insular intentive communities in which trust is unproblematic, but there is a lack of exposure to dissenting voices and different outlooks on the world. The second perspective takes into account involuntary exposure to media, whether through browsing, email, retweets or advertising, suggesting a mode of engagement defined not by iterative questioning about where to go next but a continuous stream of incited reactions to incoming messages. But there is perhaps less between these positions than there appears. While the curatorial perspective presumes media use as a coherent, goal-oriented set of practices, choice in media consumption is qualified by everything from its purposiveness (work or interpersonal communications as well as fact-finding, distraction and pleasure) and geographical or technological specificity to social expectations and even a lingering sense of public duty. Likewise, the second perspective paints a picture of what might otherwise be called serendipitous or ambient consumption as a deluge of hostile or misleading messages, when there is no shortage of evidence that unsolicited exposure to media is experienced by some as enjoyable and met with indifference by others. Further, while some might experience relentless thrownness into mediated encounters demanding responses as flatly disorientating, there exist networks of trust that may be instinctively drawn upon to assess incoming information and decide whether and how to process and potentially respond to it. Such networks may not take the form of anything like a support community but simply the ambient awareness of email contacts or Facebook friends, or the significations of grammar and punctuation, and the generalized sense one has, misguided or otherwise, of 'people like us' in online worlds. Again, there is more than one way to habituate.

For Quandt, the rub is that when presented with such an amorphous array of others, the majority of people active in social networks revert to the form of trust associated with face-to-face encounters. Individuals rely on experience and gut instinct, and this leads them to ascribe trustworthiness where they should not. In line with Bourdieu, 'people like us' does not refer to an innocent coming together of like-minded individuals: we are predisposed to judge others, we do so instinctively rather than reflexively and judgements are made according to unacknowledged rules of recognition and misrecognition that are not only obscure but implicated in various types of power relations. But it is possible that while individuals may be simultaneously careless and judgemental, the risks associated with either are not as great as Quandt, amongst others, suggests. There are real issues around media literacy, not just in terms of the intentionality that marks all media production and consumption but the consequences of data shareability, scalability and durability. Yet if users, especially younger ones, are blithely unconcerned about privacy, or are too trusting of other users, it could be that this represents a different kind of trust rather than trust misplaced. Again couched in terms of work, individuals make use of shortcuts to establish qualities such as authority in order to make life online manageable as real-time presence, but instead of interpreting this as the misascription of authority due to superficial or decontextualized engagement with a source, we can instead talk of a different mode of authority – one which is accorded lightly, provisionally. The implication is that one is not offering up oneself to the recognized authority; they merely serve a purpose that works more often than it does not. Similarly, snap judgements made about others on the basis of cues present, to consciousness or otherwise, do not amount to wholesale condemnation or objectification. For Heidegger, repeatedly finding oneself thrown into a world that already just exists and requires a response raises an existential question about one's orientation to the future and past. But what if thrownness is not experienced as subjectively overwhelming?

This is not to suggest that online spaces are superficial, but they are not discrete. They form part of a world in which one may constantly feel immersed in the always-already, but do not necessarily do the work of immersion or transportation themselves. We experience thrownness not in a self-contained act of listening to the radio or watching television, being immediately transported into another world and all it demands, but as a condition of always-already being in a world that is variously mediated. And after Bourdieu, while it remains the case that real symbolic violence is wreaked when one is put in one's place in any field, it amounts to subjective destruction only to the extent that there are agents and structures capable of calling forth and objectifying fully implicated selves. Pinpointing that extent is impossible, but looking at a specific orientation such as trust, it is possible to start to think about how, either theoretically or empirically, to establish what is at stake when someone finds themselves on a social media platform making rapid judgements about trustworthiness on the basis of learned instincts. It is always possible to argue that by doing so an individual is enfolded in discourse or disciplined into alignment with orchestrating logics and, conversely, to argue that by being sufficiently sceptical and reflexive, users can exert agency of their own towards empowering, transformative ends. But if trust is ascribed neither complicitly nor sceptically but provisionally, ambivalently, then it suggests that it is there to do work other than subjectification. Quandt shows that habituated trust orientations do not always work well, but their successes and failures are parts of ongoing, experimental work we collectively engage in, rather than critical steps on inexorable paths towards subjugation or liberation. This is a theme that will recur later in the book: the point is not to downplay the significance of coercion and transformation but to insist that they are not clinched in critical moments, because subjectification is not simply enforced or achieved but worked at over time. It is sustained through relatively stable orientations or bearings towards the world, but it is also discontinuous and sometimes inconsistent. If overall this book is arguing for the possibility of authentic experience of social change through and not despite the affective banalities of everyday life, and notwithstanding the perceptive failures that characterize most of our lives most of the time, this chapter provides us with an intriguing flipside. Our mediated experience of a changing world as provisional, ambivalent, contingent selves does not preclude the apprehension of what is going on around us; it also means that those selves are neither always-already determined nor existentially threatened by our daily encounters with that world, mediated and otherwise.

Chapter Seven

The Politics of Change

Media, Protest and Conflict

If the previous chapter was about identifying what kinds of social change we are living through, including changes in the media used in everyday life, this one is about the role that media play in shaping our understanding of those changes. In the first instance this will mean tackling some of the prevalent theories about the role that media play in society more generally, whether as a collective frame through which societies focus their attention and seek to address matters of common concern or as a set of institutions that entrench endemic power structures. In the context of the upheavals of the past decade, this takes two forms in particular: the role that media and morphing mediated relationships between people sustain notions of citizenship at the national and global levels and the representation by media of phenomena such as protest and conflict. And in line with the phenomenological bent of this book, it cannot suffice to discuss these things only in normative terms: instead, the idea is to understand how fairly abstract ideas such as global citizenship and conflict are lived in ordinary contexts, how they emerge to consciousness as objects in and through media. Rather than building a systemic theory of media power, declaiming that the media always function so as to stifle dissent, or conversely that social media can cause revolutions, the chapter aims to equip us with the tools needed to grasp exactly what happens when people encounter often distant others in differently mediated environments, whether as fellow platform users or images of suffering and hope. This has to go beyond media representation of political conflict, though, since the practice of witnessing distant upheaval is never wholly passive, while it may sometimes look that way. Media done well can effectively convey what is at stake for a protest movement and the dictator they oppose, but there are stakes too for audiences insofar as they are interpellated as subjects in shared worlds as they watch.

And the point is not simply to remind individuals of their global citizenship of a fast-changing planet but also to cast light onto the contingency of all that seems constant.

Without leaping to conclusions about media causality, it is natural enough to ask whether particular media as well as the particularly mediated condition of much contemporary life played a part in the rapid proliferation of protest in the first half of this decade. At first blush there is much to be said for the 'media contagion' argument (Cottle, 2011): simply put, that synchronous and pervasive visibility of dissent from one place can make dissent in another more imaginable, less risky or even seemingly inevitable. In the sweep of events in 2011 from Tunisia and Egypt to Spain, Israel and the Occupy camps, there is certainly a sense of cumulative momentum and mutual inspiration, though it is an emerging theme of this book that relations among mediated or co-present individuals and groups within and between movements are not inherently profound or transformative – and also that apparently superficial and banal relations can provide a meaningful basis for solidarity and citizenship. There is much disagreement about whether leaderless but self-organizing networked publics enable a kind of agency that is simultaneously greater than the sum of its individual constituents and protective of that individuality or afford mere aggregation that precludes substantive political collectivity (see, for instance, Castañeda, 2012; Costanza-Chock, 2012; Guzman-Concha, 2012; Juris et al., 2012; Morell, 2012; Pickerill & Krinsky, 2012). The approach taken here will be to map how protest cultures and their participants emerge as objects to each other and to actors such as journalists and academics – an emergence which is mediated in the broadest sense of the word – and with what preconditions, qualifications and implications. Without wishing to be pedantic, it is imperative to avoid the assumptions and commitments associated with characterizing any actions in one part of the world as a reaction to or inspired by observations of another place or time, when we can never be sure precisely what that observed amounts to for the observer. Likewise, it is unhelpful to talk about the spread, flow or virality of ideas and practices unless we are certain about the processes – technical as much as conceptual – of translation and proliferation. If we see footage of a group of demonstrators demanding universal access to education or a protestor being beaten by police, what precise object appears to different observers, and according to which technological, political and affective architectures? To prioritize the observer as subject is itself problematic, as all such mediated experiences also involve our objectification. So the question is this: Just what selves are called forth in such an encounter, and with what demands and opportunities?

Before we answer that question, it is worth pausing briefly to sketch out some of the currently conventional academic perspectives on the media's role in social change and continuity. First, as much as it is problematic to assign causality to networked media in spreading ideas and sparking global phenomena, it is similarly presumptuous to ask flat out to what extent media are responsible for everything from gendered norms, the hedonic treadmill or political disengagement. The tendency to pathologize media in this way is increasingly anachronistic, assuming as it does the existence of monolithic or mass media, though the durability of Frankfurt School perspectives (Adorno, 1941; Gramsci, 1971; Horkheimer & Adorno, 1973 [1944]; Bourdieu, 1984; Todorov, 1990 [1978]) on mass cultural production in much media education and social theory means that it is a tendency still encountered in the literature on media and protest. The way we think about domination and coercive power relations more generally has become more nuanced over the years, with Foucault in his own lifetime moving from docile bodies inscribed by discourse to interpellated subjects invoked insistently, prescriptively but also haphazardly and provisionally. Underlying this, in common with theorists from Butler (1993) and Bourdieu (1990) to Deleuze (1994) and Badiou (2001), remains a teleology of structural reproduction, the often unspoken assumption that whatever else is at stake in human interactions, whether they are individual or institutional, remote or face-to-face, the rules of engagement are calibrated towards entrenching unequal, unjust hierarchies of power. The previous chapter presented this outlook as a normative one rather than something arguable from evidence and inference, an apparently deontological position that can in fact be pulled apart. But normative claims can be valid, and the media functionalism argument relation does not reduce to simplistic evocations of moguls and hidden cabals ensuring that the industry works in their favour. Rather, it argues simply that there is something about media – usually their industrial organization, but plausibly also their cultural and technical dimensions – that naturally tends to reproduce an iniquitous status quo.

Media functionalism can do specifics as well as generalizations: the victimization of the global South, for instance, can be explained by institutionalized prejudice and skewed professional norms, but also equally by internet protocols and the affordances of screen technology. The political economy model amounts, however, to what Brian McNair (2003) dubs a control paradigm, insisting that the media are structured so as to demand and secure our consent to live under what should be an intolerable state of injustice. Against this McNair posits a chaos paradigm: in short, things are too organizationally, technologically and economically Byzantine for any group of individuals or corporations to commandeer – or even reliably benefit from. There are other critiques of media functionalism from political science, organizational psychology and linguistics, but for our purposes phenomenological caution suffices: we simply cannot know if the subject–object relation invoked by you or me watching a news item about protests in Egypt is one overdetermined by neocolonialism, nor conversely that the visibility of that object amounts to a laudable kind of agential subjective emergence. It has become more conventional (see Gledhill, 1988) to conceive of the various selves interpellated in media practices as sites of contestation, though this book maintains that while this is theoretically sound, in specific mediated encounters there is actually less at stake for viewers and viewed alike than either subjugation to coercive forces or the opportunity to achieve self-identity and wield subjective agency. It turns out that witnessing, apprehending, being implicated in and participating in historic change is as much about the stuff of everyday life as it concerns the sweep of history and the mechanics of social reproduction.

Phenomenology requires only that we are methodical in describing how things emerge to and withdraw from consciousness and what the conditions of and implications for that consciousness are – what kinds of object are conceivable in certain contexts, what selves are implicated and, finally, why. This 'why' can take many forms, from undersea cables and intellectual property to dominant economic models and the valorization of particular cultural practices and artefacts. In the case of the latter, consider the explanatory model of mediatization. Rather than asking what effects or influences patterns of representation have on society, mediatization asks what happens when the *logic* of the media field colonizes that of other fields – like religion, or art, or dissent. On one level the answer is the way that political discourse, for instance, has come to be temporally structured by news cycles, or how combatants in Syria have not only made full use of YouTube but also learned verification techniques to align their media production practices with those of the BBC Arabic news desk (Hänska-Ahy & Shapour, 2013). But it goes beyond news values to the elevated status of narrative and visuality more broadly; it is about a cultural tendency to recognize the individual embodiment of particular forms of symbolic capital, and it is about the way we discern an authentic account of events – not only in terms of validated times and places, but also according to specific aesthetics: the rough and ready look of video shot on mobile devices in chaotic motion.

Looking at social change phenomenologically, then, asks questions that are fundamentally different from political economy, but it is no less ambitious in its explanatory scope. Phenomenology aims to demonstrate that there are specific conditions under which all of the preceding examples are not only conceivable practices but in many cases experienced as self-evident. These conditions of possibility may be as political as neo-Marxist accounts of hegemonic reproduction, but power is conceived differently – certainly with implications for inequality and injustice, but immanent in practice rather than extrinsic to it, and suffused with our apprehension of the world rather than systematically determining it. Under the control paradigm it is taken as given that mainstream media, whether corporate or state, will apply a delegitimizing frame to protest movements. Others go further: Bourdieu, at least the Bourdieu of *Language and Symbolic Power* (1991), would argue that even the best journalism in the world – whether that means best informed, or lightest touch, or most sympathetic – could not help. By speaking out, disempowered groups can only reveal their powerlessness. But each claim relies on that same teleology of structural reproduction, a commitment that is no less conjectural than the belief that having or being given a voice is empowering (see also Mihai, 2016). It may well be, but it does not necessarily follow, and the tacit elision of voice and power is thinkable, naturally so, only under certain conditions, and with particular implications.

For present purposes, the salient point is that while the mediation of upheaval and protest has myriad characteristics, contingencies and possibilities, it cannot be assumed to serve specific political functions. More generally, this paves the way for analyses of mainstream media that are more incisive and lateral minded than those that begin and end with the dead hand of neo-liberal markets. It allows Castells (2009), for instance, to acknowledge the problems of concentration of ownership while exploring how, in the race to generate profits out of participatory media, predatory multinationals inadvertently created a new kind of participatory media audience possessed of formidable if imperfect political clout – a theme revisited in chapter 8. It also allows for more insightful arguments to be developed than the claim that mainstream media coverage of the Arab uprisings and social media engagement with them has been superficial. It is undeniable that there is much about that coverage which *has* been superficial and reductive, but for more compelling reasons than media control. A little further on we discuss the fact that visual representations of protest tend towards decontextualization, and this can be explained in a number of ways: it could be a matter of ingrained production techniques and ungenerous assumptions about audience attention spans; it could be that a camera operator's options are limited when it comes to framing a space such as Tahrir Square; or it could be, as Žižek (2011) playfully speculated, that there is simply something universal about such events that matter more than their specificity. The lack of backstory and grit in international television coverage of the uprisings has been widely criticized (see, for instance, Ramadan, 2014), but this criticism is predicated on the assumption that such coverage, if pervasive, *causes* superficial or ill-informed engagement with the wider world. And there are at least two problems with this assumption. First, there are competing claims of responsibility for disengagement, with political sclerosis as plausible an explanation as media malaise (Robinson, 1975). Second, the extent to which audiences in the West, say, *should* pay attention to the Arab world, its history, politics and people, is less self-evident than it sounds.

MEDIATED ENGAGEMENT WITH PROTEST

How much should people, whether conceived as publics or audiences, pay attention to, care about and act in relation to distant uprisings and conflicts? This 'should' is sometimes couched in terms of global citizenship (Dower, 2003) or cosmopolitanism (Rantanen, 2004; Robertson, 2010; Cheah, 2013; Chouliaraki & Blaagaard, 2013; Dahlgren, 2013; Fenton, 2013; Christensen & Jansson, 2015), though Castells identifies this as a minority, and elite, concern at best. More commonly, the sense of curiosity about and concern for the interests of distant others has its origins in classical Western political philosophy and the values of mutual respect, prudence (in the sense of Aristotelian phronesis) and autonomy, with the fact of colonialism pushing interest in others towards responsibility. That popular discourse should reflect these principles is less certain, and that media should actively seek to instil and sustain them is more tenuous still. But without delving into existential questions about what mediated popular culture is *for*, it is perhaps more useful to consider a concrete example: Twitter. In terms of popular engagement through Twitter with the events of the Arab uprisings, however, research on tweets using hashtags such as #jan25 tends to confirm conventional appraisals of social media as facilitating little more than applauding a media spectacle: posts show a lack of awareness of political and historical context and an attention to events which is distracted and short-lived (Lotan et al., 2011; Russell, 2011; Wilson & Dunn, 2011). And yet it is questionable how much such findings resonate with broader cultural trends. Labelling Twitter a superficial medium makes little sense, simply because it cannot be assessed in isolation: tweeting is often done in conjunction with other media practices such as watching television, and the sharing of hyperlinks makes up a sizeable proportion of tweets about recent upheavals in the Middle East, as it does with other events (Gleason, 2013).

One response to this is that while Twitter may not have caused this kind of discontinuous and uncommitted engagement with world events, it is symptomatic of a more generalized mediated orientation to the world that is fragmented and impatient. By this view, the fact that participants in social media are choosing to invest in distant developments in a desultory fashion is neither here nor there: this is the logical conclusion of what media have been doing to us for decades. But in the best traditions of ethnographic research, it often helps to stop asking what media do to people, and to ask instead what people do with media. For starters, it is important when analysing tweets to move beyond a focus on their content: apart from anything else, for many tweeting is a low-threshold activity entailing a great deal less backstage effort (Murthy, 2013) aimed at presenting an informed, polished front-stage self. The upshot is that observed failures to perform cultural competence are perhaps less meaningful than failures in other mediated and face-to-face encounters, since less is going on here than the demanded publicization and judgement of wholly implicated selves. This is not to suggest that competence is irrelevant on Twitter, and it may take distinct forms compared to other platforms: facility with hashtag humour and abbreviations, for instance, can be seen as ways of performing at-homeness. Further, Twitter is not only about participation, of reaching out and forming communities, though its passive use tends to go under-researched (see especially Crawford, 2009). The spike in users following NPR's Andy Carvin as he tweeted events in Egypt in early 2011 (Hermida et al., 2014) suggests a demand not for interaction but for access to apparently immediate, unfiltered coverage of dramatic events – the authenticity of which seems to have been enhanced rather than undermined by the fact that Carvin relied predominantly on non-journalistic sources in the region. This last point is unpacked further in chapter 8.

This could conceivably have been experienced by users as being part of something big, but not necessarily. It is entirely possible that even if audiences followed the developing stories of uprising and rebellion because they appeared to them as a nascent critical moment in world history, the experience was primarily an emotional one, or else a reaction to mass-produced, mediated spectacle. And while authors such as Liesbet van Zoonen (1994) have offered cogent defences of emotional engagement as a gateway to public deliberation, Lance Bennett (Bennett & Entman, 2001) and Chouliaraki (2006) are convincing in linking emotionalism and passivity. However, if we suspend for now the question of how media over the years have eroded active participation in various public spheres, including that of the international community, as well as the question of how media could potentially re-engage people, then the possibility remains that emotional but otherwise low-level, spectacular but relatively short-lived engagement is exactly what users expect from Twitter; this is an orientation that has been naturalized as unproblematically meaningful. Significantly, this does not mean that we as analysts are reduced to describing uncritically how people use Twitter and what meaning they derive from it. First, a Twitter feed by a particular journalist or around a hashtag can be pulled apart as a phenomenal object that appears and withdraws, ebbs and flows, and provokes, outrages, frustrates and rallies: in order to explain its attraction, the way it is experienced viscerally, in real time, is important. Next, the conditions under which this kind of engagement is self-evidently meaningful can be examined, particularly in relation to subjectification. This line of inquiry begins from the premise that all practices are, in part, oriented towards the maintenance of the seamless experience of the self – not because of deep-seated narcissism but simply how day-to-day habituation works. Rather than performing ostentatious compassion, then, the idea is that social media engagement with distant others and events will tend to reaffirm one's sense of self in an instinctive, affective way. In the narrowly political sense there is no incitement to action the failure to perform which has serious subjective consequences, no sense that not campaigning, donating or becoming as well informed as possible will undermine a sense of self that is likely, if any kind of attention is being paid, to include compassion, decency and curiosity. More significantly, it suggests that this form of being in the world does not necessitate the explicit recognition of others as agents in order for self-identity to be relatively stable. Whether or not this amounts to disengagement or alienation is arguable, but it is clear that if this form of engagement is broadly satisfactory and functional to mediated publics, then conventional notions of global citizenship appear anachronistic. We return to this claim in the final chapter of the book.

There is some support to be found in the literature for the kind of social relations that appear to fall well short of conventional notions of citizenship and solidarity, such as an implicit social contract or mutual recognition of subjectivity, but which may over time form a workable basis for the same. Benedict Anderson (1983) most famously posited that the sense of community is more about what we imagine to share rather than what we actually do share, though the sustained effort involved in building an imagined community far exceeds shared habits of paying attention. Bernard Stiegler (2013b) uses the metaphor of an ant colony to convey the idea that it is the way people just rub along together, leaving invisible traces as they go, that constitutes a social network, rather than critical encounters. Richard Sennett's (1977) argument against intentive communities is also apposite here, as well as Butler's recent writing on the ethics of care (Butler, 2004; Butler & Athanasiou, 2013): instead of definitive moments in which one is called forth to demonstrate solidarity or common endeavour, it is the way that individuals who disagree or have little to do with each other interact that constitutes the fabric of a community. However, while sense of self or of community might not be dependent on dramatic ultimatums and overt performance – most find it easy to resist (most) aid appeals, after all, or to decline the ever-present invitation to engage in autonomous research to better understand what is in the news – there are nonetheless callings forth. These are part of what was referred to in the previous chapter as the habitus of the new: not an obsession with the near future (cf. Powers, 2015) but an always-already orientation to what comes next, the perpetual procession of objects that might not demand our full attention but nonetheless elicit low-level, incremental reactions, positionings, adjustments.

Media encounters, then, have the capacity at least to call forth selves aligned to logics of production and power, even if such demands are habitually shrugged off. But routine practices of self-maintenance do not happen in isolation but with reference to the world of objects, and this kind of relational positioning will of course include mediated emergences to consciousness – at least those messages that register, some of which will have been sought out and others received serendipitously or against one's will. Consequently, while audiences are generally well insulated against mediated encounters that would disrupt their habituated sense of self (Susan Sontag's 'This is what war does, this is what you tolerate' polemic (2003) about the images of abuse in the Abu Ghraib prison is one such example), because there are potential subjective stakes for audiences in media encounters, the representation of others matters to them as well as those represented. How distant others are objectified through media is generally considered an ethical question in terms of their rights, their status. But their mediation implicates viewers in the question of how to live in a world in which these others exist, in which these things are going on. This is in line with Arendt's (1958) conception of solidarity and Dower's (2003) of global citizenship, though the distinct line this book takes is that such principles are not clinched in moments of truth or derived from metaphysical premises: they are part of the humdrum work of being. Either way, though, the mediated encounters in which these principles play out are not abstract but contingent, which means that this book's focus on the experience of media consumption and production cannot preclude the substance of media representation. As such, it is to the representation of protest and upheaval in the media that we now turn.

PROTEST IN THE MEDIA

Much of the recent literature dealing with the visibility of protest, conflict and suffering has focused on the reduction of events and people to rationalized media objects and by extension to illegitimate or inert objects of hegemonic discourse. There are various explanations of how this happens and with what aftermath, as well as broader contextualizations that point to the proliferation of screens or, with the rise of consumerism, of symbols or simulations. In Todd Gitlin's (1980) canonical account, protests are represented in mainstream media through various frames which serve to delegitimize dissent; significantly, however, this was not a function of the aesthetics of visual imagery or the flattening effect that mass reproduction of cultural forms is argued to have. Instead, for Gitlin, hegemonic reproduction is hardwired into every aspect of the news production process, from technological and editorial to the way that journalists and other media professionals are recruited. There is much to be said for this approach, and Gitlin has been careful to avoid merely invoking a system designed and operated with structural reproduction in mind. The mechanics of hegemony cannot be taken as given, and it is the compelling detail in his work – down to selection of sources and use of scare quotes – that prevents it from lurching into pontification. One aspect it deliberately underplays, though, is the capacity for autonomy and reflexivity on the part of media workers. And rather than presume that each of these individuals across the media and creative industries has been indoctrinated so as to secure their subordination to broader hegemonic functions, it is at least possible that some of them are relatively savvy about media politics, possessed of a degree of awareness of their own position in relation to elite and establishment power, and not entirely reconciled to the thwarted idealism or outright cynicism which is imagined by academics and others to be the logical conclusion of their professional socialization (Benson, 2006).

In philosophical terms, this simply means that there is no one-to-one correspondence between the way a professional subject is structured by the field she inhabits and the structuring effects of her structured practices: there is inevitably slippage, negotiation and, from time to time, critical insight. Why then, overall, do journalistic and other practices in relation to protest tend towards projecting the status quo into anticipated futures? One reason is simple groupthink: contrary to the belief that journalists are motivated by the desire to stand out from the crowd, the journalistic orientation to the world is not towards the radically new or unprecedented but to knowing what is being said by peers and authority figures at any given time (Bourdieu, 2001). This is not meant to suggest a lack of professionalism: journalism like all fields is relational, and to exist in it is to engage in constant positioning in relation to other agents, being in alignment with the right way of doing things. It does, however, produce a significant degree of homogeneity in the professional sense of felicity – that is, what just happens to be thinkable or sayable at any given juncture. In a different context this can be seen played out in real time on Twitter: posts made during a broadcast of a political discussion programme are as much acts of positioning as of expression, and the sum total of such tweets tends towards the predictable and unimaginative. The open question in contexts of populism, dissent and uprising is whether this type of popular discourse, characterized by a combination of instinctive hostility to the 'other' side of politics and blanket derision of institutionalized politics, then makes it more likely that the status quo will continue. Journalists' experience of protest and turmoil past tells us that the answer is yes, because we have seen it all before. But this is experience of the embodied, quotidian kind, the kind solidified through having made countless anticipations of future outcomes before, adjusting how one calibrates the odds of things playing out one way or another. It is a call based on shared inhabitation over time of a field, which is different from learning from history.

There is a paradox here, since despite what is widely accepted to be a professional field marred by collective amnesia (Sharkey, 2000), it is precisely history that is routinely deployed to form journalistic heuristics: in early 2011, developments in the Middle East were frequently compared to the fall of the Berlin Wall, while the civil war in Syria was likened to Bosnia. This overdetermination of narrative by historical precedent is argued (Edy, 1999) to produce not only inaccuracies in our understanding of events on the ground but also misapprehensions on the part of journalists, academics and audiences alike. We return to this question substantively in the following chapter, but for now it suffices to flag up a recurring theme: questioning whether professional or public engagement with distant events is properly authentic only gets us so far. Engagement that looks disingenuous or superficial may nonetheless be functional in how it orientates navigation through the world day to day, and it is further plausible that over time it can form the basis of public engagement classically conceived, if such principles as engagement, solidarity, care and so on are seen as things worked on in mundane contexts rather than secured in extremis. By this logic, media professionals' professed interest in history – journalists are known through their memoirs to be voracious readers of historical non-fiction – can be taken at face value, while the way they *use* history can be dissected in strategic terms. Responding to apparent dissent within a protest movement with world-weary fatalism is not necessarily motivated by an internalized will to undermine its prospects – though that might be the effect – but by an act of authoritative positioning (Markham, 2011a). Knowing where to stand in relation to the eruption of dissent abroad does not demand the same performance of resignation. Here, characterizing Tahrir as another Wenceslas or Tiananmen is about gut instinct, playing the odds by rules learned through years of anticipating, honing and recalibrating. It is a game driven more by embodied strategizing than history understood, but it is no less genuine for it.

More broadly, there has been something of a rowing back from analyses modish in the 1980s and 1990s that the spectacularization of conflict – and much else besides – has effectively emptied events as we come to know them of all ontological content (Baudrillard, 1983; Poster, 2001), that all we have is the shallow play of surfaces, endless recursions of representativity. There remains, however, an enduring vein in the literature insisting that our reliance on visual media, especially mass broadcast media, necessarily effects a superficial engagement with mediated others, not only as a result of the limitations and demands of screen interfaces but as symptomatic of a culture awash in symbols and disconnected from 'deeper' meaning. It has been suggested here that differentiating 'proper' and degraded forms of attention and engagement risks losing sight of how each is experienced in everyday life. This is not to say that all kinds of attention and engagement are equally valid but that, first, each needs to be understood in terms of the work they do in quotidian contexts that may depart from what we might think they are *for* and, second, that in comparing orientations it cannot be assumed that there is a straightforward opposition between surfaces and depths of phenomenal objects. There are ways of usefully complexifying subject–object relations that offer us more than philosophical gymnastics, and the earlier empirical chapters of this volume do not limit themselves by bracketing out all but directly observable data nor to doggedly seeking 'the thing itself'. For now, though, this approach means suspending suspicions about the paucity of relations necessitated by contemporary practices of media production and consumption in visual media. Specifically, is it possible that the spectacularization of protest is a good thing when it comes to awareness-raising and mobilization?

Cottle (2006) labels as dramaturgical those approaches that judge the opportunities afforded by mainstream media's predilection to visual images of conflict, controversy and deviance to outweigh the ideological baggage that comes with discursive framing. Proponents of protest dramaturgy are under no illusions about media bias and sensationalism, but it is thought that there is scope for sparking debate and reaction that exceeds these determining logics. Much is made of the staidness of the public sphere traditionally conceived, with aspersions now commonly cast over notions such as rationality, consensus and civility in political discourse. It has been widely noted, including here, that these terms carry a gender bias, and potentially a first-world one too. But for our purposes there are other, potentially more fruitful, ways of pulling them apart. Rather than casting aside rationality for its exclusion of emotion, for instance, it is arguable that in its Habermasian form, rationality's principal defect is that it is not political enough. Policymaking conducted according to Habermas's formulation is avowedly evidence-based, consensual and procedural, when it is conceivable that idealism, the dark arts of persuasion and charisma and the machinations of horse-trading and dealmaking are not just unwanted byproducts of politics but its beating heart. The goal of consensus in public deliberation is rightly criticized for what it precludes – radical alternatives to dominant economic logics, say, and more generally the ongoing pursuit of dissensus (Rancière, 2010) and agonism (Mouffe, 2013). Related to this, there is a long intellectual tradition of understanding violence as political agency rather than the failure of politics, as a vital form of political communication rather than its opposite (Fanon, 1963; Malešević, 2010) or as a mundane phenomenon (Staudigl, 2007). Likewise, it is possible that media that apparently act contrary to the rules of the public sphere by sensationalizing and simplifying, playing up the emotional and imaginative over the rational and factual, can be rethought as sites of dissensus or transformation.

THE PHENOMENOLOGY OF MEDIATED PROTEST

The affordances of visual media may not address all the shortcomings of the public sphere conventionally conceived, then, but for DeLuca and Peeples (cited in Cottle, 2006) the 'public screen' does offer a genuine 'alternative venue for participatory politics' and a 'striking contrast to the public sphere'. It is worth delving a little further into the aspects of visually mediated protest that they hold up as potentially fertile: 'dissemination, images, hypermediacy, spectacular publicity, cacophony, distraction and dissent'. Sontag wrote of the Abu Ghraib photographs that their particular horror, aside from the practices represented and their banal mis-en-scène, was that they were created in order to be traded, casually, as email attachments or through social media networks. The sharing, reposting and remixing of images such as that of the 'blue bra' protestor assaulted in Tahrir Square, or the 'woman in a red dress' being hosed by security forces in Turkey, can be interpreted either as a piece of political communication amplified and proliferated or as the hollowing-out of political content, the circulation of a floating signifier into which recipients are free to project whatever message they choose. Such images are as open to interpretation as any others and in their recursiveness are not categorically different from an image of Che Guevara coming to epitomize off-the-peg political consumerism or that of Klimt's *The Kiss* becoming redolent over time with the visual iconography of student accommodation. But in these cases recursivity is an effect of mass production, whereas the presumption of shareability (boyd & Ellison, 2007) in images of dissent taken on mobile devices with the intention of their being posted on social networks suggests a distinct ontological status. At stake here is not the intended message of whoever produced the visual image or footage but, after Husserl (1931), the intention behind the act of attending to such an image or footage. Attending to an object whose dissemination is integral to its status clearly posits a different subject–object relation not only to one-to-one communication but also one-to-many, in the form of traditional journalism, for instance. For advocates of the network society thesis the agency of the image is both more diffuse and potentially powerful, but it is unclear what power amounts to here unless we are talking about what other agents subsequently do with the image.

Object-oriented ontology (Harman, 2002, 2011) is helpful in this regard, in that by characterizing all constituent actors first and foremost as objects – person with camera, camera, viewer, network, digital image protocol and so on – it is relatively uncontroversial to speak of the non-human aspects of the agency of an image as it circulates. But agency does not entail efficacy, and circulation does not imply an alternative form of participation in public deliberation. Principles such as cacophony and distraction, however, are more promising insofar as they speak to encounters that disrupt the habituated experience of being in the world, but in a generalized way. Whatever someone's political sympathies, they are likely to be able to process specific messages fairly effortlessly, agreeing with or dismissing them according to taste, regardless of how these messages circulate. Faced with noise or anything else which blocks that instinctive ability to respond to incoming messages, an individual may simply be annoyed. But they may also find themselves grasping for new ways in to whatever lies behind it, engaging imaginatively or simply being more openly receptive to subsequent stimuli. Again, there is no guarantee of sustained attention or qualitatively different engagement with a political issue, but there is with distinctly mediated specularization the possibility of orientations outside of the habitual. Whether this amounts to efficacy as ever depends ultimately on articulation to action contexts, but first and foremost to how someone finds their way to an object that initially appears uncanny.

Writing about the experience of watching YouTube, David Meek (2012) offers a compelling corrective both to the idea that watching some distant other through a screen somehow transports us 'there', to the place represented, and to the opposing claim that the distance between viewer and viewed remains stubbornly uncollapsed. The latter is typically explained either in terms of the reduction of that being represented to something generic or else a failure of the cultural translation required to see that place as its inhabitants do. But what if each perspective misunderstands how we experience place? Normally we think of place as something we inhabit, or act in or observe, and while there might be much that we take for granted in places we routinely inhabit, place and self are mutually external. This is not to say they are autonomous from each other; after Lefebvre (Lefebvre, 1991) it makes more sense to think of places not as spaces that are discovered but as objects produced through specific cultures of practice, including description, exploration and mediated representation. A demonstration in Tahrir Square, then, is not something we discover and observe but an object we create through our observing, with all of the overdetermination that implies. To speak of us misapprehending the square as a place of protest is wide of the mark, because by this account our practices of apprehension will inevitably produce a different place from that produced by a protestor, journalist or other audience members. But this assumes that we are a priori selves that go around producing places, and Meek reminds us that place comes first: our being emplaced is prior to our conscious experience. Importantly, this is not a defence of historical materialism, a belief that the reality of Tahrir will resist our overdetermining ways of observing, categorizing and making sense of it. Instead, '[t]his emplacement is not in a specific material place, but an informational one, namely forged through emotional connections' (Meek, 2012: 13). The relation and tension between affect and engagement remain unresolved, but this line of thought does allow us to conceive of an always-already emplacement as located on a continuum between online and offline practices.

All protest aims at visibility. However, there is something distinct about cultures of protest seeking maximum visibility in mainstream media despite, as DeLuca and Peeples contend, corporate media's perceived tendency towards ideological discipline. The condition of such a productive protest object emerging is acceptance that with supposed media saturation, hegemonic media cannot monopolize attention. Attention is a scarce commodity, which places the viewer in a relatively privileged position and the imaginative dissenter well placed to exploit counter-intuitive attention-seeking methods. This is not to ignore those protest movements that prioritize autonomous, prefigurative action over publicity campaigns. But one criticism made against Occupy is precisely the belief widely held by its participants that 'the media' or 'the mainstream media' are determined to undermine their credibility. Public screen advocates are not presumed to be naïve but open to the possibility that the life span and quality of a tweet or a YouTube clip is not predictable or able to be straightforwardly appropriated and warped by establishment power (cf. Newsom et al., 2011: 1308). However, the commoditized conception of public attention in this approach suggests that it has adapted itself fully to the logic of mediatization (Hjarvard, 2013) and specifically the notion that whatever grabs the attention of global audiences – cacophony, theatre, violence – is justified. This overlooks the fact that attention comes in many different forms, some better articulated to engagement and action than others: that which forces audiences to think twice or engage their imaginations may enable more efficacious or sustained engagement, but then again it may not. The same perspective also overstates the scarcity of attention – a scarcity that is necessary if attention is to be conceived, in valorized market terms, as a precious product in a seller's market, but which does not match the experience of many, most even, of living in media-rich environments.

This, then, brings us to the crux of how to think about the media's role in covering the Arab uprisings and political upheaval generally: in short, what kinds of objects of protest appear to the consciousness of those involved or watching, and what kinds of relations are posited between those objects and subjects. On the one side are those (Debrix, 2006; see also Hammond, 2007) who argue that all mediated conflict, but especially the visual, posits a passive viewer because political meaning is only intelligible in material specificity and spectacle is prone to make all protests, wars or famines indistinguishable. On the other side are those (Chouliaraki, 2006; Orgad, 2012; see also Griffin, 2010) who contend that it is exactly such decontextualization which enables engagement, allowing for a relation that may be more than anything the product of projection, but which nonetheless is experienced in more personal, imaginative and visceral ways. There are lessons to be drawn from photojournalism here, with Hariman and Lucaites (2007) making the conventional point that the persuasiveness of an image has little to do with its realism, and the less conventional one that nor is it to do with its association with particular moral values. Instead, an image has to offer up the structure of a moral response 'that is adapted to the deep problems of the public culture at the time' (Hariman & Lucaites, 2007: 175). The upshot is that mediation is not *about* decontextualization or universalization, but *abstraction* within particular cultural contexts. It is true that such images lose their historicity, and that those already encoding less historical detail 'most readily lend themselves to this abstraction process' (Griffin, 2010: 18), but an image will only gain purchase if it is fixed to particular myths – national, cultural, professional. If not, depicted events are likely to be regarded as isolated and discrete, disconnected from the underlying discourse that exists around this kind of event. This is convincing: in order for protests to resonate they must be easily subsumed by audiences among the things that are naturally conceivable and 'just talkable about' as protest as we understand it.

Resonance and purchase, though, are not the same as public engagement. Griffin (2010: 29) suggests that if 'key images used to symbolize a conflict' lack historical detail, then the reactions they provoke will be limited to the personal and emotional; he is quite specific about what responses fall into this category, listing 'a generalised impression of pain, anger, terror, grief, resignation, perseverance or triumph'. These words warrant unpacking, as they reveal a fair amount about how academic discourse conceives of mediated conflict. The word 'used' in the first quotation suggests a degree of instrumentality, as though a photographer, video camera operator or editor has some scope to decide how best to capture the essence of a conflict. Photographs of the Mai Lai massacre in Vietnam failed to achieve the iconic status of, say, Accidental Napalm, but not because of a lack of richness or provocativeness in the images themselves, but because of production issues: publication of these images was delayed, and when they did emerge they did not resonate with what Vietnam had by then become in the public imagination. It is important to bear in mind the production process underpinning the recording and dissemination of such images, but in the context of digital media we also have to be mindful of the way that certain images or memes go viral, to use the common term for exponential proliferation. Virality is misleading insofar as it suggests inevitability and vitality – both questionable aspects of networked communication – but what is important about the rapidly amplified dissemination of images of conflict or protest is that they are neither arbitrary nor predetermined. Again, particular viral images may resonate, but not uniquely so; their emergence as massively circulated objects is contingent early publicization by valorized individuals and forums, serendipitous coincidence, translatability to different media and national contexts, and so on.

AUDIENCES OF PROTEST AND CONFLICT

So if certain images come to symbolize a conflict, it is not because they contain unique meaning, or that they emerge democratically through networked media, their pre-eminence the result of nothing more than their propensity to be shared. They do so because they fit specific logics of emergence, though to a degree haphazardly, as with the sheer volume of images on offer there are bound to have been alternatives that would have done the same work of symbolizing a conflict just as efficiently. As such, we need to turn on its head the question of which images come to symbolize an upheaval and ask instead what objects of upheaval these images present to us – and, again, what kinds of subject–object relations are posited. Let us consider three archetypes. First, whether through photographer, editorial or audience selection, representations of individual protestors frequently achieve the iconic status of standing for a protest movement; they can be depicted as defiant (Tiananmen Square), victimized (blue bra woman) or dead (Neda in Iran's 2009 post-election tumult). In each case, that which the protestors are ranged against is rendered simply morally wrong, rather than politically illegitimate, and the viewer is positioned in a relation of sympathy, rather than solidarity. Second, among the most circulated images of the Arab uprisings are of crowds massed in urban squares, often at night, with fireworks and banners contributing to the sense of theatre. Individuals are not usually discernible in such images, with the result that the protest appears as an undifferentiated, if unstoppable, force. It is protest that has achieved critical mass, but with its participants somewhat dehumanized in the process. Such an object conforms to Chouliaraki's (2006) 'adventure' mode of engagement, one depoliticized like the first but also rendered as viscerally thrilling rather than politically motivating.

The third category is perhaps the most complicated, but certainly iconic judging by visibility online, in the press and also on academic book covers. These are images where passionate, angry individuals are performing protest in ways that we find familiar – holding banners, chanting, making gestures in concert – but also recognizable as individuals, and as individuals in a particular place and time. Islamic dress is predominant, Middle Eastern flags are prominent and at least a proportion of the banners are written in Arabic script (it is possible that those in English are a manifestation of mediatization, adapting to the logics of emergence in Western or global media markets). What kind of protest object do such images represent, and what relations are posited in their creation, reception and dissemination? It is relatively straightforward to reach for orientalist explanations, with protests exoticized for the entertainment of Western audiences, the subtext of Arab inferiority or disorder thereby enshrined. Quantitative research carried out using the Tahrir data sets (Lotan et al., 2011; Wilson & Dunn, 2011) suggests that it would be difficult to make a case for the opposite: that is, proof of idealized, informed engagement with events in the Middle East that go beyond political interest to the full recognition of these political objects as political subjects. But we can understand the mediation of political upheaval better if we look at the work which such mediated objects do. First, this means disaggregating different audiences, as it is likely – though not incontrovertible given the limited success satellite broadcasters including Al-Jazeera and Al-Arabiya have had in building a pan-Arab public sphere (Rugh, 2004; Mellor, 2007; Hafez, 2008; Pintak, 2011) – that coverage of popular uprisings in Tunisia engendered reactions of encouragement, inspiration or solidarity in other countries across the region. But it also means moving beyond the conception of Western audiences as apathetic and self-absorbed. It is true that the quality of Western engagement with political upheaval in other parts of the world is often selective and ill-informed, but this is not the same as saying it is insincere or patronizing. Chapter 8 explores the ramifications of academic discourse in which emotional support stands in for solidarity: in short, it sustains a myth of unstructured generativity in politics and technics alike. But this just highlights the need to pay close attention to the contingencies of engagement: projection may be self-serving, but it does not follow that this proves an absence of engagement. The emotive content of such engagements – excitement, fear, hope, despair – are not sufficient conditions for participation in public deliberation or activism, but nor are such emotions absent when participating in talkback radio, or a protest march, or voting in an election.

A considerable amount of work has gone into assessing whether and how mediated representation can prompt Chouliaraki's ecstatic response, literally one which takes one out of oneself, or in the terms of the present discussion breaks through the seamlessness of everyday conscious experience and the contingent conditions of possibility which sustain it. This is often described rhetorically as pushing audiences out of their comfort zones, but 'comfort' need not connote the blinkered, cosseted lives that audiences live, blithely unaware of the horrors unfolding elsewhere. In phenomenological terms, comfort refers to the givenness of most conscious experience, the effortless way that an object such as a protest, protestor, tear gas or chant appears to us, and we experience a sense of positioning in relation to it. If the desire is for audiences to really apprehend what recent events in the Middle East are about, and to engage in issues of intervention, aid, diplomacy and globalization in critical and informed ways, all things that they currently fail to do, then it follows that this sense of comfort needs to be disrupted. The constituent upheavals of the Arab Spring need to be understood on their own terms – not just as distinct from each other but, crucially, distinct from all the other events that appear to consciousness. In order for this kind of undiluted apprehension to occur, the logic goes, then either the distance or layers of mediation that intercede between subject and object need to be overcome: what needs to be grasped are the things, the events, themselves. However, what if the problem is not one of distance, or mediation, but one of *orientation*? The focus then shifts away from the obstacles that lie on the path to some ideal of full, unmitigated perception to the embodied responses to objects of politics or protest, injustice or suffering to which audience members are predisposed.

We have seen already that part of this orientation is subjectification: individuals will instinctively position themselves in relation to a mediated object usually such that their sense of continuous selfhood – as compassionate, or dispassionate, or principled, or world-weary – is sustained. This is not the same as solipsism: subjectification happens in all kinds of ways and is usually a low-stakes practice for subject and object alike, the stuff of habit rather than a practice which carries the ability to traduce another's being in the world. Beyond that sense of self, the emergence of a distant, mediated other to consciousness is constrained not so much by incomplete apprehension, marked by what is missing of the full subjectivity of that other, as constituted as that which we are actively primed to recognize as meaningful. After Foucault, this might be thought of as a will to knowledge – the opposite of censorship, being invited to apprehend but in mandated forms that exceed our individual agency. This is less circumscribed than it sounds, leaving us the task of assessing extant modes of objectification and, rather than seeking their elimination, asking what work they do for us and what alternatives there are. The more normative claims about what orientations *should* yield which reaction are evident enough in the academic literature on distant suffering (Boltanski, 1999), and especially in the journalism of attachment (Bell, 1998) or charity campaigns that seek to harness emotion and direct it towards instrumental ends. However, while haphazardly effective, such efforts largely fail to grasp the seriously limited scope that exists for shaping the way that an object appears and is recognized, for overcoming the sheer givenness of most apprehension. The objectness of a protest movement or political tumult does not come from the thing itself. Neither does it come straightforwardly from wishful projection: it is instead a matter of what we are habituated to recognize as a valorized symbolic form. Valorization is not a measure of objective meaningfulness – the distorted calculus by which deaths in different parts of the world are weighed makes this clear (Moeller, 1999) – but the manifestation of what we are used to recognizing as meaningful, and what that recognition affords us. Van Dijck (2013) describes this as what we have learned to discern as truth in the media we use, but it extends to our very ways of knowing about the world and our being in it.

It is significant that this conception of how objects appear to consciousness is rooted in Giddens' (1984) model of structuration: structures exist only insofar as they are enacted in practice, and while they might have durability they have no logical priority or ontological stability. In concrete terms, this is an attempt to move on from those accounts which would characterize the uprisings of 2011 – all uprisings, in fact – as interchangeable: whatever political upheaval is depicted, the viewer's response is predetermined, and the outcome – what the viewer thinks of distant others, what they think of themselves or the imagined communities to which they belong – is unshakeable. Such arguments were fairly common in the context of the various conflicts of the 1990s that came largely to be understood and acted on as ethnic or interethnic in essence: for Hammond (2007), this reduction reflected the primacy of the West's need to assert liberal, humanitarian values over the facts on the ground. As was seen in the previous chapter, there are also parallels in electoral politics, with populist figures from Donald Trump to Boris Johnson described in such flatly functional terms, empty vessels in which audiences with starkly differing world views can find reflections of those views. Projection itself is not the problem if the whole idea of perception is understood as being intentive rather than a process that starts with the world out there and ends in our minds. But as Ruddock (2006) has argued, media cultures in which diametrically opposed audiences can find validation of their existing prejudices and thus affirmations of their senses of self in the same media texts substantively undermine the viability of a public sphere – they are not a benign reflection of audiences' ability to decode media on their own terms. Ignorance, deep-seated orientalism and projection bode ill for any kind of global community, let alone polity.

However, while rhetorically this is compelling, in fact audiences are neither hardwired to recognize certain meanings or symbolic forms whatever they are exposed to nor can they wilfully project whatever they choose onto an object such as a pro-democracy march. These claims are two sides of the same coin, the first cleaving to a monolithic articulation of structuralism, the second in the phenomenological sense idealistic. In practice, even in contexts where for cultural or technological reasons the appearance of an object is seemingly short-circuited and overdetermined, mediation between subject and object is nonetheless multifarious and iterative. By way of illustration, and to link this discussion to its potential policy implications, let us consider one of the ways in which individuals and institutions seek to effect a particular kind of objectification of political upheaval, one which positions the viewer in such a way that action is conceivable: deploying celebrity advocates to front humanitarian campaigns (Brockington, 2015; Scott, 2015). It is easy to be cynical about such manoeuvres, characterizing them as nothing more than dressing up complex issues according to a populist logic that a dumbed-down audience might just respond to. More generously, celebrity advocates can be seen as an attempt to disrupt the ritualized habit of watching the news, a habit that might be seriously engaged but entirely passive, the absence of action perfectly compatible with a humanitarian sense of self.

UNICEF has recruited several celebrities in recent years, from David Beckham and Ewan McGregor to George Clooney and Angelina Jolie – it will be seen in the following that the choice of celebrity is critical, with audiences quick to turn against spokespersons seen as inappropriate (Geri Halliwell) or sanctimonious (Bono, Sting). In the context of the Syrian civil war, the British comedian and UNICEF advocate Eddie Izzard visited refugee camps across the border in northern Iraq, making a series of appeals for donations to support the humanitarian effort. Izzard identifies as transvestite and is best known for absurdist-inflected stand-up comedy while also known for 'serious' acting roles and, increasingly, charity work. While nothing can be assumed about how different audiences respond to Izzard as a celebrity, it is possible to gain some insight into how he appears as a mediated object, and what assumptions are made about his audience, by examining the video of one particular appeal (UNICEF, 2013) as a text and, in the manner of Chouliaraki (2010b) and Zelizer (2010), extrapolating possible audience experiences from its visual content, frames of reference and underlying symbolic economy. The latter term is not intended as recourse to *political* economy but rather the usually unacknowledged criteria by which symbolic value is ascribed in any given context.

Whether successful or not as an entreaty to donate, the campaign's strategy in encouraging a different quality of phenomenal relation to humanitarian crisis is projecting a simple lack of pretence. The choice of Izzard is telling, with a style of delivery that is meandering and shambling rather than polished or rehearsed. Beyond the obvious attraction of using someone affable to represent a humanitarian campaign, the broader implication is that the target audiences of this appeal are predisposed, or presumed to be predisposed, to trust someone who is seen as somewhat subversive, irreverent or anti-establishment. That recognition does not simply happen but is discerned – at the individual level by a combination of symbolic markers from the actor's facial expressions, chaotic body language and a voice that switches repeatedly from mumbling to declarative, and at the cultural level by a shift towards the valorization of unofficial, non-professional authority. The pervading tone of the appeal can be summed up as an acknowledgement of the artifice and absurdity of the media most of the time, as well as an indication that this is not most of the time: this is real. In part this is achieved through the visual design of the appeal – a straight-to-camera piece with no apparent filters or edits and Izzard dressed in a black UNICEF T-shirt and baseball cap. This is interesting in itself as it suggests we recognize authenticity in the explicit absence of production values, with little in the way of obvious preparation and a quality of sound and vision that could be emulated by many mass-market mobile devices. This simultaneous drawing of attention to and disavowal of the producedness of the appeal might then be thought of as akin to the way authenticity was often indicated in the cinematography of the French New Wave, using rough jump cuts to draw attention to the producedness of a scene. In any case it flatters the audience and draws them into a relation of complicity: we know that you know that this is a piece of media, and you will instinctively and rightly respond with scepticism, but because we're both in on it we can get past the bullshit and cut to the truth.

Although delivering information of straightforward meaning and seriousness (the need to provide shelter, food, medicine, schooling), Izzard's delivery is marked by distractedness, trailing off and sudden bursts of clarity and zeal. The effect is a tone that is unaffected (lack of affectation being, again, something whose performance and recognition has to be learned) and slightly quizzical (his default countenance is sceptical, curious), which invites an ironic reaction to the appeal. It is not difficult to construct the anticipated impact of his performance, an acknowledgement that usually when you see him on screen you expect subversive, surreal humour – but this is different. However, this could prompt multiple responses, again according to what different groups of individuals are predisposed to recognize in media, and the work this recognition does for them in everyday contexts. Thus, for those instinctively looking for an authentic account of what's going on in the world there may well be a felt commitment to follow the advice about what to pay attention to and how to act upon it. For others instinctively primed for confirmation of their reflexive, ironic relationship with the media, this is what they will experience. There seems little scope for a loss of credibility on Izzard's part – he has established both credentials for charity campaigning and a recognized sense of the perversity of the entertainment industries that insures him against any perception of self-importance. On the audience's part, there is the option of taking pleasure in the invitation of complicity *as well as* declining to answer the appeal to donate to the campaign, the knowingness of the experience ensuring that one's own compassionate subjectivity is not challenged.

EXPERIENCING DISTANT WORLDS WITH, AND THROUGH, MEDIA

To round out this chapter, it bears turning our focus back to social media and the role they played in objectifying the Arab uprisings as loci of attention and often action, the latter conceived broadly enough to include tweets and likes. In doing so, two opposing arguments need to be confronted. The first returns to a form of media instrumentalism in emphasizing the increased efficacy that social media afford, in particular the democratization that ensues from the deinstitutionalization and deprofessionalization of communication and engagement in social media networks, in the West as much as the Middle East. The second builds on the functionalist perspective set out above in relation to more established mediums and extends the same logic to social media: all it has done is lower the threshold for engagement, requiring negligible awareness or commitment, leading to a thoroughly degraded and self-serving relation between, especially, Western audiences on Facebook, YouTube and Twitter and those active in protest movements in the Arab world. Chapter 8 addresses the implications for our understanding of protest and political change of the tendency to overstate the self-organizing productiveness of global networked cultures of protest and activism. Before arriving at these bigger debates, though, it is worth spending a little time dwelling on the mechanics and context of social media use: how social mediated phenomenal objects appear and withdraw, what relations between user and social media are posited, as well as subject–object relations between users, other users and the people and events they post about.

First of all, in order to comprehend the givenness with which everyday life is lived, it is important to understand how people come to feel at home in social media contexts. There are broader questions here about cultural competence – not just digital literacy but facility with the unspoken rules of social media, such as hashtag humour, acronyms and cultural references – as well as the ethics and aesthetics of practices like trolling and flaming, often occurring where user identity is anonymized. But there is also the bodily experience of social media that at first appears self-evident but, like all experience, is in fact contingent on certain conditions of possibility – and this matters not only as an additional layer of observable behaviour but at the cultural and political level too (Liberati, 2016). It is simultaneously obvious and striking how quickly people become accustomed to the various swipes and prods that control an iPad's functionality, or typing with thumbs on a Blackberry, as they no doubt will easily adapt to touchscreens that are increasingly able to afford textured sensations. Shaun Moores (2017) has written eloquently about the experience of fingers being at home on a touchpad (see also Pink et al., 2016), drawing on Merleau-Ponty's phenomenology of typing. There is more to this than attempting to describe a naturalized, unreflexive practice in as much detail as possible. The point is that the practical knowledge required to type or use a trackpad is only present when the corporeal effort is made to do so; it is the body that understands how to navigate this environment. Further, it is not simply a matter of muscle memory, since that which the body apprehends is not only physical. As Moores puts it, the hands behave spellingly. The same logic can be applied to tweeting: as well as behaving spellingly, or perhaps with less of an orientation to the demands of grammar and spelling, the body also behaves in a manner adapted to communicating in massively networked online environments. This is not to suggest that conscious intention plays no part in tweeting – one often actively moulds one's words according to anticipated responses, after all – but there is also a non-conscious intentional understanding of the constraints and affordances of Twitter: its brevity, certainly, but also its possibilities for replicability and scalability. The meaning of a tweet consists at least as much in its circulation as its content, a logic the adaptation to which is corporeal, technical and cultural as well – that is, adapting to collective schema for reading a tweet and (maybe) its owner, as well as assessing the status of each.

It was argued earlier that while it is true that the experience of the temporal present is always oriented towards what comes next, this does not amount to a fetishization of the new or the dissolution of discrete microscopic encounters into something ontologically different – an undifferentiated flow as phenomenal object. Experience itself is usually seamless and as such flow-like, but it does not work logically to reverse-engineer a claim that social media objects are also flow-like: we make seamless experiences out of discrete stimuli all the time. Understanding this allows us to move beyond a proposition often applied to social media and the way that distant others encounter global events such as the Arab uprisings, based on the proliferation of messages and the apparent absence of at-hand criteria for assessing them: that audiences feel inundated, disorientated, more at-sea than at-home. It is patently true that social media engagement can be superficial and fickle, but this is not ascribable to the platforms themselves. Looked at phenomenologically, the experience of social media is not predominantly a bewildering one. At-homeness is still the norm, as is the at-handness of tools to navigate social media encounters. This means that where there are interactive practices and cultures that might be condemned on ethical grounds – incitement to violence, apathy, discrimination – there is little to be gained from blaming the supposed volatility and transience of social media. Neither can be assumed about the nature of social media as mediums, still less as experiences. And a corollary to this is that nor can it be reliably postulated that social media have an innate capriciousness that is ideal for producing new ways for distant selves to connect in ethically superior ways. This remains a valid goal, but one to be pursued incrementally through the ongoing self-work of everyday life rather than by way of transformative technology. But insofar as something like mediated distant solidarity is likely to be sustained by mutually partially implicating encounters amid quotidian routines, there is no reason why social media should not play a part in this pursuit.

After Foucault, it is often argued that it is where power is invisible that it is most profound, not through an idea being silenced but by its becoming so self-evident as to be inarticulable. And after Heidegger, it is where media withdraw from consciousness that they are most powerful, no longer objects of consciousness but part of its conditions of possibility. As the architectures of social media withdraw from consciousness, there is a tendency to think of it as ambient, and *as such* to think of its impact on our experience of being in the world as profound. Harman (2017), however, reminds us that to posit depths of withdrawal is to perpetuate a dualism of materialism and idealism that does not stand up to scrutiny; more pertinently, he reminds us that surfaces, too, have meaning. Social media literacy is a laudable aim, and there are admirable campaigns to promote coding and awareness of privacy and commercial concerns. There is a limit, however, to the usefulness of problematizing a lack of awareness of the hidden deep meanings that social media contain, given first that there is nothing ontologically special about these depths we conjure and secondly that the lack of awareness is a condition of all experience. By declining to overstate the importance of awareness, then, fragmented, distracted, ambient and delegated attention in social media start to appear more benign, leaving us to examine those moments where social media act as interfaces between surfaces and depths, or surfaces and surfaces, rather than as withdrawn background.

The shift towards what Harman calls realism without materialism can be seen as a historical one, much in the way that Scannell (2014) has described a move over the past four decades or so in phenomenology away from a political commitment to uncovering ideology in everyday practices to addressing the what and the how of an experiential world that by and large works, always, continuously and without interruption. However, this is by no means an abnegation of critical or normative analysis. Couldry et al.'s (2016) research into social analytics, for instance, makes the case that it is only through a phenomenological lens that analytics can be foregrounded as a site of contested agency; other approaches that simply assume that algorithmic cultures foreclose agency preclude the possibility of critical reflexivity by collapsing epistemology into ontology. Phenomenological perspectives on/of social media are also compatible with ideological accounts. What makes Andrejevic's (2011) work in this area compelling is that it goes beyond conventional arguments about participation in social media amounting to nothing more than the exploitation of free labour, setting out the consequences for subjectification: namely, the estrangement that ensues when one's own activity appears as something turned back against us as a kind of 'alien power' (see also Caraway, 2016). In each case the point is that exploitation and coercion are not assumed but posited as conditions or implications of conscious experience. To return to Scannell, the reason we are generally unaware of those conditions is because of the 'unfathomable complexity' of everything that underlies our experience of givenness, not some origin of determination driven by a teleology of domination. In other cases the results are decidedly less political. A translation of Goffman's analysis of how radio announcers manage to master informality to other media contexts (Ytreberg, 2002: 490) tells us much about the work that goes into appearing at home on Twitter: just as in the studio, '[p]articipants must produce illusions of fresh talk while accommodating a range of technical and logistical factors'. There are wider forces at play here in terms of the growing informality of public communication, and maybe a political dimension too, insofar as certain individuals and groups will find it easier than others to master such identifiers of felicity. But there are also benefits to not assuming that adopting these practices entail incitement, or indeed democratic affordances.

Let us turn to the bigger picture, of which there are two main aspects. The first is that by pulling apart the different orientations that audiences may have towards media, social or otherwise, it becomes readily apparent that they will often be different than those assumed from a media pathology perspective, or that we would like them to have if our normative leanings are more sanguine about public engagement. In the latter case the corollary is that when faced with such a mismatch between either hypothesis or observed reality, the most plausible explanation is simply that public engagement is not what social media are for. The second point is that by attempting to understand what underpins the experience of being in the world as seamless, we can start to develop an analysis of how the continuities of everyday conscious experience either afford or occlude the emergence of longer-term, systemic change to consciousness. In short, we can begin to understand how history itself withdraws from conscious experience in prosaic everyday contexts, without starting off from an assumption that in a multiply mediated age individuals are either trapped in an overwhelming present continuous or fixated on the immediate future. We turn in the next chapter to the possibility that social media have transformed not only the way we understand change as it unfolds around the world but also potentially the nature of social change itself. In line with the thesis threaded throughout this book, it will be seen that any such transformation in the way that history and politics happen is unlikely to be the product of a decisive rupture with what we have hitherto understood as the historic and the political, or the revelation of new possibilities of the same. The conditions of intelligibility of the lived present and as such of the possibility of alternative futures do shift, but they do so amid the messy, inconsistent, affective patterns of everyday life. And in the concluding chapter it becomes clear that rather than adding up to a call for incrementalism at best and ambitionlessness at worst, it is precisely social life understood as being experienced as provisional and ambivalent that holds the potential for the at-hand grasp of the stakes at play in the present, the potential for change in the future and the possibilities this opens up for journalists and the rest of us.

Chapter Eight

Facebook Revolutions?

Understanding the Work That Social Media Do

The journalistic reduction 'Arab Spring' can be explained away easily enough as a manifestation of premediation (Grusin, 2010), a congenital inability to see events afresh but only through the prism of what has come before. But even as a simplistic handle it was from the beginning a fairly reflexive one, with most print media continuing to couch it in scare quotes and the mainstream journalistic discourse around the democracy movements characterized by scepticism as well as excitability. That scepticism was as much the product of received wisdom about the intractability of the Arab world's problems as of journalistic rigour, but aside from some of the rolling news broadcasters – CNN in particular – there was more to the journalistic coverage of the uprisings in the media than simple celebration. Nonetheless, there was also a palpable sense of emotional investment by journalists and commentators in the protest movements and a concatenated projection of political values onto them. And that elision of politics and emotion fed directly into how the uprisings came to be recognized from afar as well as within the region itself. One might argue that coverage driven by wishful thinking is no better than that emanating from flat prejudice, but there was more to it than a Huntingdonian (1993) assumption that Western democracy is the inevitable final stage towards which all societies will eventually evolve. This was something more visceral, the thrill of an irresistible swelling that promised to sweep away not just the injustice of authoritarian regimes but the stale, compromised institutions perceived to stultify politics everywhere. Moreover, this projection extended well beyond media froth into the tide of academic publications that followed soon after the fall of Ben Ali and Mubarak.

Projection is never entirely arbitrary, and it is collectively sustainable only in relation to certain objects and within contingent contexts. In the case of the Arab uprisings, the perceived arrival of a new politics appears to have been predicated on the conception of social media politics as spontaneous and self-organizing. The aim of this chapter is to pull apart this collective phenomenal recognition, and the chapter proceeds by way of a discourse analysis of around two hundred academic journal articles on the uprisings and the role social media played in their growth and spread. Three specific claims will be unpacked. First, the prevalence of ecological and biological metaphors used to characterize social media is linked to a wider misattribution of vibrant agency to social media platforms, an agency that enshrines a political teleology of generativity – the creation of novel and intrinsically progressive political spaces. Second, a connection is drawn between these imaginings of social media and conceptions of protest cultures more broadly, also increasingly associated with norms of structurelessness, organicism and creativity. This is by no means to argue against the efficacy or ethics of protest or to discount the very real achievements of recent movements but rather to posit that there is nothing about the horizontal or rhizomatic structures and dynamics of contemporary protest that is necessarily generative of new or ideal forms of political subjectivity. Further, this notion that new political identities and cultures can only emerge in the absence of structure and constraint is used – usually implicitly but sometimes explicitly – to maintain that nascent democratic movements in the Middle East need to be protected not just from the authoritarian regimes they oppose but the overdetermining hegemonies of Western media and academic discourse. The latter is manifest most frequently in calls to resist the application of European political theory to recent events, but it also raises questions about the complicity in global regimes of domination by all contributions made by non-Arab academics. The chapter's third principal claim is that while there are valid arguments against privileged others speaking on behalf of political activists, there is in much of the literature an aversion to objectification as such that misunderstands its centrality to the conscious experience of continuity and change alike.

The feverish debate over the role of social media in the Arab uprisings has more or less coalesced around a view that Facebook and Twitter were important but not instrumental in sparking, escalating and spreading cultures of protest. In straightforward terms of organization there is ample evidence of the efficacy of social media conventionally conceived. Tufekci and Wilson (2012) demonstrate, for example, that Twitter users were more likely than non-users to have attended the first day of mass protests in Cairo in January 2011, though causality cannot be reliably established and other explanatory variables for action may have been excluded from their analysis. In qualitative terms research by Howard et al. (2011), among others, paints a vivid picture of the subversive ends towards which social media is particularly well suited, such as documenting police brutality and arbitrary detention through practices of 'sousveillance', or the recording of protests and other events from the citizens' perspectives (Andén-Papadopoulos, 2014) – though the easy accessibility of footage of this nature could as easily serve to inhibit as incite engagement in protest movements (Bassel, 2012). Next, social media are not an all-or-nothing proposition in protest cultures: each of the Arab uprisings was characterized by a distinct mix of platform use depending on pre-existing communicative cultures, platform penetration and a degree of serendipity (Robertson, 2013). Facebook dominated the social mediation of the Tunisian protests (Marzouki et al., 2012); Twitter was prominent in the anti-Mubarak protests (Bhuiyan, 2011) – no surprise, given the deep roots of blogging culture in Egypt – while the early years of the Syrian civil war saw rival groups waging media campaigns on YouTube. For all of the content and data within easy grasp, however, its politicality is far from self-evident. Rinke and Röder (2011) see the 2011 tweets and posts in and about Egypt as a continuation of five years of blogging that originated in the Kefaya movement opposing the nomination of Mubarak's son as his successor – a blogging culture that despite its origins was largely, conspicuously apolitical. Others weigh in against the reduction of social media outpourings to 'futile chatter' (Hofheinz, 2011) on the basis of a nuanced understanding of what political engagement actually looks like in everyday contexts: political communication in action is not all about slogans and press releases but socializing, joking and just passing the time, too. Archives like the Tahrir Data Project show that even when people tweet about a politician or a political movements there is often more to their words than an unequivocal, illocutionary political act. As much as it might constitute a political act by signalling affiliation, expressing solidarity or seeking to mobilize others, it might also be explicable as status-seeking, or mimetic, or learned interaction rituals (Murthy, 2013).

All communication is similarly complicated, and the upshot here is that evidence of something other than political authenticity in a tweet or an entire social media discourse should not be interpreted as political vacuity. It is not difficult to find thousands of #jan25 tweets that suggest a lack of awareness of the history and political context of unfolding events, or that speak a naïve romanticism about liberty and equality, but these are not representative of whole interpretative communities – or even of individuals, as social media users are frequently adept at switching deftly between the serious, mundane and profane. It will be seen in the final chapter that since the same is true for journalists and activists working in conditions and towards goals that are unquestionably politically serious, there may well be grounds for something like viable political engagement and solidarity among the banalities and superficialities of social media routines. The previous chapter argued that neither the socializing functions nor profit-seeking motivations of a platform such as Facebook preclude its being used for political ends, at the same time as there is nothing about its networked structures that are inherently politically transformative. Lewiński and Mohammed (2012) demonstrate how readily apolitical comments on social media can become politicized by the responses of others, while on the other hand Kuebler (2011) shows how following ostensibly political blogs is as much about just keeping up with whatever friends or consecrated others are saying as a conscious act of political engagement. In short, the distinction between the political and apolitical is both ontologically unsound and epistemologically fraught, and that is a state of affairs we should be comfortable to live with. Rinke and Röder (2011) draw the analogy of public spaces like shops and cafés in the Arab world that frequently feature televisions or radios blaring out news and debate programmes, with conversations between proprietors, customers and passers-by ranging effortlessly from the comical to the critical.

The language used on social media, then, takes all the forms it does elsewhere: ambiguous, ambivalent, argumentative, humorous, outraged, baffled, contradictory, conciliatory, never uniquely expressive or exempt from conventions and norms. It was seen in chapter 3 that Egyptian journalists tweeting the downfall of Mohammed Morsi exhibit a similar tendency to switch between straight reporting, high rhetoric and mundane expressions of support or opposition, though others (Papacharissi & Oliveira, 2012) have suggested that Egyptian journalists found it difficult to adapt to the kind of mixed-mode performance demanded by social media. The point is that whatever their words on these platforms look and sound like is not fully a product of those platforms: journalists may try to make the most of the affordances of one space or another and to meet perceived expectations, but they are also acting through an epistemological orientation to the world learned through professional experience, and maybe cultural experience as well. A distinct political subjectivity may be at work in such socially mediated interactions, but it is not realized there in its fullest form. It can only be grasped in the light of all the habits and affordances, pleasures and pressures of everyday life in which a journalist's professionalism and politicality are inevitably subsumed in the mechanics of work and the social networks threaded through it. The same logic applies to amateurs, activists and onlookers: their political identities are various in origin and never play out in pure form but only amid the constraints, expectations and internalized rules that characterize any discursive forum. So as much as it is valid to question exactly what object a viewer recognizes when they see spectacles of protest on television screens, it makes sense to ask what or who, precisely, social media interlocutors might feel solidarity with.

This question is particularly pertinent, considering the words used by academics, both Western and Arab, to describe the social media protest cultures that emerged around and through the events of 2010 and 2011: 'empowering'

(Kuebler, 2011), 'galvanizing' (Lynch, 2011), 'liberating' (Christensen, 2011), 'energizing' (Agathangelou & Soguk, 2011) – in each case the participial adjective ascribes a form of agency to social media. If that form is difficult to pin down, that is the essence of it: it is intangible, organic in its genesis and evolution and elusive and fleet-footed in an ever-changing present. Further, it is precisely the apparent absence of constraint and especially of objectification – by conventional, establishment or mainstream narrative, professionalism or official discourse – that enables a distinct mode of subjectivity to come into being. There is a parallel to this in the widely cited, radically alternative political subjectivities that can emerge from the vacuum produced when an authoritarian regime is overthrown (Elseewi, 2011; see also Arditi, 2008) – drawing on Charles Taylor's (2004) notion of social imaginaries (see also Grant, 2014), the idea is that truly transformative or authentic subjectivities cannot be designed but rather be allowed to develop on their own terms in spaces maximally free from political, academic and journalistic determination. It is not that the literature or even a minority of it reads transformativity into actual tweets and timelines, but there is an undeniable current that apprehends the seemingly unchecked flow of communication – notwithstanding character limits, bandwidth and literacy – as productive of *something*: freer discourse, more creative activism, different and better ways of inhabiting mediated worlds. It makes sense that different kinds of interactive spaces allow for different ways of doing politics and being political – but only different, and not inherently more radical, and not more authentic expressions of the cultures and aspirations of individuals and populations. Social media platforms are anything but an absence of structure, and political subjectivity does not emerge sui generis ex nihilo: it consists precisely in objectification by and of the world within all its oppressive, overfamiliar ordinariness.

It bears restating at this point what political subjectivity amounts to from a phenomenological perspective. In broader terms, phenomenology starts from the premise that a lot, even most, of everyday life is experienced as given, habituation meaning that most stimuli are comfortably responded to unthinkingly, corporeally. But given that despite this seamlessness there are real stakes in how situations play out – this is Heidegger's sense of care – the scholar's job is to unpack what that givenness is contingent on. This in turn hinges on revealing radical contingency: if one looks at ordinary experience from the right angle, it becomes possible to apprehend how unlikely it is, given all the conditions of possibility of experience that this would be the one that, over time, comes to be the 'just is', the always-already present that overwhelms with its obviousness. More than an exercise in disruption, then, the phenomenological approach has the aims both to explain how we got here through recourse to structural changes and to establish what futures are possible – though ordinarily unthinkable – and with what stakes and for whom.

Where this becomes political subjectivity is in the shift of analytic focus from the individual to collective selves, the self-evidentness of 'people like us' and 'people like them', the enveloping inevitability of relations within and between groups that is actually anything but. The aim of phenomenological analysis, then, is to uncover the precarious pasts and futures of social relations that appear to consciousness as solid, unchanging second nature. This takes on a real urgency in the case of social media politics, written about as weightless, unconstrained by old ways of being political and with innumerable possible futures. By depicting objectification as a thing of the past, irrelevant in a world of new and self-generating political cultures, we lose sight of how ways of being political emerge in a world that remains stubbornly material. In practical terms, this manifests as an unwillingness to take seriously the role that political institutions, processes and norms still play – as well as economic and technological constraints – in the evolution of political identity and movements.

MASS SELF-COMMUNICATION

One dominant theme in the literature is the durability of the individual in social media politics – not in the neo-liberal sense of competitive individualism but the merits of an individual identity that can survive engagement with collective cultures without fear of annihilation. For Stiegler (2013b; see also Crogan, 2010, 2012), indeed, this is precisely what enables people to resist the flattening forces of market capitalism when they use mainstream social media platforms, their discontinuous, patchy investment in network cultures a sign not of their lack of commitment but of their personal authenticity. Seen one way, this is similar to one of this book's main theses: that political engagement that looks fickle and unserious nonetheless has the capacity to sustain substantive political relations between distant others over time. That claim, though, is not built upon deontological individualism, which is inconsistent with the phenomenological take on how we emerge as conscious selves only insofar as we are objects for various – and variously grouped – others. The supersession of the individual subject is not just a basis for political values like solidarity; it is how one comes to experience one's individuality. This book's defence of the politically banal, ambivalent and provisional is not about celebrating the unique authenticity of individuals free to connect and disconnect, aggregate and disaggregate, but rather a temporal claim. Political principle and its experience as political subjectivity is never the expression of who an individual really is; it is something she works at – sometimes fitfully, distractedly, reluctantly – over time in everyday contexts.

For totemic figures such as Castells (2009), though, it is very much the creativity and expressivity afforded to individuals by social media that allows for a new kind of radical transformativity. His mass communication of the self paints a picture of an organic whole very much bigger than the sum of its parts – a creative audience capable of collective intelligence – but one which is special precisely because its parts remain discrete. This goes against the grain of any political model with historical materialist origins, and specifically the tenet that all identity, political and otherwise, is collective before it is individual. This is at the root of the accusations of narcissism sometimes hurled at social media cultures, a vain insistence on individual priority seen as fundamentally corrosive to the emergence of political movements. It is worth asking, however, whether Castells's mass self-communication is as uncollective as all that, the equivalent of a silent flash mob in which participants are co-present but dance to music only they can hear through their headphones. There is a meaningful distinction to be drawn by actions which are merely simultaneous and those which amount to something like common endeavour, but it is one which tends to be made on the basis of values that are frequently elusive in observations of human behaviour: commitment, seriousness, collectivity. This is at the heart of Jeff Juris's distinction between logics of connection and logics of aggregation, though he is careful to compare the two in ways that are not just normative, looking instead at the observable outcomes of movements that organize themselves alternately around squares, listservs or social media sites.

It is true enough that collectivity is easily romanticized, and it is worth taking seriously the notion that something distinct emerges when individuals interact and work with each other in less constrained, less prescriptive ways. For Fenton and Barassi (2011), though, something is irrevocably lost when structured deliberation – requiring time, effort and sacrifice – is removed from the political equation. This goes beyond efficacy: the very viability of political subjectivity depends on structures and forces – coercion even – that subsume the individual within the ideals, rules and institutions of a collective agenda that came into existence in particular historical moments that are in turn the product of longer histories of struggle, conflict and progress. The opposition is not a neat one, since the disciplines and constraints they have in mind are present in some form on social media – internalized rules of performance and recognition, learned competences, group policing of perceived immorality and deviance. But these are invoked spontaneously and often invisibly, in contrast to the publicly avowed principles and aims of the kind of political movement Fenton and Barassi have in mind. The political for them requires public visibility as well as solidity in time and space, two factors which for Stiegler as well as Castells are antithetical to living authentically. For Stiegler and Castells authenticity requires autonomy, which rests on the possibility of both mutability and invisibility. Anything else threatens to coerce or delimit the political imaginaries that would otherwise have been possible.

A direct consequence of Stiegler's prioritization of subjective fluidity over consistency is that, politically, the act of expressing oneself becomes more important than what is expressed. This emphasis on speaking out, rather than on having views or principles, is the basis of what he terms singularity (Stiegler, 2011; cf. Beardsworth, 2010), the dimension of individuality that is stifled in the old politics but flourishes in the new. From this it is easy enough to infer galloping solipsism, but he is careful to point out that speaking out does not equate to self-actualization, the full becoming of a subject. As in previous models, the viability of singularity depends on there being others engaged in similar practices, but where it departs from traditional phenomenology is that subjectification does not depend on thoroughgoing mutual recognition of subject- and objectness – indeed, it *requires* something less than the full glare of recognition by and of others, which can only be oppressive and inhibiting. Visibility (Casper & Moore, 2009) to others does not amount to publicity, the latter requiring a more durable kind of presentation and recognition of self, the former consistent with the privacy, anonymity, even furtiveness Stiegler sees as integral to individual autonomy. Further, it prioritizes modes of interactions with others in which one's subjectivity is not fundamentally at stake: affective and transient rather than scrutinizing and deliberative. In such an environment, unconstrained self-expression allows simultaneously for uncoerced self-actualization as well as the formation of collectivities that are creative and unpredictable, not dogmatic or tiredly familiar. This is what distinguishes the new politics from the old.

It can sound anachronistic to argue against a political culture this organic and free-wheeling, especially as Fenton and Barassi (2011) stress the importance of physical co-presence and agreed rules for deliberation for efficacious political mobilization. However, they back up their critique with a compelling case study that speaks to the same transition described by Juris (2012) and Bennett and Segerberg (2012, 2013) that sees movements gain in visibility but in so doing undermine any sense of a coherent collective identity. The identity of any movement can be a nebulous thing, which threatens to render any argument about its resilience or decline impressionistic or speculative. In the case of the Cuban Solidarity Campaign (CSC), though, that decline was manifest in distinctly real-world terms: the loss of a more prescriptive and public group identity was concomitant with an inability to constrain and direct their members' attention, interaction and communication, and that in turn made it impossible for the movement to achieve what had been one of their main stated aims. This was to spark a debate bigger than Cuba – about the radical contingency of neo-liberalism – that was undeniably ambitious but just about possible in the sweaty, smoky context of protracted and focused seminars and debates. Only with such dedication, rigour and sacrifice was it possible to plant the seeds of solidarity and, through it, substantive political subjectivity. Instead, what they got when they traded a planned political programme built around co-presence for an online discussion forum was sympathy. For Stiegler this need not be a dead end, with the kind of mass individual participation in affective, symbolic production the CSC witnessed carrying with it the potential to evolve into something else, a benign political imaginary unshackled by manifestoes and respectful of individual autonomy. But for Fenton and Barassi this is naïve: though it may achieve some specific aims, there is no basis for presuming that networked communication will deliver systemic change, and no reason for having faith that it will generate new political subjectivities, new ways of being political.

The debate over the political generativity or depoliticizing tendencies of social media thus taps in to the long-running arguments about the status of the public and private, the collective and individual, in politics (Sennett, 1977; Fraser, 1990). The organizational fluidity of the models that Castells and Stiegler theorize is in step with more recently dominant conceptions of identity more broadly, and, likewise, the individualistic, affective interactions they place at the centre of their conceptions of the political resonate strongly with the emphases on intimacy and personal experience in identity politics. Much of the emergent academic discourse around the Arab uprisings also cleaves to the individual, expressive and quotidian as the natural locus for the political. When Elseewi (2011: 1197), for instance, describes the impact of satellite television on the protests, it is not cast in terms of a pan-Arab public sphere or global solidarity but 'a revolution in individual subjectivity'. For Wall and El Zahed (2011: 1339), YouTube is *creating* new political selves, and thereby novel forms of citizenship, not through deliberation or mobilization but because as a medium it is 'visual and intensely intimate'. These and other scholars are comfortable using the word 'revolution' in relation to the role of social media, but this is a revolution of the imagination rather than being about the overthrow of autocracy as such, or an ideological assault on hegemony. This is certainly appropriate, given these authors' emphasis on the new ways of being that social media afford, but they remain steadfastly individualistic. Revolutionary change consists not in a collective rethinking of what is possible in the world we inhabit but in an individual's ability to think their way out of their habituation towards the more creative and thus more authentic selves that may, as others perform similar feats of self-imagining, also generate innovative ways of coming together.

IMAGINATION, CREATIVITY AND PERFORMANCE

This can sound like nothing more than a celebration of daydreaming, but in the case of Elseewi at least the focus is on thinking creatively about and through aspects of everyday life – travel and finance as well as technology – that have become so mundane as to be invisible and unquestionable. How this would ideally be perceived is telling in its derivation from Appadurai's 'prisms of the possible' (1996), in which the realm of possibility is defined according to the ability of the disconnected, autonomous mind to think up alternatives. Where this turns problematic is its reliance on a particular conception of creativity that consists in a combination of instinct and spontaneity. These are not in themselves bad things, or even ineffective ways of reflecting on and changing one's habits, but the last thing they are is unstructured – and it is the supposed lack of determination in instinct and spontaneity that is relied on to open a door to new political imaginaries, subjectivities so different that we would struggle to recognize them as such. Looked at phenomenologically, instinct and spontaneity are contingent modes of practice that are like others learned, internalized and forgotten as contingent. Creative thought is not unstructured cognition but embodied and pre-reflexive, oriented by structured anticipation learned through prior individual experience and collective history. Imagination is not purely productive; it is also reactive and responsive. There is a sense that for Elseewi as well as for Castells and Stiegler interactive networks and political cultures should have respect and esteem for what individuals imagine in the privacy of their own minds, but this valorization is based on a questionable notion of individual ownership of anticipation and meaning-making.

Creativity is at the heart of much thinking about contemporary practices of protest, dissent and activism (see Mustafa Tagma, 2011; Rahimi, 2011a and 2011b; Wall & Zahed, 2011; Khamis et al., 2012). This framing device has its roots in Laclau and Mouffe (1985), though unlike in the latter's meticulous dissection of the demands of agonism (Mouffe, 2013) it is routinely assumed that the two are one and the same thing, that being creative is a reliable way to disrupt structural realities and spark productive conflict. Writing about the Iranian post-election protests of 2009, Rahimi (2011a: abstract) describes internet activism as a 'creative configuration of complex networks that primarily interact through meaning-laden performances that carve out spaces of dissent'. Strikingly, here the political agent is the network itself, the performances it engenders not a matter of skills and competences honed over time but un- or underdetermined acts capable of creating a distinct kind of political space. The noble intentions of individual activists is unquestioned, but what makes this new politics uniquely weightless and fruitful is the possibility that, notwithstanding intention, networked media enable the emergence of unpredictable, unprescriptive practices that will, if nurtured and allowed to develop in whatever way they will, culminate in a transformative politics unlike any that has gone before. Importantly, this way of thinking about recent protest cultures remains committedly humanistic; its conceptions of social networks do not draw on actor network theory. As with Stiegler, the generative power of social media does not entail the subsuming of the individual by the collective. That social media communication and interaction are the products of free self-expression is pivotal, and the collective that evolves and mutates as communicative content is spread, aggregated, remixed and mashed up is powerful precisely because it does not demand submission, discipline or compromise.

The commitment to humanism in online protest cultures is at odds with a lot of other theorizations of digital media; for Deleuzians it is not usually about transformative spaces being carved out but selves being carved up by algorithms (Lazzarato, 2014). Greene and Kuswa (2012: abstract) explicitly cite Deleuze when they write that 'as a political subjectivity, the protestor emerges in the crease of a regional fold of protest places as these places make and unmake maps of power', a conspicuously sanguine reading of enfolding that to other eyes encapsulates the alienation wrought by the digital. Such optimism rests on the characterization of particular spaces as teleologically transformative, and not only that but also teleologically progressive. This notion appears in Sassen's writing on the political 'street' (2011), a space where protest can spontaneously emerge free from the malign fingerprints of ideology or a suspect hunger for power. The less salubrious human traits that can otherwise sully a nascent political movement are mitigated by the ascription of political agency to the space itself, a space in which protests just happen and protestors innocently 'emerge'. There is a principled reluctance to detail what that space will look like and how we will get there from here, a firm belief in something higher than the grubby politics we have known and faith in the possibility of human progress. But it is something altogether different than the Spirit that emerges out of Hegel's phenomenology, through a dense, conflicted and endlessly iterative series of objectifications of and by other people and the material world, as well as history itself. The hands-off approach to transformative subjectivity by comparison looks less humanistic than it first appeared, as well as less optimistic about systemic change in the everyday worlds we inhabit.

As with protest spaces, the idea of protest as performance also rests upon a transformative teleology: it is transformative *because* it is a performance (see also Allam, 2014). This points back to the discussion in chapter 6 of what forms of political practice are illocutionary, capable of producing political realities in their enactment. In its academic usage performance is not quite deontological; implicitly or explicitly there is another norm or value underpinning it. In some cases this is, again, creativity: the more imaginative a protest performance is, the greater its transformative force. For others it is about the feeling behind a performance: Rahimi (2011a) writes that that the politically 'contentious' nature of performances of protests consists in the intensity of its emotion, in line with a broader view that interactions within protest cultures are not about deliberation or making common cause but the mutual display of emotions and 'narratives of protestation'. Relations between individuals in networks are characterized as affinities (derived from social psychology; see Giles, 2002), suggesting serendipity and fleetingness in conscious distinction against heavier-handed, more demanding notions of group membership. As such it could be thought to be similar to the claim made in this book that solidarity is not about conspicuous self-sacrifice and the loud declaiming of allegiance but the discontinuous, ambivalent stuff of everyday routines. It is not, however, for two reasons. First, this book conceives of individuals not as authentic selves using media to express themselves but as already deeply and multiply implicated in collective structures and forces. A corollary to this is another line threaded throughout: we are summoned up as particular selves whenever we use media, but these selves are not fully implicated in the media worlds demanding attention and apprehension. Subjective implication is not clinched as neatly as that. And second, the literature discussed in this section conceives of progressive political change, under the right conditions, as something simultaneously weightless and unstoppable; here, by contrast, it is seen as work whose experience is usually mundane, sometimes risky and often less than enjoyable.

In any case, there is something revealing about the characterization of dissent as art form and performance (Lim, 2012), whose narrative arc exceeds any individual activist through its evolution in networked media, that brings us closer to the implicit conceptualization of progressive political change current in this corner of academic discourse. This is a new kind of politics that has a life of its own, a vivified, organic politics innocent of contamination by either ideology, institutionalization or personal lust for power, and benign in its respect for individuality. Cultures of practice like hacktivism (Rahimi, 2011b) are not only subversive and agonistic but generative of 'vibrant' public spaces. The belligerent or profane nature of dissenting voices is sufficient to *create* and not simply describe new political realities that are innately dangerous and progressive, realities that have a lifespan beyond discrete political acts because they combine, morph and evade through generative networks that are often likened to organisms and ecosystems. Elsewhere, Rahimi (2011b: 160) describes dissent as dynamic and porous and writes that 'such an ephemeral process carries the element of spontaneous creative interaction in the ways individuals can carve out new domains of communication through which dissent can be articulated and enacted in diverse ways'. Tacit in this language is the idea of dissent as a fragile kind of life that if nurtured and protected from both state and conventional powers, establishment political discourse can develop into something more resilient, more authentic and eventually transformative. It is this insistence on the *vibrancy* (Bennett, 2010) of dissident cultures that suggests wishful projection onto the Arab uprisings and other high-profile mass mobilizations, a vibrancy derived not from recent theoretical innovations in materialist philosophy but from something more like faith. It is only with such a normative commitment to how things will – eventually – play out for the better that the language of radically better political spaces 'opening up' or being 'carved out' by the agency of social networks is self-evident, likewise the foretold 'emergence' of a new political subjectivity that is sanctified, precarious but ultimately inexorable.

It is easy enough to criticize the romanticization of protest cultures but more productive to seek to unpack them by resisting the illocutionary conception of political expression, suspending the belief that practices of dissent and their political effects are one and the same thing. This elision is evident in the extrapolation from activist practices in authoritarian states that are necessarily agile and furtive to an ideal political subjectivity that is inherently fleet-footed and wily, unable to be pinned down by political regimes or academic ones. Such a subjectivity may coagulate over time in particular, contingent conditions, but it is by no means guaranteed. And to connect back to a recurrent epistemological theme, observable dissident political acts are not straightforwardly equitable to a distinct political ontology. The collapse of one into the other is sometimes manifest in the reduction of complex political situations to a game of cat and mouse, albeit one with life-and-death implications, with the lumbering bulk of the state pitted against the guile not only of actual dissenters but of dissent itself. References to agonistic practice are not couched so much in terms of the insistent, incessant contestation of extant power hierarchies but more in a disembodied kind of creativity: 'newer forms of social media have complicated the agonistics of political life in the articulation and staging of new contentious performances in the public sphere' (Rahimi, 2011b: 161). Whereas for Mouffe agonism encapsulates a dogged commitment to political struggle and a refusal of spontaneous consensus to the status quo, in this quotation it is reduced to something latent and conventional, transformed into praxis only through the addition of contentiousness to the mix. It is hard not to cheer the sheer cheek as well as bravery of many contemporary activists in the Arab world; to elevate contentiousness itself as politically productive, and productive in a progressive sense, is to reify transgression as a transcendental act of illocutionary politics. During his lifetime Foucault (1993) came to reject such a reading of transgression, ignoring as it does the inevitable complicities and unintended consequences of all political acts; in more prosaic terms, it simply loses sight of the distinctly unvivified, endless slog that comprises the work of protest.

Foucault's trajectory shows that concepts are not preserved in aspic. The same could be said for Butler's performativity, which has come to stand for a considerably more voluntarist and instrumentalist conception of practice than the stricter model of incitement detailed in *Bodies That Matter*. This is the kernel of that move to imagining politics as illocutionary: whereas according to its original delineation performativity spoke of the coerced activation of selves that already exist in the realm of the social – and of history – it has come to signify, or at least to accommodate, practices productive of the new and, crucially, better. The Butler of *Bodies That Matter* held out hope for progressive change no further than in the inevitable slippages of incitement. Through its reinterpretation, if performativity has not quite become fully willed and transitive, the distinct forms it takes is given to enable us to speak fairly confidently of performance as a harnessable resource with predictable effects. According to this reading, for activist performativity to be illocutionary it needs only to be dissenting, imaginative or counter-intuitive. Once such speech or other acts are made, new political realities are not just constituted but continue to develop autonomously, exercising agency and becoming self-sustaining. Butler always allowed for the possibility of radically distinct subjectivities, but not as reliably foreseeable outcomes of certain ways of doing politics. This is a phenomenological injunction rather than an exercise in cynicism: due to the corporeal embeddedness and overwhelming givenness of most everyday experience, radical alterity is rarely thinkable, let alone viable. Ascribing a generativeness to performativity ignores all the other generative structures that give rise to and shape subjective experience over time. And finally, this interpretation of performativity appears to be normative at base: dissident acts have a special ontological status because they are right.

THE MYTH OF GENERATIVE STRUCTURELESSNESS

The flipside of the conception of radical political imaginaries as sui generis phenomena whose form of emergence is an expression of their purpose is the pervasive characterization of domination – both political and discursive – as extrinsic. This is difficult to reconcile with phenomenological accounts deriving ultimately from Hegelian subjectification that proceeds through and not in spite of the constraining structures of materiality, economics and power. But depicting authoritarian political regimes as well as the official discourses of politics and mainstream media as exogenous forces acting to thwart authentic expressions of democratic will effectively enables an othering of those regimes and discourses. They come to be defined negatively, as everything that is inhuman, infertile and monolithic, wholly constraining and never constitutive. At the same stroke anything dissenting, alternative or unofficial is accorded a different, valorized teleology on the basis of its perceived structurelessness. And again the result is an elision of observable, laudable acts of ingeniousness and temerity on the part of activists, and theorizations of the nature of protest itself that necessitate its efficacy. This is not quite the same as foretelling particular outcomes of protest campaigns; nonetheless it presents as irresistible the emergence of novel, transformative political spaces and identities. To illustrate this chain of logic from extrinsic power to postulated resistant agency, consider the claim made by Mustafa Tagma (2011) that states and their institutions will always try to 'tame' protest movements. First, this necessitates that protest is wild in its natural state. And second, it implies that protest *has* a natural state, a protean fecundity that exists in idealized form in isolation from – and defined in opposition to – politics as it is habitually lived. It assumes contra-Foucault that there is an outside of political determination, and that getting there is only a matter of alterity.

It is notable that this hopefulness often sits alongside an aversion to detailing what form such an alternative politics would take, circumscribed by the risk of complicity that all academic discoursing entails. It is important not to overgeneralize, though, and there are notable exceptions in the literature that seek to establish how new subjectivities might emerge in concrete situations and what they might look like. Ismail's (2011) contribution to a special issue of *Third World Quarterly* assessing the relevance of Norbert Elias's work in the post-2010 Arab world enlists the concept of civility to think through the distinct subjectifications endemic to authoritarian and post-authoritarian societies. This is a light-touch application of civility, with Ismail warning against the wholesale importing of Western notions of civilization as well as the imposition of Western political methodology, but she maintains that nonetheless it remains a useful tool for interpreting the selves observed in particular social interactions, and especially the usually unacknowledged negotiations of appropriateness that go on when citizen meets agent of the state. There is a clear-cut refusal in this account to cast the state as the other of ordinary life: the state cannot be thought of as an abstraction since individuals' understanding of it is not grasped through their imaginations but in real-world dealings with institutions and their employees. However, for all it sets out to demystify the state, as it is revealed it is again as an exogenous force demanding the performance of particular subjectivities, neo-liberal as much as authoritarian. The state is ascribed the agency to make selves and impose them on us as it summons us to play out particular official scenarios. This is not quite consistent with Butler's claim that selves come into being through submission; it is saying instead that we are selves, we have selves that are annihilated by official ones. To think of subjectivity as the product of state procedures is to posit a relationship of interiority and exteriority between the two, which Butler has explicitly sought to avoid. The state–individual relation is unequal and unjust in all sorts of ways, but neither side of the dyad is originary. This is more than a philosophical nicety: by adhering to the interiority of the self and exteriority of the state, the only possible readings of concrete interactions are instrumental and mechanistic in their conception of state power.

Ismail homes in on the specific official practice of *ishtibah wa tahari*, police stop-and-search practices that form a highly visible and much resented embodiment of official suspicion and investigation policies. Beginning with a Foucauldian elucidation of power as being at its most disciplinarily effective when dispersed and invisible, Ismail moves quickly – as Foucault often did – to the tangible artefacts of power, including military uniforms and compulsory ID cards. She writes that the experience of *ishtibar wa tahari* 'informs subjects' understandings of and feelings about state power as exercised by its agents' (Ismail, 2011: 849), which makes sense: subjective understanding is affected but not effected by state power. But this is followed by an inferred political subjectivity thus brought into being, pushing aside the myriad contingencies that determine our daily experience of the world, most of which are habituated to the point of insensibility, and the totality of which is messy, unknowable and, to a degree, indeterminate. This is expressed in bluntly instrumentalist terms, surmising that stop and search exists *primarily* in order to enact subjectivities, where in reality those subjectivities are at most imperfect translations of an official template of obedient citizenship, by dint of the vicissitudes of structuration. This is encouraging insofar as it establishes that states do not have the straightforward power to summon compliant subjects into existence at will, but it also makes resistance to authority more difficult to imagine. In everyday life it is impossible to step outside of subjectification, as it is what constitutes conscious experience in the first place. This is not really a problem, and nothing like the functionalist proposition that the always-already priority of discourse is the ultimate disciplinary regime: it is true that there is no outside of subjectification, but since it is multifarious this does not amount to the incitement of selves that are cookie-cutter subjects or endlessly exploitable workers – or helplessly gullible consumers, for that matter.

For Ismail though (see also Fuchs, 2015) there is a simple dichotomy of discrete self and othered state that exaggerates the determining force of the latter to the extent that it is ascribed a villainous kind of agency, singling out a youth for his posture and demeanour. More importantly, this reduction of the self/state relation to one of simple, antagonistic opposition means that resistance to authoritarianism is also oversimplified, ultimately denoting *anything* contrary to official edict. This is consistent with the line of argument that since subjectification is political, then anything which disrupts its disciplined unfolding amounts to resistance. But given that we are constituted through subjectification and not acted on by it from without – again, this is much more complex than doing what the state tells us to do – we do not just become dissidents by deciding to disobey an official rule. This is the nub of the fallacy of characterizing the state not just as corrupt and dysfunctional but also as nefarious, and it can be summed up in three propositions. First, it rests on the assumption that official representatives such as police straightforwardly embody the state with neither slippage nor codetermination by other political, cultural and social forces. Second, a one-to-one correspondence is posited between the policies of a state enforced by its agents and the determination of an individual's subjectivity – how she sees herself as well as what she thinks of the state. Third, and most significantly, this position rests on the claim that coercive subjectification can be resisted by the simple act of refusal.

The politics of refusal (Hardt & Negri, 2000) has been the focus of prolonged and often heated debate (see, for instance, Thompson, 2005), rightly so as it hinges on the question of under what conditions an individual can refuse to be the structured effect of neo-liberalism or neocolonialism. For the sake of consistency it pays to stick with the Arab world, and specifically to look at what is given to constitute refusal. It is compelling that Ismail is keen to push beyond the usual iconography of protest discussed in chapter 7 – banners, slogans and chants that risk collapsing into overfamiliar spectacle. She alights on the observations of youths slouching and dressing scruffily, fully aware that this will be construed by police officers as suspicious. Again there are echoes of Butler here in asking what agency one has over how one's gait and attire are recognized by others, and the repercussions that might follow if one is perceived to move or dress aberrantly. The difference is that for Butler dressing in drag and mincing cannot amount to a refusal of subjectification: each is a reflex that may well end up reinforcing subjectification's dominant mode, entrenching it as a naturalized axis of orientation. The coercive part of becoming a subject is that which feels like the most natural thing in the world, rather than that which is demanded from an authoritative other and, maybe, denied. Here, though, bad posture and untidy attire are described explicitly as a refusal to perform a docile subjectivity. Extrapolating outwards, acting uncivilly is elevated to the status of a resistant political act. Though Ismail is careful to stipulate that this does not automatically constitute political efficacy, as with many of the authors discussed above a space is opened up by incivility in which a coherent culture of resistance may emerge. This is consistent with historical arguments that the only way to effect systemic change is to break the basic social contract, challenging the assumptions on which all social relations are predicated in order to force a fundamental reassessment of the social and political order. But this also threatens to diminish political subjectivity, what it means to be political, suggesting that when faced with an uncivil state it is sufficient and moral to respond by acting uncivilly oneself. There is doubtless a case for upending the norms of appropriateness that govern social interactions, though this will not in itself deliver less or differently structured political subjectivities, let alone coherent political resistance.

THE COMPLICITY OF ACADEMIC DISCOURSE

Ismail is also indicative of an argument encountered widely across the literature on political activism in the global South, namely that nascent democratic movements need to be protected not only from the state apparatuses that seek to suppress them but the overdeterminations of Western academic discourse as well. This claim takes a variety of forms, the most familiar being that to assume that history is universally a one-way journey towards Enlightenment political principles and European kinds of democratic states is both arrogant and complicit in the reproduction of iniquitous global power structures. Newsom et al. (2011), for instance, state bluntly that Western scholars writing about the Middle East, all of them, begin from the premise that all Arabs are oppressed and, worse, that they are incapable of apprehending their oppression because they are the products of authoritarianism. For one, this exhibits a lack of imagination about the way that academics think and engage with the people and regions they research. It is easy enough to posit that with the best of intentions othering still goes on when academics analyse and compose, but in fact the day-to-day practices that underpin the subject–object relationship are not so neatly delineable. In this way academic scholars are little different from journalists, doctors and campaigners: there is probably a power dynamic that consists in the privileged position the professional occupies as well as the cultural status their work is accorded, but the experience of work is uneven. Rather than speaking about the blanket objectification of the researched, it is more productive to think in terms of the way that researched individuals and groups appear amid the routines and regulations of work, sometimes distanced, sometimes intimate, sometimes conflicted. The forms of subjective recognition that go on as this work proceeds are likewise varied: not all of it will be Hegelian, but nor is it all a flat imposition of a preformed other. And when Newsom et al., turning their attention to global broadcast media, opine that 'the West receives rhetoric and reframes it to suit itself' (2011: 1308), there is a similar lack of nuance in their grasp of what media work is like – full of conflict and competition and ambition, as well as deadlines and inboxes and paperwork. This is not to say that news work is innocent, and the way that it comes to be experienced as a natural mode of being in the world is undoubtedly contingent upon the naturalization of norms that are politically implicated. But it is inconsistent and unruly, and to characterize 'Western media' as a discrete subject is as clumsy an othering as that alleged of Western imperialists. In more concrete terms, the agency of the phrase posits that the West and/or its media can collectively 'do something' to what is assumed to have been an authentic, local communication – a level of instrumentalism that far exceeds what mainstream frames are capable of effecting.

For Newsom et al. as for others, Western media and academia alike cannot help themselves, hardwired as they are by histories of colonialism and capitalism to enforce the will of the power centres they serve. There is no scope for these professionals reliably doing a better job, and the only ethical alternative is that they desist from producing and thus imposing discourse about and on the Arab world as elsewhere, leaving a space for indigenous narratives to develop unmolested. While elsewhere (Soguk, 2011) consideration is given to the changing forms that orientalism has taken across time and space, more commonly media and academic discourse are conflated and conceived as monolithic and single-mindedly antagonistic towards newly emergent Middle Eastern voices. Volpi (2011) exemplifies this theme, affirming that Westerners in the business of generating and disseminating knowledge are incapable of overcoming their deep-seated belief that Arabs are incapable of democracy because of their congenital preoccupation with tribalism and religion and that the polities they inhabit are unreformable because a state's claim to a monopoly on violence is always illegitimate when that state is an Islamic one. There are clearly strains of these prejudices in mainstream media discourse, though it is by no means all-pervasive, and there are corners of political science and international relations that invoke the end-of-history thesis, intentionally or otherwise. They are not hegemonic and are routinely criticized by other academics and journalists as well as activists, think-tankers and the denizens of social media.

For Volpi, however, the takeaway is that we should go further and reject wholesale the political concepts and frameworks used by academics in these disciplines. Instead, we should content ourselves with passively observing rather than trying to interpret and explain events like the Arab uprisings. The call to Western academic scholars is to get over their fixations on Montesquieu and Tocqueville and to stop obsessing over deviations from established abstract models of civil society and to look instead at how civil society is actually constituted in the daily life of Arab cities and nations. It is counterproductive by this view to look for evidence of or scope for the type of civility that has developed over centuries in the history of ideas and the political institutions of Western Europe and North America. If such preconceptions were pushed to one side, we would see that there are of course forms of functional civility underpinning Arab politics and culture, but they are more about communication and display in everyday rituals, for example in rhetorically elaborate expressions of respect. This seems an appropriately phenomenological response to a genuine dilemma of working with necessarily abstract concepts like objectification and subjectification in academic research practice, keeping an open mind when looking for evidence of the 'everyday subjective'.

But there is a subtle yet important elision here. Volpi is right to warn against the blind imposition of ontological and normative frameworks on cultures and societies that may have distinct and possibly incompatible organizing principles, and many others have sought to establish solid ground on which universal and relative values can be ethically reconciled. However, in the same way that resisting conventional definitions of resistance or dissent can lead to an interpretative model in which whatever is observed is taken to be evidence thereof, it does not follow that by refusing to explain the makeup and development of Arab civil society using Western academic units of measure and theories of social change that whatever is then observed is evidence of a locally authentic civility and politics more broadly. Epistemological fallacies aside, this ethos works from the essentialist assumption that each society – usually referring to nations, but sometimes cities and geographical or linguistic regions too – has distinct and intrinsic political values and uniquely appropriate mechanisms for instituting them that will naturally surface and take shape once the constraints of both authoritarian government and Western discursive determination are eliminated. Being open to different ways of thinking about and doing politics is just good politics, but this does not mean that political and discursive vacuums are naturally generative of radical or transformative alternatives – and certainly not that whatever actually appears in the absence of the old structurations is radical or transformative. It is sensible to assert that the political system best placed to deliver the collective will of, say, Egyptians may well not resemble European models of socialism, social democracy or neo-liberalism. All that follows from this is that scholars should be sensitive, open-minded and flexible when engaging in political diagnosis and prescription – not that their conceptual toolkits are at best irrelevant and at worst complicit in global oppression.

As for macropolitics, so too for the micropolitics of identity. It is common to encounter cautionary advice about transposing Western discourses of gender, sexuality, ethnicity and religion to the contemporary Arab world, though here it is worth pausing to consider *which* discourses of gender and the rest these authors have in their sights. And it is usually the classically liberal kind built around notions of personal freedom and autonomy, though also criticized for being individualistic and, to some, patriarchal. There is less of a perceived problem in transposing theories of identity currently accepted as progressive and morally defensible, including those that centre on performativity and intersectionality. Consistency demands that the same circumspection should apply to radical Western theorizing as to the canon, though really the point here is that there is nothing wrong with conceptual transposition so long as it remains reflexive and subject to critique. The alternative, to step back and watch as authentically local ways of thinking about identity, does not hold water against the injustices the cultural relativist is obliged to excuse. In fact, identity discourses – that whole set of what is just thinkable and sayable about identity in a particular context – neither emerges innocently in the local nor is imposed hegemonically. Moreover, they can be dissected and interpreted and those interpretations can be contested; tweets and demonstrations can be read for first- and second-order meaning, expressing the voices of protestors but also saying much about the constitution of the everyday experience of politics that is *not* part of the at-hand discourse of those activists. Done with critical transparency and robust peer review, it is both possible and ethical to talk about what speech acts mean, other than their in vivo content, without just putting words into the mouths of distant others.

The pre-uprising work of Tarik Sabry (2010) is exemplary in this regard, drawing on Heidegger's phenomenology to flesh out how the condition of modernity comes to be experienced in all manner of quotidian circumstances. In relation to political activism this means asking how individuals experience an encounter like a demonstration as immediately, overwhelmingly present, throwing them not only into a physical environment but also a historical one full of embodied experience, felt relations to co-present and distant others, learned rules of interaction and negotiation, and orientation towards possible futures. We have seen that, for Heidegger, authentic being in the world is precisely about the intelligibility of possibilities present in the situation in which one finds oneself. The upshot for academic research is that it is appropriate both to reconstruct the conditions that made that experience of a demonstration immediately apprehensible as all the things it is, as well as to infer the implications of contingent experience for possible future worlds and possible future political subjectivities. Talking about the future as it is constrained by the experience of the past and present is not the same as imposing a conceptual straightjacket on the political imaginaries of the Arab world's future. This amounts to the objectification of protestors, professionals and citizens, and some objectifications are better than others; the fact of objectification is itself morally neutral. Similarly, asking research participants in the Middle East to speculate about the future is not to incite them to thus subject themselves to discursive discipline. Indeed, it was seen in chapters 4 and 5 that most respondents are neither resigned to political continuity nor blithely optimistic about the future, but they are keenly aware of the stakes involved in how things play out from here and their role in them.

For now, however, it is apposite to end this chapter by highlighting some of the ways in which academic researchers have experienced the Arab uprisings as overflowing presents grasped in real time, especially in work produced as the movements continued to spread and achieve victories. And what is revealed are our own political imaginaries, the immediately at-hand instincts for perceiving and talking about oppression and resistance, authoritarianism and popular will. Ismail's refusal of docile subjection displays a commitment to resistance conceived as stubborn and belligerent – undoubtedly a precious attribute in the face of seemingly intractable inequality and injustice, though not necessarily a good fit for the compromise and sublimation that conventionally theorized collectivist politics requires. For Khondker (2011) the state is personified first as sneaky and then clumsy, doing harm inadvertently. Conceiving of a state as something to be outwitted is evocative, and potentially a good way to mobilize dissent, but it also runs the risk of conflating acts of guilefulness with the idea that dissent is naturally guileful. Sometimes this is manifest in the gleeful celebration of acts that appear clever and wily, that embarrass authorities by showing them to be slow on the uptake. This invites an emotional response, which might express camaraderie but could also be mere cheerleading, and which may well be less effective than more prosaic acts of resistance. It is amply evident in Khamis et al.'s (2012) work on creative resistance that when confronted with tales of audacity and evocative political expression – everything from hacking Google maps to dyeing a fountain's water red – it is difficult not to feel compassionately invested in the protestor's plight, and nor should that be the aim. It is human to feel catharsis and delight in response to the breaking of stuffy taboos or the mocking of authority through satire. Yet it remains important to understand what exactly is being recognized in such moments, the role that intention plays in the recognition of others and the conditions of possibility that shape the forms recognition can take. Joy at the minor victories of an underdog may resonate with genuinely felt humanitarian compassion and a principled commitment to democracy, but it can also indicate a keenness to recognize political transformativity – a keenness met all too easily through at-hand symbolic forms familiar to us from popular culture, half-remembered history and our own experience of watching the world.

None of this is to suggest that academic engagement with popular uprisings and all the hope and sacrifice they entail should be drily calculating. But the emotive language found in writings on the Arab uprisings, reaching for words like 'dreams', 'tragedy' and 'almost unbearably poignant' (Axford, 2011: 682), points us towards the affective work done by these phenomenal protest objects (Benski & Langman, 2013). This work is normative, too, perceiving political transformativity in individual and creative acts rather than the institutional and procedural machinations through which political change is conventionally wrought. Principled projection onto these events is unavoidable, but worth making clear all the same, and the uprisings appear to enable something often lacking in domestic political orientations: unironic engagement with noble political actors. Moreover, if Western projections of political subjectivity are rooted in a hardwired orientation towards instinctive recognition of authenticity that is naïve about the contextual complexity of the protest movements, so too are nativist perspectives that assume that if only Western delegates would stop thinking and writing about events in the world that are not their own, then something politically authentic will emerge. That the former is so often framed around the affordances of social media when it comes to political mobilization means that both are predicated on the perceived generativity of structurelessness. But subjectivity emerges through structuration and not in its absence, pushing us away from imagining what might happen in a political vacuum towards investigating the myriad factors that shape the experience of the political in encounters in the world that are as continuous as they appear unprecedented, as mundane as they are extraordinary.

Chapter Nine

Living in Interesting Times

The Work of Experience, Engagement and Identity

This book is situated against the backdrop of a broader dialogue in recent media research that turns the spotlight away from the content of media texts towards practices of media production and consumption. Ong's (2014) review of the literature maps this shift in relation to media witnessing of conflict, bringing into sharp relief not only the different methodologies but also the distinct ethos motivating investigations of texts, audiences and production contexts. Maltby's (2013) ethnography of media professionals working at the United Kingdom's Channel 4 News exemplifies the latter approach, going beyond a descriptive account of working practices and also simply giving these employees a voice, seeking to understand the practical contingencies that underpin the ethical decisions they make. This is a productive move, especially as it militates against functionalist accounts in which 'the media' represent distant others in irresponsible or damaging ways. It gels with most production-side research (Born, 2008) in that whatever the strengths and weaknesses of individual reporters and producers, most feel they can account for their actions and are not unthinking cogs in a coercive media machine. The point, though, is not simply to humanize journalists, producers and technicians. Instead it is twofold. First, to demonstrate that media ethics are not a matter of abstract principle but decisions taken amid the routines and rhythms of everyday professional life. Second, it is thought that by opening up production contexts to public view, audiences will be able to imagine their way into a more live, less flat relationship with those featuring in news coverage of uprisings and conflicts.

This chapter likewise takes the insights into the working lives of contemporary Arab journalists and asks what these can tell us about the way that audiences around the world pay attention, if at all, to seismic events. It will be seen in what follows that this is about more than coming up with new ways to engage viewers and readers with distant revolutions and wars. It is about questioning the very point of witnessing (Ellis, 2000, 2009; Peters, 2001; Chouliaraki, 2010a): on what grounds it is important to acknowledge geographically remote experiences of suffering, injustice and euphoria, what form that acknowledgement should ideally take and whether the role of witness is ethically best assumed by individuals, media delegates or mediated publics as a whole. Mortensen (2015), for instance, floats the possibility of connective rather than collective witnessing, while Gregory (2015) writes of ubiquitous witnesses. The aim here is not to relativize or dismantle the whole normative grounding of media representing humans to other humans (Silverstone, 2006), but it is important to make clear the implications of the fundamental and usually unspoken normative assumptions we make about subjects on either side of the production process.

MEDIA WITNESSING AND SUBJECTIVE RECOGNITION

The professional media industries have a chequered history when it comes to bearing witness to global upheavals and calamities, personified on the one hand by heart-on-sleeve self-appointed saviours (Bell, 1998; Seib, 2002) and on the other by mercenary gadflies, unified only by a limited understanding of the history and politics underlying whatever they are there to cover (Knightley, 1975). In reality, while the field produces conspicuous sanctimonious moralizers and war junkies, the range of approaches to representing political upheaval, conflict and disaster is too heterogeneous to be reduced to one or two ways in which the media, or Western media, look at the rest of the world. Some of this comes down to the talent and initiative shown by particular filmmakers, reporters and media houses; in part it is because of the oversight provided by media watchdogs, NGOs and scholarly research. Either way, the question of how good or bad a job media professionals do of representing events distant from their audiences is a live one, especially as there is considerable debate around what criteria should apply in the first place. Ong's research is indicative of how conflict journalists have come to be recognized – popularly, as well as by academics – not simply as messengers but as delegated witnesses of human suffering, injustice and jubilation. With all of the power implications that come with one group or another claiming a particular valorized role, the journalist is recognized as an embodied authority on the important stuff, entrusted by the rest of us to ensure that no significant human experience goes unseen and undocumented (see also Wilkins, 2016).

This applies regardless of whether particular journalists or media organizations are trusted, or whether those occupying the role are increasingly unpaid amateurs or PR spokespeople. As discussed in chapter 7, the role is a consecrated position and can be understood on those terms; the question of who claims and occupies that role it is a secondary one. The cultural value of witnessing, though, is not therefore deontological. For one, it is contingent on the efficacy of visibility – whether documenting revolutions and atrocities constitutes recognition of their champions, accountability for their perpetrators and solidarity with their victims. The current consensus (Tester, 1994; Chouliaraki, 2008; Orgad, 2011; Kyriakidou, 2014; Maier, 2015) in the distant suffering literature is that visibility is insufficient, and maybe even deleterious: increasing coverage defined not only in terms of column inches and airtime but also in screen resolution and ubiquity of accessibility might correlate *negatively* with audience engagement. And this raises profound questions of media morality. The normative imperative at the heart of this deliberation is a basic one: since media are inextricably morally implicated in that they are in the business of representing people to other people, it is not enough that suffering is seen but that we as individuals and publics respond to it the right way, morally speaking. That, then, is the normative cargo that the conflict reporter bears, and the same logic applies to those covering protestors, dissidents and activists.

The distinction between media producer and consumer may have been thoroughly blurred by social media and user-generated content (Jenkins, 2006), but if anything this just demonstrates how broadly recognized the role of delegated witness is (Ellis, 2009): consider the effortlessness with which bystanders to crimes and accidents assume the role of witness on camera or on Twitter, knowing instinctively how to play the part (see also Papacharissi, 2015). We saw in chapter 8 that while some scholars see scope for radically new kinds of subjectivity and intersubjectivity in social media, others detect only the loss of what was good about solidarity as it was historically conceived, or worse, subjection to ever more invidious forms of neo-liberalism. There is no need to rehearse the debate over collectivity, connectivity and aggregation, but what is particularly salient here is how political subjectivity – not just being political, but being political in relation to others (Isin, 2002) – is conceived in terms of weight and solidity, or their absence. For some, the promise of socially mediated subjectivity lies precisely in its weightlessness, worn lightly and endlessly motile. For others, the blood, sweat and tears involved in old ways of protesting are fatally lacking in the new politics. This book has refused both imaginings of political subjectivity, insisting that it is not something wrangled and delivered in critical moments of pain and revelation, nor does it emerge naturally out of an absence of constraints. Specifically, this means that the normative principles underpinning the media's role in sustaining ethical relations between non-copresent people – witnessing, accountability, scrutiny, resistance, reform – need not necessarily demand personal toil and tenacity, but nor is there some pure form of these that would appear if only we could remove the overdetermining structures of journalistic and academic discourse. As with Graeber's ethnographies of activism (2009), however, this book maintains that meaningful political principle can be sustained by much more banal everyday routines.

This matters because it is against these alternately arduous and idealized conceptions of caring that contemporary audiences are being compared and found wanting (Moeller, 1999; Orgad, 2011). Individuals getting involved in political issues on social media are derided as slacktivists, but there is a cogent response in asking exactly what would count as caring enough to amount to substantive engagement and what would constitute evidence of solidarity. Acting politically is generally sufficient for the political scientist, and while there is disagreement about thresholds of politicality, templates exist for recording political behaviour. But acting politically is categorically different from being political: political subjectivity demands not just certain behaviour but a particular experience of political engagement. This is not commonly explicated, but its presence under the discursive surface is clear enough: the experience of acting politically has to be effortful or transcendent to count as meaningful. Likewise, the ordinary viewer of mediated distant suffering and tumult does not attain the status of a witness who really recognizes what is going on unless they also suffer – whether emotionally, or through time given to paying attention, or by acting on what she has seen. Just how much pain and cost must accrue in order to constitute proper witnessing of faraway misery? How much of a jolt does someone need to have experienced in order to have really registered the magnitude of a popular revolution? If, however, it can be demonstrated that politically principled practices of media production and activism can also be experienced as ambivalent, mundane or even fun, then it should be possible to imagine different criteria for assessing mediated public engagement with upheaval and suffering.

There is no reason to doubt the sincerity of the participants in this research when they describe what motivates them – a keen sense of public duty, a passionate commitment to human rights and social justice, an unwavering belief in the importance of deliberation. It is always technically possible to reduce all expressions of altruism to self-interest and expressions of any kind to performative practice, but this makes little practical sense in the face of interviewees who were able to seamlessly speak to personal principles both in the abstract and in the toing and froing of everyday life. This is where the meaningfulness of principled practice is sustained or not, after all. And diving in to those banal practicalities tells us a lot about what it means to be political, to be principled, to care. Social media, for instance, were more often than not referred to as a drain on time rather than something which transformed the interviewees' political agency; covering demonstrations on the other side of town wiped out the possibility of getting anything else done, while emails piled up mercilessly; interfering editors were criticized not for impinging on journalistic integrity but for creating needless extra work. Respondents consistently reported a proliferation of political activism in both cities in recent times, and while it was usually implied that this is a good thing, it too was talked about in terms of work: the time taken to report protests, the resources required, staying up late, getting up early, being constantly on the phone, having less of a social life, not spending enough time with the kids. The point, though, is that all of these experiences should not be thought of as competing demands on one's being in the world but as complementary ones. Political subjectivity is sustained through all of these things and not in spite of them. It is possible that the sense of constant busyness that journalistic work affords is at the core of the respondents' generalized experience of meaningfulness. Importantly, this does not hollow out professional and political principle. It is the regularity and frequency of practices from writing and campaigning to texting and checking Facebook that sustain the meaningfulness of principle, as much as principle sustains the meaningfulness of these practices.

Something similar can be said for the routine social practices respondents engage in. From a more strictly Bourdieusian (1994) perspective this might be characterized as the collective suspension of disbelief about meaningfulness that goes on in all professional and cultural fields. But this only holds if *all* social practices are at some level oriented towards the conservative reproduction of structures, and this is a normative claim rather than one that can be inferred. It is entirely plausible that, as with busyness, social activity sustains professional and political meaningfulness, as much as any deeply held conviction about what counts as meaningful sustains cultures of socializing. While there was evidence that both paid and unpaid work can crowd out some social practices, it was also clear that whether at work or out on the streets being political was itself very sociable, and often outright fun. In one sense this is obvious: at least exchanging pleasantries is one of the unspoken rules of professional interaction, while attending a demonstration in Lebanon or San Francisco invariably entails as much catching up with acquaintances, sharing cultural references and easy jokes as it does chanting slogans. But it was also apparent that life in newsrooms allowed for more socializing than is the case in, for instance, Nick Davies's (2008) account of contemporary British journalism. There were snarky asides about colleagues who were lazy or domineering or sexist, but plenty of comments too about colleagues being like a second family or just enjoyable to be around. It was also evident at the headquarters of *As-Safir* and *Al-Ahram*, with co-workers routinely sticking their heads around each other's doors, making humorous observations, exchanging gossip and making plans for dinner. Conventionally, we would see such conviviality as a natural outgrowth, what happens when individuals who share a pre-existing professional passion and political commitment come together. But it works the other way, too: affectively enjoyable daily routines sustain that sense of passion and commitment over time. The latter is contingent on the former: principles are not innate, after all, but experienced as integral to one's identity only to the extent that conditions exist in which their iterative, habituated enactment is effortless. Principles are not hardwired and wielded in spite of external constraints; they are subjectively meaningful only insofar as there are contexts in which they are just thinkable and just doable.

The interviews are full of talk about politics, activism and journalism, but also sport, technology, shopping and, notably, food. When pressed to say more about their colleagues, friends and interlocutors, respondents tended to focus more on personal traits rather than their political outlook, including when the relationship was otherwise clearly predicated on shared beliefs and commitments. Instead of casting judgments on someone's values and dedication, then, approval more commonly took the form of references to their children, sense of humour or status, and disapproval, the form of their meanness, arrogance or unimportance. The picture that develops is of a sprawling network of ties strong and weak, built around a plethora of routine engagements and encounters that are sometimes distinctly political, but mostly just human. It is worth noting that reported interactions were often abstracted rather than actual, perhaps not surprising given that the practice that unified all respondents was writing, and writing usually involves imagining an audience. The network to which they belonged appeared to subsist through a constant ongoing conversation between comrades, colleagues, readers and followers, but one that was often experienced as hypothetical and speculative, an internal dialogue. In any case, the central point is that it is this web of social interactions, often enjoyable, usually humdrum, that allows for the collective meaningfulness of political principle to solidify and endure – rather than the inherent meaningfulness of abstract principle inspiring that web into existence.

If this image of communicative camaraderie appears cosy, informal and collaborative, it should be emphasized that discord, mistrust and fatalism are also threaded through several transcripts. Especially among older interviewees, there was a strong belief that the conflicts underpinning the Lebanese civil war had not been resolved but merely papered over, and that they threatened to re-emerge at any time. In Cairo the most experienced reporters were also the most jaded, seeing corruption and cronyism as intractable and their own agency as journalists hopelessly circumscribed. The risk, as ever, is to cast journalists and activists in this part of the world as noble warriors, doggedly continuing their struggle in spite of everything. There are real dangers involved in being politically active in Egypt and Lebanon, and these should not be underestimated. Journalists have been killed and imprisoned in large numbers in Egypt, and for all the talk of the ineffectuality of government censors, intimidation is experienced regularly in both countries. But the interviews do not reveal reporters and campaigners tirelessly clinging to political principles in the face of enormous obstacles. Instead, they show principles made meaningful by shared cultures of practice that, whatever the backdrop, are often routine and affect-driven. Principle is not predicated on a *happy* workplace or social network. All kinds of affective routines can nurture it, from simple familiarity to, counter-intuitively, resignation: wearily or wryly conceding and continuing to concede that things will never change is a way to enact principled subjectivity in everyday life; it is not a matter of holding determinedly on to inner principle in the absence of contexts in which it can be externalized.

One final assumption that warrants unpacking is that groups of professionals or amateurs united by a common political cause will tend to be horizontal in their organization, resisting hierarchy in the name of consolidating tribal identity (Wapner, 2002; Juris & Pleyers, 2009). The Beirut cohort in particular largely explicitly referred to their work as activism, and across the two cities these media professionals were extensively networked with reform-minded others, networks that combined a high degree of social media engagement with other kinds of mediated and face-to-face communication. Chapter 8 showed how some theoretical perspectives predict that the fluid, multifarious connections afforded by network cultures tend towards a greater degree of individualism in political movements, as opposed to the supremacy of the collective favoured by politics done the old way, with manifestoes hammered out in smoky rooms through clearly defined organizational structures and processes. Individualism by this view does not connote competitiveness, though, but rather its opposite: individuals committing themselves only as much as they are comfortable with, linked in such a way as to effect a collective agency that is simultaneously greater than the sum of its parts and undirected, leaderless (or leaderful). No one wields disproportionate influence, and nor does any ideological commitment or historical legacy. And there was precious little evidence to support this model – most closely associated with the Occupy movements, but readily transposed to the Arab uprisings at the time – in our sample population. A large majority rejected both the role of passive documenter of events and of public servant, there to inform but not influence their audience. From chapters 4 and 5 it is clear that they resisted indoctrinating their readers and viewers, but influence is precisely what they aimed to cultivate.

Those most immersed in activist movements – the ones who organized and participated in demonstrations rather than just covering them – were also quick to dispel any notion of an organic, self-organizing collective. All in some way saw themselves as leaders, and the way they presented themselves as such demonstrated unequivocally that ego matters. This falls a long way short of egomania: the assumed role is not about recruiting disciples or forming a political vanguard as such, but nor is it the passive curating of other people's thoughts and opinions. In short, most derived palpable satisfaction from their role as authorities, not dictating what others should think but guiding them, coming up with new ideas and arguments, creating new discursive spaces that others could participate in. This, too, could be seen as something sustained by personal conviction, and there was certainly a good deal of confidence and passion on display. Importantly, though, occupying a privileged position was not experienced so much as a burden or solemn duty, but frequently very enjoyable. And this enjoyment derived as much from the sense of doing worthy work well as from the buzz of getting a lot of likes and retweets. This last statement could be read as an accusation of frivolousness, but really it is not: regular, affective pleasures can be just as instrumental in nourishing conviction as deeply held principle. Detailed awareness of audience reach and impact on social media, and obvious delight at having a lot of approving followers, is not at all inconsistent with unwavering political commitment; indeed, it might underpin it.

Consistent with Butler (1993), enduring political subjectivity for this cohort was contingent on the mastery of a repertoire of practices, some more banal and affective than others. Reflexivity was conspicuous: most displayed a heavily ironic perspective on their own status, fully aware that a good deal of performance and identity management is required to achieve recognition and status. Talk of the absurdity of media activism was frequent, with the requirement for believable sincerity always undercut by the desire to be famous and influential. But it is a game worth playing, not only because of the political stakes but personal ones too. More specifically, confident enjoyment of the game spoke to a shared though implicit feeling that everything was always to play for, for them if not for the country as a whole. This in no way casts their activism as narcissistic; it is precisely what provides the day-to-day momentum of their work. This is significant in itself, but in what follows it will be seen to have real implications for how we think about audiences of upheaval and suffering as well, the experience of the self seen not as comprising stable, established beliefs and values but very much as work in progress. The pleasure this group of professionals derive from their work comes not from simply expressing what they think but from participating in an environment in which how they are seen and what they can do with that are always up for grabs.

The implications, then, are fourfold. First, affect matters when it comes to political engagement (Barnett, 2008; Crociani-Windland & Hoggett, 2012). Pivotally, this is not the same as well-established and compelling calls for emotion to play a more substantive role in public life (Arendt, 1958) – this is affect in the sense that is more often than not used pejoratively, referring to how things are experienced amid routines of everyday practices, things that are merely felt and not fully apprehended. Second, social capital is potentially just as potent as solidarity when it comes to being political; that is, coordinating with others towards political ends, opposing malignant forces, challenging structural injustice and coming up with new ideas for organizing society. And this is social capital not in the bonding, collaborative sense of Putnam (2000) but the more strategic, Manichean terms of Bourdieu (1990), capital that is won through game-playing as much as merit and used to accrue power and status. However, while for Bourdieu this was about how entrenched power secures its place in a field and how its structures are reproduced, the analysis here suggests that game-playing and principle are not mutually exclusive – indeed, the former might sustain the latter in everyday contexts. The way respondents spoke of principle often came across as heavily ironic, playful and even self-serving, but their principles were no less genuine for it. This is because, third, principle is experienced not as the expression of some innate core of identity but as ongoing work to do, necessary to achieve political aims but also self-management. Politics is part of the daily grind, sitting among myriad other routines, regular but also discontinuous. Political engagement may frequently appear to lack intensity, consistency or even seriousness, but this is the rub: it is not the externalization of a deep-seated, originary political subjectivity but part of the never-ending work of political subjectification, work that plays out in the dance of everyday life. Finally, the experience of social change is not about revelation, of grasping the enormity of things going on out there. It is about an orientation to the everyday world experienced affectively, habitually, as given. The point, however, is the way we experience the present does not necessarily hinder grasping what is at stake in it for the individual, group and society as a whole: on the contrary, it is – or can be – the routines and felt experiences of daily life that sustain such an awareness and active engagement in environments in which one's subjectivity and what that affords are not always and already foreclosed. This is not to say we get it right a lot of the time: after Bourdieu, structured misrecognition is the norm in most encounters in the world. But subjectivity – not just how we see ourselves but how we see other objects, human and otherwise, and how we appear to them as objects – is temporally open-ended, something we work at through and not in spite of the way we experience the small stuff.

PROVISIONAL SELVES: IMPLICATIONS FOR AUDIENCE ENGAGEMENT WITH DISTANT OTHERS

There are clearly limits to the generalizations that can be made about the publics of different countries and regions on the basis of a dedicated, self-selecting, professional cohort. But this can be put another way: surely, if the experiences of a group so self-evidently politically engaged and motivated can be full of pleasure and anguish and all the affective registers in between, then we should not expect audience engagement with suffering and upheaval to be uniformly sombre and sober. This is by no means acquiescence in the face of apathy, but rather a reframing of what form an ethically defensible recognition of suffering takes in everyday practice. It was seen in chapter 7 that writers from Kundera (see Hammond, 2007) to Carruthers (2008) and Sontag (2003) share a view of audiences, mostly conceived as mass Western news audiences for news, which verges on the contemptuous, casting them as cold, self-involved and feckless. Chouliaraki and Boltanski are less openly scathing, diagnosing a lack of public solidarity with faraway victims as a symptom of a broader malaise of alienation, itself an understandable reaction to a contemporary society awash in spectacle and superficiality. But they share with the others a common endeavour, to explore alternatives for rediscovering empathy and ultimately solidarity, to find ways of making publics care as much about the experiences of distant others as they – and dedicated journalists and activists – do. There is doubtless something of a status claim in this, in the way that the rise of the campaigning journalist acting as the world's conscience is both intended by its practitioners as a force for good and a bid for cultural authority. But it is also apposite to the politics of recognition debate in political theory, applying theorizations of the conditionality of mutual subjective apprehension to the malignant forces standing in the way of global solidarity: for our purposes, the commercialization of news, overfamiliar narratives of human experience, the warping of social relations by capitalist logics and, maybe, the very practice of mediation. We know from Silverstone that overcoming these obstacles is not about obliterating everything that mediates between subjects but establishing an ideal relational positioning from which mutual understanding and perspective are possible. Chouliaraki (2013) takes this one step further, positing that not only distance but also a certain mode of regarding the other – an ironic one – is both rational and potentially constructive. This is an important intervention since elsewhere irony is given to be a toxic condition of postmodernity, a distorting optic that makes any discussion of truth and morality impossible. But irony can take many forms, and Chouliaraki has in mind a refusal to take apparent meaning as self-evident, which is sceptical rather than cynical (see also Burgers et al., 2016). Rather than immediacy, then, a questioning detachment is the necessary precondition of someone thinking their way towards the experience of others. For journalists and campaigners, the message is clear: rubbing an audience's face in suffering and insisting that they acknowledge it in all its horror, declaiming that history is being made in Tahrir Square and demanding recognition of the momentousness of what is happening, is pointless. And more futile still is the demand that audiences not only care but do so in the right way – that is, not voyeuristically, or narcissistically, or merely affectively.

In many ways this is familiar territory, chiming with Adam Smith's line (in Chouliaraki, 2013: 29–30) that imagining what being in the world feels like for others is a skill that needs to be nourished over time, and with Taylor's that this cannot be achieved prescriptively. There is also an echo of Sauter's (2014) theorization of the fruitful externalizations of the self enacted through social media narratives, which she places in the historical tradition of self-writing going back through Foucault, Rousseau and Pepys to the Epicureans. This work serves as an effective bridge between healthy scepticism about one's encounters with the world, which might reduce to simple media literacy, and scepticism about how we appear to the world, all too imaginable when we see our tweets and posts out of their intended context. As well as refusing to take facts at face value, the ironic orientation to the world is a refusal to take the self as self-evident. This might mean nothing more than not taking oneself too seriously, a decent antidote to engaging with distant suffering and drama piously or in a moralizing manner. It also invokes Hegelian subjectification, that epic dialectic of subject and object that is ultimately about human history in the material world. But irony suspends this profundity, allowing for a better understanding of being in the world with others as it is experienced at the level of the routine and banal.

One readily observable manifestation of irony is the lurid performativity of much media witnessing by ordinary citizens: the way that many people instinctively know how to go into witness mode when a reporter's microphone is thrust before them in the street or that live-tweeting an unfolding event, drawing on learned narratives and rhetoric, comes as second nature to some. It is corporeal as much as moral, going on the way that television news witnesses speak and hold themselves as though in character, and social media witnesses spontaneously access authorized ways of speaking about familiar events and spaces. This could be interpreted simply as spitting out discourse, regurgitating internalized practice configurations on cue. But Sauter suggests that there is enough slippage and suspension in self-writing on social media to suggest that it is both governmentality in action and an awareness – on whatever level – of performances to be performed. Likewise, the moment of self-recognition sometimes seen in vox pops when a speaker becomes aware of the strangely authoritative voice they have adopted when asked to speak for a crowd of protestors or recount the details of a shooting. And this opens up new territory: the possibility that audience engagement with distant others is neither simply incited nor artless but a semi-knowing response to what is expected of people generally or people like them in particular. A phenomenological perspective goes further than the political theoretical postulation of what is expected of citizens according to, say, an implicit social contract. It allows for a felt awareness that an individual's sense of self and their place in the world is not all or nothing – it needs to be practised iteratively, worked at, in ordinary situations. This does not annihilate empathy or solidarity. This kind of ambivalence towards, or even deliberate distancing from, remote human experience sits well with a principle like solidarity once it is accepted that such principles never just are, and are never just expressed or enacted. Instead they are sustained through routines that necessitate a certain detachment; an enduring awareness of their mundaneness ensures that everyday contexts never quite withdraw. The point is that their withdrawal is not, as Orgad (2012) has it, the condition of the emergence of political subjectivity; everyday experience is itself the condition of that subjectivity.

In pragmatic terms, this means that there is little point in wringing our hands over the apparent fact that the ready visibility of violence and misery does not seem to induce empathy and solidarity in audiences. Nor is it sound to suggest that mediation is itself the problem, that visualization perverts that which motivates it – either by hollowing out the ontological content of political upheaval and human suffering or, after Rousseau, by inevitably resorting to techniques of performance (see also Miller, 2016). It also means arguing against Sontag's call for visual media in particular to try to break through the mediated fug that people are thought to wallow in, ultimately forcing them to twig that this is what suffering *really* is and these are the real people experiencing it. There is nothing about mediation per se that makes that which is represented less real, though of course some accounts are better at conveying human experience than others. The flipside is that nor should media aim to break through whatever stands between viewer and viewed – complacency, distraction, cultural remoteness – to provoke some kind of revelatory recognition of the humanity of those depicted, since recognition is about iterative, embedded practices rather than eureka moments. Further, this approach offers a way around the politics of pity debate. For Arendt (1958) pity reduces victims to 'nothing but men', or in Rancière's (2009) words 'a monotonous moan', nothing but needs and lacks, wounds to be treated, mouths to be fed – the archetype of Foucault's biopolitics. For Rancière as for Boltanski, the essential weakness of pity is that it prompts private responses to what should be recognized as public problems; Chouliaraki's 'emergency' response to distant suffering highlights the same issue with emotion sincerely felt but which goes nowhere. Few argue these days that emotion should be totally excluded from public deliberation, but pity specifically is characterized as innately passive, an emotion without articulation to spheres of action. Butler counters in *Precarious Life* (2006) and elaborates in *Frames of War* (2016) that pity can be marshalled towards solidarity if we understand our own vulnerability to be the same as that of the victims on our screens, if we acknowledge not just the sad fact of a life lost but of the futures also extinguished, futures we can better imagine to be as precious as our own. This, however, again relies on a breakthrough moment, the kind of lightning bolt of realization that does not tally with the way that recognition is felt, practised and embodied over time.

The politics of recognition debate flagged up at the beginning of this book (see especially Fraser & Honneth, 2003) has fanned out in several directions over the past fifteen years or so, with theorists exploring the intersubjective possibilities of voice (Couldry, 2010), visibility (Casper & Moore, 2009) and listening (O'Donnell., 2009; O'Donnell et al., 2009). The question of whether identical subjective recognition – recognition of another as that other fundamentally is – is an unshakably metaphysical one, and as such is bracketed out of phenomenological accounts in favour of an analysis of how recognition works in everyday contexts. This is of a piece with the idea that the texture of a society is defined not by critical encounters between people but by what enables them to more or less rub along even when they are in conflict and when they interact indirectly, ambiently or by way of glancing blows. Goffman's earlier work (1963) studies how what he dubbed civil indifference operates at the microscopic level of social interactions, but there is scope for scaling this up the better to capture what kind of recognition exists between people in a polity or imagined community – in particular, how it develops or atrophies over time. The same might be said about social relations at the global level, with recognition contingent not on intense confrontations revealing an other's undeniable, overwhelming humanity but on a more generalized awareness of others' subjectivity and what their suffering means. Orientation towards others is like everything else embodied practice, usually experienced as instinct but with some room for reflexive positioning. This might not amount to epiphany, and certainly not on an equal scale for all others encountered, but irony, ambivalence, resistance, annoyance and all the other conceivable responses to mediated upheaval and suffering may in habituated form afford sufficient space and solidity to sustain substantive recognition.

This was certainly the case with the participants in this research, for whom there was no sense that the gravity of the events engulfing their worlds was lessened when they became the stuff of their work with all the petty affect that entails. What we learn from these practitioners is that their political principles and moral values are not for the most part clinched in specific critical encounters but seen as ongoing work, experienced as a generalized orientation towards others sustained with less than intense engagements with others in the world, including those experiencing revolution, injustice and deprivation. Rather than seeking out creative ways to disrupt the seamless lifeworlds of media audiences, the same logic can apply here: what is needed is a sustained but uneven and generalized orientation towards the political and social phenomena transforming the lives of others for better or worse. This is not to suggest that both the invisibility of others' misery and its over-familiarity cannot breed indifference – and as such thinking imaginatively and counter-intuitively about the representation of others in specific, concrete circumstances remains important. But engagement with the world around an individual is an incremental process, and giving her space to develop a principled, liveable and adaptable orientation to it means allowing for specific responses that are ambivalent, or inconsistent, or that just do not amount to much. This is the way with most reactions to most encounters: they are just liveable with, enabling the individual to sustain a passably consistent idea of who they are and the world they cohabit. It is not heartless, at least when seen in the round. It is how solidarity is lived, not usually as a full-throated declaration of one's humanity or global citizenship, or a decisive action that proves one's moral character, but as practical choices made in time and space.

The question of how we relate to distant others is thus unmistakably ethical, but as with Simone de Beauvoir it can only be an ethics that embraces ambiguity rather than reaching for ontological certainty:

> Only, unlike Kant, we do not see man as being essentially a positive will. On the contrary, he is first defined as a negativity. He is first at a distance from himself. There is within him a perpetual playing with the negative, and he thereby escapes himself, he escapes his freedom. And it is precisely because as evil will is here possible that the words 'to will oneself free' have a meaning. Therefore, not only do we assert that the existentialist doctrine permits the elaboration of an ethics, but it even appears to us as the only philosophy in which an ethics has its place. For, in a metaphysics of transcendence, in the classical sense of the term, evil is reduced to error; and in humanistic philosophies it is impossible to account for it, man being defined as complete in a complete world. Existentialism alone gives – like religions – a real role to evil, and it is this, perhaps, which make its judgements so gloomy. Men do not like to feel themselves in danger. Yet, it is because there are real dangers, real failures and real earthly damnation that words like victory, wisdom or joy have meaning. Nothing is decided in advance, and it is because man has something to lose and because he can lose that he can also win. (de Beauvoir, 1948: 34–35)

De Beauvoir's phenomenological insistence that existence precedes essence is consistent here with the suggestion that we embrace the failures that most of us enact in everyday life. Failing to live up to a hypothecated global citizen or cosmopolitan witness is inevitable, though this is not simply to advocate pragmatism. For de Beauvoir, freedom consists in there not being an essentially good choice to make in any given situation, since the present is finite in its facticity – in line with the claim made in this volume that selfhood is not wholly in the balance in any discrete encounter with a distant other.

This is distinct from arguing that the infinite realm of abstract morality and the ethics of day-to-day life should be subject to different registers of scrutiny; instead it means effacing the opposition of finite and infinite, against the German idealist tradition. By doing so it becomes clear that values can still emanate from will, but that their doing so is particular rather than universal – and certainly not heroic.

This could sound a little like Heidegger's dictum that we should let being be, but as with Heidegger it is important not to lose sight of what is up for grabs when selves are, incrementally, disclosed. The crux for de Beauvoir is that we do not begin with abstract values and then find objects on which to project them, but nor, pace Sartre, is the answer to start with nothing so as to achieve full, moral selfhood. Whereas Sartre proposes that we make ourselves a lack in order that we can be, de Beauvoir effectively calls that out as presumptuous, even pompous: we do not own our lack in a live-or-die fashion; lack is part of the furniture, something that motivates the things we do in quotidian arenas, actions which can be generated by and in turn generate values without being part of some universal mission to become. The notion of lacking and pursuing being in order to complete ourselves only makes sense in religious contexts or with a strong notion of self-mastery that is at odds with how our encounters in the world are experienced temporally.

> Therefore, in the very condition of man there enters the possibility of not fulfilling this condition. In order to fulfil it he must assume himself as a being who 'makes himself a lack of being so that there might be being'. But the trick of dishonesty permits stopping at any moment whatsoever. One may hesitate to make oneself a lack of being, one may withdraw before existence, or one may falsely assert oneself as being, or assert oneself as nothingness. One may realise his freedom only as an abstract independence, or, on the contrary, reject with despair the distance which separates us from being. All errors are possible since man is a negativity, and they are motivated by the anguish he feels in the face of his freedom. Concretely, men slide incoherently from one attitude to another. (de Beauvoir, 1948: 35)

The upshot is that philosophers should not view people, and media scholars should not view audiences, as a means to an end of idealized solidarity. Disclosing being as a work in progress is an activity, not a metaphysical or historical drive towards ultimate subjectivity. That which is desirable for publics or audiences is not something that can be argued from first principles and then nurtured in situ, but rather something that springs from desire itself. That distinction between desire and the desirable is one way of expressing the distinction between disclosure and being, and it is also the basis for arguing for the possibility of morality beyond self-interest and hedonism. Put simply, values emerge through and not in spite of desires. As with Sartre, the basic existential condition of freedom creates the lack in which desire appears, but there is more to desire than either sensual satiation or the profound pursuit of identity. Put another way, part of what is desirable consists in being right, but this can simply mean being right in one's own eyes and maybe that of one's intimates or a generalized sense of others; it does not have to be right in the eyes of God, let alone the theorist. The fantasy of being will always fail, but this is not a cause for despondency: while we may never arrive at the ideal self, it is precisely in the dynamism of selfhood, including all the inevitable failures, reversals and compromises, that ethics become possible.

Later in the same book, de Beauvoir goes on to argue that the pursuit of existential selfhood is a fantasy of absolute freedom, of reaching a point at which there is no longer anything at stake; one's self is unimpeachable, and there are no wrong choices to make. This, she points out, is childish, and to act as though it were possible is potentially dangerous. There is still plenty of room for passion, because again it is through constructing projects around one's passions that values become thinkable and actionable. The 'sub-man' refuses to contemplate the implications of his freedom; the nihilist blithely assumes that there are no such implications; while the 'serious man' attempts to absolve himself of the responsibility of freedom by submitting to immutable universal truths. 'Serious man' is intended as a term of derision, but her point is not to mock earnestness, only what she sees as the infantile wish to surrender one's freedom to dogma. Seriousness as an end in itself is at best pointless and at worst destructive, but seriousness as lived experience – conflicted, haphazard, distracted – is another matter. De Beauvoir's wider call here is to avoid mistaking outward manifestations of universal values for universal values themselves. Another way of putting it is to understand that learned, recognizable performances of virtue are just that – not necessarily disingenuous, but not incarnations of abstract truths – with the corollary that analysts of publics, mediated and otherwise, should be wary of diagnosing right and wrong kinds of self on the evidence of observable behaviour. We need not go as far as de Beauvoir in delineating the conditions of genuine freedom, but the basic point remains salient: being responsible for one's selfhood means recognizing that one is responsible to the selfhood of others; what is at stake for me in how things unfold from here is also at stake for others. The selves disclosed in such encounters are partial, provisional and discontinuous; they are not instantiations of an intrinsic or universal self but part of the work of selfhood – work that is freighted with consequences, but not always and not consistently, and which like everything else reduces to things to do and time to do them in.

HARNESSING CHANGE: THE POSSIBILITIES OF DISSENSUS

We have seen that having a grasp of what is at stake in the way the world around us is changing, for ourselves as well as for others, is something which is worked on over time and not achieved absolutely in moments of particular intensity. There is no reason to assume that this would just happen organically, however, a natural consequence of large numbers of individuals interacting or just inhabiting common geographical or mediated spaces – the same applies to social media platforms as it does to the citizens of a large and heterogeneous country. That means that against the model of algorithmically orchestrated politics and the more thoroughgoing, leaderless articulations of grass-roots politics, there remains a specialized role to be performed in coordinating and orchestrating attention and orientation. This need not take the form of a new kind of political leadership as such, but it does entail a defence of cultural authority in an age when such a concept has little currency. The interviewees here did not see themselves as mere overseers of information and enjoyed the status that comes with wielding influence over an audience won over across several years. The line they drew was between indoctrination and creating space for debate – not a vacuum, but an arena whose parameters they drew up themselves. This sounds merely benign, but for several it also entailed provocation: refusing to tell your readers what they want to hear, challenging their assumptions, furnishing them with alternative ideas and questions and asking that they respond. Journalists, commentators, activists and scholars are all in the business of doing this in one way or another, which suggests that there are more general questions to ask about what kind of authoritative, organized practice is best suited to nurture intersubjective recognition. Away from strategies that aim to shake people out of their complacency and confront them with the world as it really is at this precise moment, what could sustain piecemeal, iterative recognition that, over time, might amount to solidarity? This final section teases out the possibilities of dissensus, a kind of organized disruption of the conditions of intelligibility in everyday life, in order to do just that.

The first thing to say is that this is different from arguing that journalists and academics should be more active political campaigners, assuming leading roles in protest movements. Instead of political activism, then, the role envisaged here is more concerned with the contestation of that which is tacitly accepted in particular cultural and professional contexts, consensuses that have become unspeakable because of their sheer self-evidence to insiders and opacity to those on the outside. In theoretical terms such a role draws on Rancière's (1998, 2010) characterization of dissensus as the organization, even institutionalization, of critical dissent. Where it differs from agonism is that it is not so much about disrupting congealed conflicts in the political status quo but routinely upsetting the obviousness that attaches to the power arrangements of any social order. It is, then, a question of the mutual intelligibility of different social worlds and professional fields, beginning as Amir did by establishing what we do not currently know about each other and, crucially, cannot know because we do not possess the means of translation (see also Ascher, 2011). That last term has frequently been deployed to capture what it is that journalists do for societies as a whole (Fürsich, 2002): beyond holding power to account, helping different groups understand each other. Helping groups recognize each other, however, is a distinct prospect, entailing engagement with the contingent underpinnings of their largely taken-for-granted experience of the world, establishing the limits of mutual intelligibility. Rather than grabbing people by their lapels and demanding that they recognize these others as subjects, the question becomes how best to facilitate emergences to consciousness of others that are often fleeting and tangential, yet embedded well enough in the rhythms of quotidian life to sustain recognition of the distinctness and plenitude of others' experience of the world. If this sounds abstract, in practical terms it boils down to the role that language plays in different lifeworlds. Regarding politics, for instance, it is about the fact that different groups have different ways of talking about it – not just rhetorical differences or cultural inflections, but ways that are fundamental to the very conceivability of the political.

If one looks at the news media across the Western world there is clearly no shortage of coverage making the most of differences between different groups in society, with disagreements amplified and the usual array of narrative techniques for drawing a line between 'people like us' and 'people like them'. Underneath this, though, is a well-established consensus about the basic principles of how societies are organized and the principles according to which they operate. Conspicuous but superficial conflict is known to all and sundry as the stuff that sells: slanging matches and personal betrayals in politics, the perceived deviance from cultural norms by one subculture or another, lurid crimes that make one fear for one's family. This is all familiar territory, but it is notable that understanding why these assumptions are made usually go no further than positing that audiences respond to sensation and fear. But those responses are not only visceral; like any other practices they are associated with position-taking and distinction-making and thus underpin an individual's orientation to the world in a temporally incremental manner. The same logic applies to the journalist and commentator, too, habitually used to positioning assorted others as part of the daily grind of work. Collectively, these media practices make it naturally meaningful to look for differences of opinion and identity, status and morality, while rendering less thinkable that which underpins the experience of most things as easily talked about.

How far to take this contention is debatable, though there has been considerable rowing back over the past twenty years from the strict Foucauldian reading that naturalized ways of talking and thinking are causally implicated in the reproduction of specific power hierarchies in society. The limitations of such a view are, first, that its detection of iniquitous power everywhere leaves little room for distinguishing between its nefarious and harmless manifestations. And second, it means that any institutionalized discourse of knowledge, such as journalism, is stripped back to amount to little more than a vehicle for structural reproduction – regardless of distinct organizational cultures and individual efforts. Examples are easy enough to locate: the way journalists write and broadcast about finance draws attention towards nefarious individuals and groups – be they bankers or people on benefits – not playing by the rules, but it makes less intelligible a questioning of the deeper economic changes that have taken place over the past thirty years and what alternatives exist for the next thirty. Or the way that coverage of military invasions fixating on individual politicians and the gaudy spectacle of war works to the detriment of public understanding of international politics, economics and history.

Pleasing symmetries aside, the relationship between cultures of practice of media production and consumption are nothing like that straightforward. Journalism and the media broadly cannot simply be blamed for public apathy and disengagement from the profound questions facing us as societies and globally. More specifically, journalism's habitual focus on the present is not the force preventing better understanding of long-term, systemic shifts. The same fallacy is evident in some critiques of consumerism that draw a direct line from the superficial choices we are invited to make everywhere we go to the lack of deep thinking about fundamental questions of social justice and what it means to live authentically or ethically. The two may be linked, but to cast one as the cause of the other is to posit consumerism as exogenous, a corrupting other to who we really are. It is not, however, an external force, but as integral to and constitutive of our subjectivity as our physical surroundings. For better or worse, it is who we are and not a distortion of our true nature. But that does not necessitate fatalism: it means simply that rather than insisting that people recognize the reality of the world however defined and by whomever, we question the limits of intelligibility of the way the world appears to us and how we experience it. It is, then, about worrying away at the edges, making them less seamless.

Who is best placed to do this worrying at the seams remains an open question. Journalists do not have a good track record when it comes to challenging conventional wisdom – maybe because of an innate conservatism borne out of precariousness (Hesmondhalgh, 2006), or maybe because of the conundrum raised at the beginning of this book, with an orientation towards the immediate past and future crowding out more awareness of systemic change and continuity. Sociologies of journalism do not, however, tend to reveal a trade lacking in self-confidence, with generalists and specialists alike generally at home offering grand explanations about society's ills and reflecting on politics from well above the fray. Apparently trapped inside the Beltway or the Westminster bubble in daily professional routines, journalists are in fact comfortable transcending these closed worlds with far-reaching networks, toes dipped in all kinds of literatures and discourses and a readiness to take on all comers in social exchanges and research interviews. This, though, is the journalist as meta-critic rather than dissident, the authority who stands above it all without committing to specific campaigns and agendas. That is in line with chapters 4 and 5 in which participants spoke of a long-term role for journalists as authoritative deliberative leaders rather than a political vanguard, but it falls short of dissensus, still less Mouffe's agonism. A willingness to confront and engage with all and sundry is different than a preparedness to face structural issues; to ask the big questions about why things are the way they are is to risk appearing naïve and earnest. A professional cultural disposition of argumentativeness is one thing, but trying to apprehend the contingency of the status quo that pervades the experience of everyday life can appear sophomoric.

Naïve, earnest, sophomoric: these are obviously not failures of professionalism but failures to understand the unspoken rules of the journalistic game, that learned instinct for what is appropriate and inappropriate to talk about with peers and actors in different fields. In Singer's (2005) research on journalistic interactions with non-professional others online, this observed lack of fit is one of the weapons at a journalist's disposal for maintaining boundaries between valorized and lay practitioners. It is above all an orientation that refuses to take things too seriously, to regard the objects of one's work through an ironized distance, much as happens in other trades. This does not preclude journalists being dogged in pursuit of the truth or proclaiming morally on the rights and wrongs of the way things are, but this is part of the game – a self-aware performance that goes with the territory and is, to many, one of the daily pleasures of the job (Protess, 1992). Interviews with Western reporters (Markham, 2011b) show that enjoyment stops precisely at the point when core ethics and world view are probed, anything necessitating a discursive shift away from the irreverent and sceptical. However, it was noted in chapter 2 that a sceptical disposition is arguably a prerequisite of engaging in the world in a manner that might underpin the subjective recognition of others and, perhaps, solidarity with them. And chapters 4 and 5 showed that this kind of engagement is perfectly compatible with daily life experienced largely through small pleasures and petty frustrations; it is not a matter of demanding the unironic, unmediated grasp of the world as it really is and a proclamation of political principle in confronting it. Put in terms of subjectivity, not taking things seriously is not the same thing as not being serious.

This is not to say that not taking things seriously is innocent, and as with any field disposition it is strategic, a role that feels like a second skin to insiders but is alien to outsiders. It can be counterproductive as regards public engagement, associated with a blindness to new forms of politics coalescing in unexpected quarters and authorizing ambivalence and difference towards the old forms. There is a world of difference, however, between being dismissive or cynical and engaging with specific encounters with the world provisionally. Rather than experiencing each moment of thrownness as something demanding full apprehensive and subjective enactment, the journalistic disposition is particularly, though not uniquely, suited to maintaining a critical scepticism, committed to sizing the moment up but resisting the idea that it is a replete, always-already reality. This disposition refuses to see everything as being at stake in each encounter with the world, at stake for that world and for oneself; it pushes against the phenomenal incitement that this is how the world is now and that you must fully commit to apprehending and positioning yourself in relation to it. When faced with apparently monumental change for better or worse, the provisional orientation accepts that this could be how things are going to play out from now on – but perhaps not, let us see. This applies to the environment in which one finds oneself, but also to that self: not taking oneself seriously, then, is not an appeal to personal humility but a matter of taking oneself provisionally. Whatever self is invoked and performed in the encounter, it is not a final self but a work in progress. And it is in that work that serious engagement, the kind capable of grasping radical contingency and the experience of the other as identical to our own, subsists.

If this sounds lofty, in practical terms it simply means journalists or any other committed witnesses being committed to irreverence towards their own status as much as to others. It need not be experienced as an all-encompassing mission to capture the truth or to transform society – it could, but just as tenable is an unfussy, workmanlike willingness to push at the boundaries of intelligibility. This in turn means two things: a readiness to ask questions of different groups that leaves oneself vulnerable to exposure as ignorant or naïve and a willingness to prod at the bleeding obvious of one's own social milieu, with the same risk attached. That does not amount to a call for journalists or amateurs to embrace worthiness, or to become personally more politicized, or to personally commit to changing the world. Nor is it to suggest that we all should speak more authentically or sincerely. For starters, authenticity is always contextual and reliant on embodied practices of enactment and recognition (Goffman, 1959); it is not something that can simply be willed, like Aristotelian good faith. Instead, it means a readiness to try to understand other professional fields – politics, economics, philosophy – on their own terms, confident about questioning why things are the way they are there and without fear of being outed as inexperienced or ingenuous. As was seen above, for Rancière establishing the limits of mutual intelligibility is precisely the point, encapsulated by Phillips through the metaphor of translation: the real impetus for improving intersubjective recognition between groups is not the learning of equivalent terms in each of their languages but reaching the point where one 'no longer recognises in the other's language any shared object that one can present in one's own' (Phillips, 2010: 50). It is in these absences of intelligibility that Rancière locates the possibility, over time, of a properly political engagement with the world.

The role of the journalist or any other delegated witness in this model is not to fill these absences but to give them form, to translate the discourses of professions and disciplines and cultures as far as possible, but more importantly to set out explicitly what we outsiders cannot even begin to conceive of translating into our own words. This position is adjacent to Badiou (2005), for whom democracy is conceived as that which does not 'take persons into account', aiming instead at some universal truth, or more appropriately, a commitment to an iterative process of divulging, questioning and being brought up short by truths. What remains central is that dissensus is about disagreement over the conditions of understanding, rather than the sentiment. Instead of shackling ourselves to showing the world as it really is, or to giving authentic voice to another, the remit of the committed witness is instead the enunciative modalities (Phillips, 2010) of speaking and the conditions of possibility that govern them – the 'distribution of the sensible', as Rancière puts it in *The Politics of Aesthetics* (2004; see also Ross, 2009; Robbins, 2015).

For Rancière, it is art which is situated closest to the 'precipice' and thus best placed to give us a glimpse of the unspeakable. It has long been argued (see, for instance, McNay, 2000) that Foucault's preoccupation with the transgression of discursive boundaries rests on an unsustainable distinction between the inside and outside of discourse, while Butler forensically sets out the problems associated with positing interiorality and exteriorality of subjectivity (Butler, 1997). Here, though, the risk is that the outer, that unintelligibility we seek to tease out and prod at amid the routines of daily life, is normatively loaded as something elusive and tantalizing. This allure of unknowability is at the heart of all claims about the new politics based on deontological normative commitments, or tenets of faith – faith that deinstitutionalized or de-professionalized media practices will be less constrained and hence more truthful or pure, or that algorithmically organized communicative networks will generate new and currently unimaginable political subjectivities. In each case there is a gap between the status quo and the desired outcome; the conceptual work required to breach that gap is given over to metaphors – structural, spatial, biological, systems-based – that give form to projected alternatives to current realities but do little to establish probability or direction of travel. The iterative, provisional teasing out of contingency might by contrast appear to lack a commitment to a radically transformed future, but that need not be the case: it is simply that such a commitment is sustained through the rhythms of everyday practice rather than avowed.

Going around pointing out how arbitrary locally universalized systems of thought are, worrying at the edges of seamlessness, disrupting what is experienced as an ontological solidity – all of this could also be argued to be merely nihilistic. Why should it be assumed to encourage engagement? In short, because it is not a revelation of the way the world is and you are, but a methodical reminder of the contingency and thus open-endedness of each. It is an elucidation of stakes. The aim of disrupting what are experienced as whole and seamless symbolic worlds is, rather than proposing possibilities for how different things could be in a utopian sense, to establish how radically different groups experience the world at an everyday level. The overarching goal may then be to foster intelligibility between lifeworlds, but the immediate effect of highlighting the fragility of givenness is to demonstrate how narrowly conditional and provisional those worlds are. The implication is not necessarily one of existential gloom. In the context of journalism, the benefit is not so much in establishing the arbitrariness of intelligibility in different fields, but rather in showing that there is nothing outside of intelligibility and thus there are stakes in how different phenomena – politics, aesthetics, knowledge – come to have meaning. If there is an existentialist inflection to this, it is simply the notion of meaning as something always in a state of becoming, rather than inherent or final.

However, this raises potential problems. First, we have seen that if the broader intelligibility of a field is conditional on it being a game worth playing, then it reduces to Bourdieusian *illusio* (2000: 11): the collective, and collectively misrecognized, sense that that being invested in an essentially arbitrary symbolic economy is worthwhile. Concepts such as solidarity or community then run the risk of becoming merely functional: they exist to make living in society meaningful; they are a necessary condition of the seamless experience of the lifeworld and thus, possibly, secondary to the demands of subjectivity. This is not intended to be pedantic. The metaphors of space, organisms and systems mentioned above, whatever networks and processes they are intended to explain, also carry connotations of solidity, vitality and productivity, which should give us pause. These metaphors and the thinking they represent are functional, in that they contribute to the unproblematic experience of everyday life. But it is then arguable that it does not matter what form ideas like solidarity and community take so long as they serve this function: since they amount to little more than a reaction against the possibility of nihilism, then whichever provides comfort and stability is sufficient. However, thinking about critical journalism and witnessing in terms of the disruption of the obviousness of social orders is not to advocate the evacuation of these or any other concepts. The point of understanding and communicating contingency is to establish that when it comes to the meaning of ideas, for the self and for society at large, everything is to play for.

It can always be argued that all routines are existential comfort blankets, ways of imposing meaning on a meaningless universe. Even routinized witnessing, with its catalogues of suffering and injustice, can be refracted in this way, a culture of practice that can sustain a collective orientation to something solid, stable but essentially arbitrary. But while such practices contribute to the experience of everyday life as given, if fully critically engaged they can also draw attention to that givenness and the habits, assumptions and structural conditions that make it so. The result is not to point to an existential void, to posit that meaning is either present or absent, but that meaning is both superficial and full, contextually constituted all the time and with tangible consequences. The point of witnessing change then reduces to something other than either a wide-eyed desire to make a difference or a romanticized embrace of existential futility. It is the awareness that things are in a real sense precarious, in flux and unresolved; this applies equally to the world and the self, not just in terms of what the latter can get out of the former but how we are seen and how we see ourselves. We all – professionals, activists, audiences – have a very real stake in how things play out.

References

Aday, Sean. 2010. 'Chasing the Bad News: An Analysis of 2005 Iraq and Afghanistan War Coverage on NBC and Fox News Channel'. *Journal of Communication* 60 (1): 144–64.

Adorno, Theodor W. 1941. 'On Popular Music'. *Studies in Philosophy and Social Sciences* IX: 17–48.

Agathangelou, Anna M., and Nevzat Soguk. 2011. 'Rocking the Kasbah: Insurrectional Politics, the "Arab Streets" and Global Revolution in the 21st Century'. *Globalizations* 8 (5): 551–58.

Allagui, Ilhem, and Johanne Kuebler. 2011. 'The Arab Spring and the Role of ICTs: Editorial Introduction'. *International Journal of Communication* 5: 1435–42.

Allam, Nermin. 2014. 'Arab Revolutions: Breaking Fear Blesses and Curses: Virtual Dissidence as a Contentious Performance in the Arab Spring's Repertoire of Contention'. *International Journal of Communication* 8. http://ijoc.org/index.php/ijoc/article/view/2271/1107.

Alterman, Jon B. 2011. 'The Revolution Will Not Be Tweeted'. *The Washington Quarterly* 34 (4): 103–16.

Andén-Papadopoulos, Kari. 2014. 'Citizen Camera-Witnessing: Embodied Political Dissent in the Age of "Mediated Mass Self-Communication"'. *New Media & Society* 16 (5): 753–69. First published in 2013.

Anderson, Benedict R. 1983. *Imagined Communities: Reflections on the Origin and Spread of Nationalism.* London: Verso.

Anderson, Christopher W. 2013. 'Towards a Sociology of Computational and Algorithmic Journalism'. *New Media & Society* 15 (7): 1005–21. First published in 2012.

Andrejevic, Mark. 2008. 'Theory Review: Power, Knowledge, and Governance'. *Journalism Studies* 9 (4): 605–14.

Andrejevic, Mark. 2011. 'Social Network Exploitation'. In *A Networked Self: Identity, Community, and Culture on Social Network Sites,* edited by Zizi Papacharissi, 82–102. London: Routledge.

Ang, Ien. 1991. *Desperately Seeking the Audience.* London: Routledge.
Angella, Marco. 2016. 'Work, Recognition and Subjectivity: Relocating the Connection between Work and Social Pathologies'. *European Journal of Social Theory* 19 (3): 340–54. First published in 2015.
Aouragh, Miriyam. 2012. 'Framing the Internet in the Arab Revolutions: Myth Meets Modernity'. *Cinema Journal* 52 (1): 148–56.
Appadurai, Arjun. 1996. *Modernity At Large: Cultural Dimensions of Globalization.* Minneapolis: University of Minnesota Press.
Archetti, Cristina. 2012. 'Which Future for Foreign Correspondence?' *Journalism Studies* 13 (5–6): 847–56.
Arditi, Benjamin. 2008. 'Arguments about the Left Turns in Latin America: A Post-Liberal Politics'. *Latin American Research Review* 43 (3): 59–81.
Arendt, Hannah. 1958. *The Human Condition.* Chicago: University of Chicago Press.
Ascher, Anat. 2011. 'Thinking the Unthinkable as a Form of Dissensus: The Case of the Witness'. *Transformations Journal of Media & Culture* 19. http://www.transformationsjournal.org/issues/19/article_01.shtml.
Aslanidis, Paris, and Cristóbal Rovira Kaltwasser. 2016. 'Dealing with Populists in Government: The SYRIZA-ANEL Coalition in Greece'. *Democratization* 23 (6): 1077–91.
Austin, J. L. 1962. *How to Do Things with Words.* Oxford: Clarendon Press.
Axford, Barrie. 2011. 'Talk about a Revolution: Social Media and the Mena Uprisings'. *Globalizations* 8 (5): 681–86.
Back, Les. 2015. 'Why Everyday Life Matters: Class, Community and Making Life Livable'. *Sociology* 49 (5): 820–36.
Badiou, Alain. 2001. *Ethics: An Essay on the Understanding of Evil.* London: Verso.
Badiou, Alain. 2005. *Handbook of Inaesthetics.* Stanford: Stanford University Press.
Bady, Aaron. 2012. 'Spectators to Revolution: Western Audiences and the Arab Spring's Rhetorical Consistency'. *Cinema Journal* 52 (1): 137–42.
Baker, Stephanie Alice. 2011. 'The Mediated Crowd: New Social Media and New Forms of Rioting'. *Sociological Research Online* 16 (4). http://www.socresonline.org.uk/16/4/21.html.
Barker, Stephen. 2009. 'Transformation as an Ontological Imperative: The [Human] Future According to Bernard Stiegler'. *Transformations Journal of Media and Culture* 17. http://www.transformationsjournal.org/issues/17/article_01.shtml.
Barnett, Clive. 2008. 'Political Affects in Public Space: Normative Blind-Spots in Non-Representational Ontologies'. *Transactions of the Institute of British Geographers* 33 (2): 186–200.
Barnett, Steven. 2002. 'Will a Crisis in Journalism Provoke a Crisis in Democracy?' *The Political Quarterly* 73 (4): 400–8.
Barr, Robert R. 2009. 'Populists, Outsiders and Anti-Establishment Politics'. *Party Politics* 15 (1): 29–48.
Bassel, Leah. 2012. *Media and the Riots: A Call for Action: Conference Report 2012.* London: Citizen Journalism Educational Trust.
Baudrillard, Jean. 1983. *Simulations.* New York: Semiotext(e).
Bauman, Zygmunt. 2000. *Liquid Modernity*. Cambridge: Polity.

Beam, Randal A., Bonnie J. Brownlee, David H. Weaver and Damon T. Di Cicco. 2009. 'Journalism and Public Service in Troubled Times'. *Journalism Studies* 10 (6): 734–53.

Beardsworth, Richard. 2010. 'Technology and Politics: A Response to Bernard Stiegler'. *Cultural Politics* 6 (2): 181–99.

Becker, Lee, and Tudor Vlad. 2009. 'News Organisations and Routines'. In *The Handbook of Journalism Studies*, edited by Karin Wahl-Jorgensen and Thomas Hanitzsch, 59–72. London: Routledge.

Bell, Martin. 1998. 'The Journalism of Attachment'. In *Media Ethics*, edited by Matthew Kieran, 15–22. London: Routledge.

Bellin, Eva. 2012. 'Reconsidering the Robustness of Authoritarianism in the Middle East: Lessons from the Arab Spring'. *Comparative Politics* 44 (2): 127–49.

Bennett, Jane. 2010. *Vibrant Matter: A Political Ecology of Things*. Durham, NC: Duke University Press.

Bennett, W. Lance. 2012. 'The Personalization of Politics: Political Identity, Social Media, and Changing Patterns of Participation'. *The ANNALS of the American Academy of Political and Social Science* 644 (1): 20–39.

Bennett, W. Lance, and Robert M. Entman. 2001. *Mediated Politics: Communication in the Future of Democracy*. Cambridge: Cambridge University Press.

Bennett, W. Lance, and Alexandra Segerberg. 2012. 'The Logic of Connective Action: Digital Media and the Personalization of Contentious Politics'. *Information, Communication & Society* 15 (5): 739–68.

Bennett, W. Lance, and Alexandra Segerberg. 2013. *The Logic of Connective Action: Digital Media and the Personalization of Contentious Politics*. Cambridge: Cambridge University Press.

Benski, Tova, and Lauren Langman. 2013. 'The Effects of Affects: The Place of Emotions in the Mobilizations of 2011'. *Current Sociology* 61 (4): 525–40.

Benski, Tova, Lauren Langman, Ignacia Perugorría and Benjamín Tejerina. 2013. 'From the Streets and Squares to Social Movement Studies: What Have We Learned'. *Current Sociology* 61 (4): 541–61.

Benson, Rodney. 2006. 'News Media as a "Journalistic Field": What Bourdieu Adds to New Institutionalism, and Vice Versa'. *Political Communication* 23 (2): 187–202.

Benson, Rodney, and Erik Neveu. 2005. *Bourdieu and the Journalistic Field*. Cambridge: Polity.

Berger, Miriam. 2013. 'A Revolutionary Role or a Remnant of the Past? The Future of the Egyptian Journalist Syndicate after the January 25th Revolution'. *Arab Media & Society* 18. http://www.arabmediasociety.com/?article=835.

Berry, David M. 2012. *Understanding Digital Humanities*. Basingstoke: Palgrave Macmillan.

Best, Kirsty. 2010. 'Living in the Control Society: Surveillance, Users and Digital Screen Technologies'. *International Journal of Cultural Studies* 13 (1): 5–24.

Bhuiyan, Serajul I. 2011. 'Social Media and Its Effectiveness in the Political Reform Movement in Egypt'. *Middle East Media Educator* 1 (1): 14–20.

Bird, Elizabeth. 2003. *The Audience in Everyday Life: Living in a Media World*. London: Routledge.

Blackman, Lisa. 2008. *The Body: The Key Concepts*. Oxford: Berg.

Block, Elena. 2013. 'A Culturalist Approach to the Concept of the Mediatization of Politics: The Age of "Media Hegemony"'. *Communication Theory* 23 (3): 259–78.

Bloom, Pazit Ben-Nun. 2013. 'The Public's Compass: Moral Conviction and Political Attitudes'. *American Politics Research* 41 (6): 937–64.

Blyth, Mark. 2002. *Great Transformations: Economic Ideas and Institutional Change in the Twentieth Century*. Cambridge: Cambridge University Press.

Boczkowski, Pablo J. 2005. *Digitizing the News: Innovation in Online Newspapers*. Cambridge, MA: MIT Press.

Boltanski, Luc. 1999. *Distant Suffering: Morality, Media and Politics*. Cambridge: Cambridge University Press.

Born, Georgina. 2008. 'The Normative, Institutional and Practical Ethics: For an Anthropological Ethics of Media'. *Ethics of Media Conference*. CRASSH, University of Cambridge, UK, 4–5 April.

Born, Georgina. 2011. *Uncertain Vision: Birt, Dyke and the Reinvention of the BBC*. London: Random House.

Borri, Francesca. 2013. 'Woman's Work: The Twisted Reality of an Italian Freelancer in Syria'. *Columbia Journalism Review*. http://www.cjr.org/feature/womans_work.php.

Bourdieu, Pierre. 1977. *Outline of a Theory of Practice*. Cambridge: Cambridge University Press.

Bourdieu, Pierre. 1984. *Distinction: A Social Critique of the Judgement of Taste*. Cambridge, MA: Harvard University Press.

Bourdieu, Pierre. 1990. *The Logic of Practice*. Cambridge: Polity.

Bourdieu, Pierre. 1991. *Language and Symbolic Power*. Cambridge: Polity.

Bourdieu, Pierre. 1993. *The Field of Cultural Production: Essays on Art and Literature*. Cambridge: Polity.

Bourdieu, Pierre. 2000. *Pascalian Meditations*. Cambridge: Polity.

Bourdieu, Pierre. 2001. 'Television'. *European Review* 9 (3): 245–56.

Bowskill, Matt, Evanthia Lyons and Adrian Coyle. 2007. 'The Rhetoric of Acculturation: When Integration Means Assimilation'. *British Journal of Social Psychology* 46 (4): 793–813.

boyd, danah m. 2011. 'Social Network Sites as Networked Publics: Affordances, Dynamics, and Implications'. In *A Networked Self: Identity, Community, and Cultures on Social Network Sites*, edited by Zizi Papacharissi, 39–58. London: Routledge.

boyd, danah m., and Nicole B. Ellison. 2007. 'Social Network Sites: Definition, History, and Scholarship'. *Journal of Computer-Mediated Communication* 13 (1): 210–30.

Boyle, Raymond. 2006. *Sports Journalism: Context and Issues*. London: Sage.

Brants, Kees, and Yael de Haan. 2010. 'Taking the Public Seriously: Three Models of Responsiveness in Media and Journalism'. *Media, Culture & Society* 32 (3): 411–28.

Brants, Kees, Claes De Vreese, Judith Möller and Philip van Praag. 2010. 'The Real Spiral of Cynicism? Symbiosis and Mistrust between Politicians and Journalists'. *International Journal of Press/Politics* 15 (1): 25–40. First published in 2009.

Briziarelli, Marco, and Susana Martínez Guillem. 2016. *Reviving Gramsci: Crisis, Communication, and Change*. London: Routledge.

Brockington, Dan. 2015. 'Celebrity Advocacy: International and Comparative Perspectives'. *Celebrity Studies* 6 (4): 393–98.

Burgers, Christian, Elly A. Konijn and Gerard J. Steen. 2016. 'Figurative Framing: Shaping Public Discourse through Metaphor, Hyperbole, and Irony'. *Communication Theory*. http://dx.doi.org/10.1111/comt.12096.

Burkeman, Oliver. 2013. *The Antidote: Happiness for People Who Can't Stand Positive Thinking*. London: Macmillan.

Butler, Judith. 1993. *Bodies That Matter: On the Discursive Limits of 'Sex'*. New York: Routledge.

Butler, Judith. 1997. *The Psychic Life of Power: Theories in Subjection*. Stanford: Stanford University Press.

Butler, Judith. 2004. *Precarious Life: The Powers of Mourning and Violence*. London: Verso.

Butler, Judith. 2006. *Precarious Life: The Powers of Mourning and Violence*. London: Verso.

Butler, Judith. 2016. *Frames of War: When is Life Grievable?* London: Verso.

Butler, Judith, and Athena Athanasiou. 2013. *Dispossession: The Performative in the Political*. Cambridge: Polity.

Cammaerts, Bart, Alice Mattoni and Patrick McCurdy. 2013. *Mediation and Protest Movements*. Bristol: Intellect.

Campante, Filipe R., and Davin Chor. 2012. 'Why Was the Arab World Poised for Revolution? Schooling, Economic Opportunities, and the Arab Spring'. *Journal of Economic Perspectives* 26 (2): 167–87.

Cappella, Joseph N., and Kathleen Hall Jamieson. 1997. *Spiral of Cynicism: The Press and the Public Good*. Oxford: Oxford University Press.

Caraway, Brett. 2016. 'Crisis of Command: Theorizing Value in New Media'. *Communication Theory* 26 (1): 64–81. First published in 2015.

Carruthers, Susan L. 2008. 'No One's Looking: The Disappearing Audience for War'. *Media, War & Conflict* 1 (1): 70–76.

Casper, Monica J., and Lisa Jean Moore. 2009. *Missing Bodies: The Politics of Visibility*. New York: NYU Press.

Castells, Manuel. 2009. *Communication Power*. Oxford: Oxford University Press.

Castells, Manuel. 2012. *Networks of Outrage and Hope: Social Movements in the Internet Age*. Cambridge: Polity.

Chant, Sara Rachel, Frank Hindriks and Gerhard Preyer. 2014. *From Individual to Collective Intentionality: New Essays*. Oxford: Oxford University Press.

Chari, Anita. 2016. 'The Embodiment of Conscience'. *Philosophy & Social Criticism* 42 (10): 1015–27.

Cheah, Pheng. 2013. '"The World is Watching"'. *Journalism Studies* 14 (2): 219–31.

Cho, Charles H., Martin L. Martens, Hakkyun Kim and Michelle Rodrigue. 2011. 'Astroturfing Global Warming: It Isn't Always Greener on the Other Side of the Fence'. *Journal of Business Ethics* 104 (4): 571–87.

Chouliaraki, Lilie. 2006. *The Spectatorship of Suffering*. London: Sage.

Chouliaraki, Lilie. 2008. 'The Symbolic Power of Transnational Media Managing the Visibility of Suffering'. *Global Media and Communication* 4 (3): 329–51.

Chouliaraki, Lilie. 2010a. 'Ordinary Witnessing in Post-Television News: Towards a New Moral Imagination'. *Critical Discourse Studies* 7 (4): 305–19.

Chouliaraki, Lilie. 2010b. 'Post-Humanitarianism: Humanitarian Communication beyond a Politics of Pity'. *International Journal of Cultural Studies* 13 (2): 107–26.

Chouliaraki, Lilie. 2013. *The Ironic Spectator: Solidarity in the Age of Post-Humanitarianism.* Cambridge: Polity.

Chouliaraki, Lilie, and Bolette Blaagaard. 2013. 'Introduction'. *Journalism Studies* 14 (2): 150–55.

Christensen, Henrik Serup. 2011. 'Political Activities on the Internet: *Slacktivism* or Political Participation by Other Means?' *First Monday* 16 (2). http://firstmonday.org/article/view/3336/2767.

Christensen, Miyase, and André Jansson. 2015. *Cosmopolitanism and the Media: Cartographies of Change.* Basingstoke: Palgrave Macmillan.

Cisneros, J. David. 2008. 'Contaminated Communities: The Metaphor of "Immigrant as Pollutant" in Media Representations of Immigration'. *Rhetoric & Public Affairs* 11 (4): 569–601.

Clifford, Michael. 2001. *Political Genealogy after Foucault: Savage Identities.* London: Routledge.

Clough, Patricia, and Jean Halley. 2007. *The Affective Turn: Theorizing the Social.* Durham, NC: Duke University Press.

Colander, David, Michael Goldberg, Armin Haas, Katarina Juselius, Alan Kirman, Thomas Lux and Brigitte Sloth. 2009. 'The Financial Crisis and the Systemic Failure of the Economics Profession'. *Critical Review* 21 (2–3): 249–67.

Costanza-Chock, Sasha. 2012. 'Mic Check! Media Cultures and the Occupy Movement'. *Social Movement Studies* 11 (3–4): 375–85.

Cottle, Simon. 2006. *Mediatized Conflict: Developments in Media and Conflict Studies.* Maidenhead: Open University Press.

Cottle, Simon. 2011. 'Media and the Arab Uprisings of 2011: Research Notes'. *Journalism* 12 (5): 647–59.

Couldry, Nick. 2003. *Media Rituals: A Critical Approach.* London: Routledge.

Couldry, Nick. 2010. *Why Voice Matters: Culture and Politics After Neoliberalism.* London: Sage.

Couldry, Nick. 2015. 'The Myth of "Us": Digital Networks, Political Change and the Production of Collectivity'. *Information, Communication & Society* 18 (6): 608–26.

Couldry, Nick, Aristea Fotopoulou and Luke Dickens. 2016. 'Real Social Analytics: A Contribution towards a Phenomenology of a Digital World'. *The British Journal of Sociology* 67 (1): 118–37.

Couldry, Nick, Sonia M. Livingstone and Tim Markham. 2010. *Media Consumption and Public Engagement: Beyond the Presumption of Attention.* Basingstoke: Palgrave Macmillan.

Crawford, Kate. 2009. 'Following You: Disciplines of Listening in Social Media'. *Continuum* 23 (4): 525–35.

Crociani-Windland, Lita, and Paul Hoggett. 2012. 'Politics and Affect'. *Subjectivity* 5 (2): 161–79.

Crogan, Patrick. 2010. 'Knowledge, Care, and Trans-Individuation: An Interview with Bernard Stiegler'. *Cultural Politics* 6 (2): 157–70.

Crogan, Patrick. 2012. 'Editing (and) Individuation'. *New Formations* 77 (1): 97–110.

Crossley, Nick. 2014. 'Embodied Actors, Sociability and the Limits of Reflexivity'. *Body & Society* 20 (2): 106–12.

Curran, James. 2010. 'The Future of Journalism'. *Journalism studies* 11 (4): 464–76.

Curran, James, and Jean Seaton. 2010. *Power without Responsibility: Press, Broadcasting and the Internet in Britain.* London: Routledge.

Dahlgren, Peter. 2013. 'Online Journalism and Civic Cosmopolitanism'. *Journalism Studies* 14 (2): 156–71.

Dalacoura, Katerina. 2012. 'The 2011 Uprisings in the Arab Middle East: Political Change and Geopolitical Implications'. *International Affairs* 88 (1): 63–79.

Darmon, Muriel. 2016. 'Bourdieu and Psychoanalysis: An Empirical and Textual Study of a Pas De Deux'. *The Sociological Review* 64 (1): 110–28.

Davies, Nick. 2008. *Flat Earth News: An Award-Winning Reporter Exposes Falsehood, Distortion and Propaganda in the Global Media.* London: Chatto & Windus.

De Beauvoir, Simone. 1948. *The Ethics of Ambiguity.* New York: Philosophical Library.

De Blasio, Emiliana, Matthew Hibberd and Michele Sorice. 2011. 'Popular Politics, Populism and the Leaders: Access without Participation?' *Centre for Media and Democratic Innovations 'Massimo Baldini' Working Papers.* http://eprints.luiss.it/1211/1/CMCS-WP-2011-05.pdf.

De Rivera, Joseph. 1991. 'Emotional Climate: Social Structure and Emotional Dynamics'. In *International Review of Studies on Emotion Volume 2,* edited by Kenneth T. Strongman, 197–218. Chichester: Wiley.

De Smet, Brecht. 2014. 'Revolution and Counter-Revolution in Egypt'. *Science & Society* 78 (1): 11–40.

Debord, Guy. 1970. *Society of the Spectacle.* Detroit: Black & Red.

Debrix, François. 2006. 'The Sublime Spectatorship of War: The Erasure of the Event in America's Politics of Terror and Aesthetics of Violence'. *Millennium: Journal of International Studies* 34 (3): 767–91.

Deleuze, Gilles. 1994. *Difference and Repetition.* London: Athlone.

Dencik, Lina, and Oliver Leistert, eds. 2015. *Critical Perspectives on Social Media and Protest: Between Control and Emancipation.* London: Rowman & Littlefield.

Dent, Chris. 2008. '"Journalists Are the Confessors of the Public", Says One Foucaultian'. *Journalism* 9 (2): 200–19.

Deuze, Mark. 2008. 'The Professional Identity of Journalists in the Context of Convergence Culture'. *Observatorio* (Obs*) 2 (4). http://dx.doi.org/10.7458/obs242008216.

Diamond, Larry Jay, and Marc F. Plattner. 2012. *Liberation Technology: Social Media and the Struggle for Democracy.* Baltimore, MD: Johns Hopkins University Press.

Dower, Nigel. 2003. *An Introduction to Global Citizenship.* Edinburgh: Edinburgh University Press.

Eco, Umberto. 1994. 'Does the Audience Have Bad Effects on Television?' In *Apocalypse Postponed,* edited by Umberto Eco and Robert Lumley, 87–102. Bloomington: Indiana University Press.

Edy, J. A. 1999. 'Journalistic Uses of Collective Memory'. *Journal of Communication* 49 (2): 71–85.

El Issawi, Fatima. 2013. *Libya Media Transition: Heading to the Unknown.* POLIS, London School of Economics and Political Science. http://eprints.lse.ac.uk/59906/.

El-Nawawy, Mohammed, and Sahar Khamis. 2013. *Egyptian Revolution 2.0: Political Blogging, Civic Engagement, and Citizen Journalism.* Basingstoke: Palgrave Macmillan.

Elahi, Manzur. 2013. '"They Are Not Different from Others": Ethical Practices and Corruption in Bangladeshi Journalism'. *Journal of Mass Media Ethics* 28 (3): 189–202.

Ellis, John. 2000. *Seeing Things: Television in the Age of Uncertainty.* London: I. B. Tauris.

Ellis, John. 2009. 'Mundane Witnessing'. In *Media Witnessing: Testimony in the Age of Mass Communication,* edited by Paul Frosh and Amit Pinchevski, 73–98. Palgrave Macmillan.

Elseewi, Tarik Ahmed. 2011. 'A Revolution of the Imagination'. *International Journal of Communication* 5: 1197–206.

Erickson, Emily, and John Maxwell Hamilton. 2006. 'Foreign Reporting Enhanced By Parachute Journalism'. *Newspaper Research Journal* 27 (1): 33–47.

Ermisch, John, Diego Gambetta, Heather Laurie, Thomas Siedler and S. C. Noah Uhrig. 2009. 'Measuring People's Trust'. *Journal of the Royal Statistical Society: Series A (Statistics in Society)* 172 (4): 749–69.

Ettema, James S., and Theodore L. Glasser. 1994. 'The Irony in, and of, Journalism: A Case Study in the Moral Language of Liberal Democracy'. *Journal of Communication* 44 (2): 5–28.

Fairclough, Norman. 1992. *Discourse and Social Change.* Cambridge: Polity.

Fanon, Frantz. 1963. *The Wretched of the Earth.* London: MacGibbon & Kee.

Farías, Victor, Joseph Margolis and Tom Rockmore. 1989. *Heidegger and Nazism.* Philadelphia, PA: Temple University Press.

Fenton, Natalie. 2008. 'Mediating Hope: New Media, Politics and Resistance'. *International Journal of Cultural Studies* 11 (2): 230–48.

Fenton, Natalie. 2013. 'Cosmopolitanism as Conformity and Contestation'. *Journalism Studies* 14 (2): 172–86.

Fenton, Natalie, and Veronica Barassi. 2011. 'Alternative Media and Social Networking Sites: The Politics of Individuation and Political Participation'. *The Communication Review* 14 (3): 179–96.

Fiske, John. 1989. *Reading the Popular.* Unwin Hyman: London.

Foucault, Michel. 1972. *The Archaeology of Knowledge.* London: Tavistock.

Foucault, Michel. 1990. *The History of Sexuality.* New York: Vintage. First published in 1984.

Foucault, Michel. 1993. 'About the Beginning of the Hermeneutics of the Self: Two Lectures At Dartmouth'. *Political Theory* 21 (2): 227–198.

Foucault, Michel. 2008. *The Birth of Biopolitics: Lectures at the Collège De France, 1978–79.* Basingstoke: Palgrave Macmillan.

Franklin, Bob. 2010. 'Introduction'. *Journalism Studies* 11 (4): 442–63.

Franklin, Bob. 2011. 'Sources, Credibility and the Continuing Crisis of UK Journalism'. In *Sources, Credibility and the Continuing Crisis of UK Journalism*, edited by Bob Franklin and Matt Carlson, 90–106. London: Routledge.

Fraser, Matthew. 2009. 'Five Reasons for Crash Blindness'. *British Journalism Review* 20 (4): 78–83.

Fraser, Nancy. 1990. 'Rethinking the Public Sphere: A Contribution to the Critique of Actually Existing Democracy'. *Social Text* 25–26: 56–80.

Fraser, Nancy, and Axel Honneth. 2003. *Redistribution or Recognition? A Political-Philosophical Exchange.* London: Verso.

Friedman, Sam. 2016. 'Habitus Clivé and the Emotional Imprint of Social Mobility'. *The Sociological Review* 64 (1): 129–47. First published in 2015.

Frisch, Hillel. 2013. 'The Egyptian Army and Egypt's "Spring"'. *Journal of Strategic Studies* 36 (2): 180–204.

Frosh, Paul, and Amit Pinchevski. 2009. *Media Witnessing: Testimony in the Age of Mass Communication.* Basingstoke: Palgrave Macmillan.

Fuchs, Christian. 2014. *Social Media: A Critical Introduction.* London: Sage.

Fuchs, Christian. 2015. 'Anonymous: Hacktivism and Contemporary Politics'. In *Social Media, Politics and the State: Protests, Revolutions, Riots, Crime and Policing in the Age of Facebook, Twitter and YouTube*, edited by Daniel Trottier and Christian Fuchs, 88–108. London: Routledge.

Fürsich, Elfriede. 2002. 'How Can Global Journalists Represent the "Other"? A Critical Assessment of the Cultural Studies Concept for Media Practice'. *Journalism* 3 (1): 57–84.

Gause, F. Gregory. 2011. 'Why Middle East Studies Missed the Arab Spring: The Myth of Authoritarian Stability'. *Foreign Affairs* 90 (4): 81–90.

Gerbaudo, Paolo. 2012. *Tweets and the Streets: Social Media and Contemporary Activism.* London: Pluto.

Giddens, Anthony. 1984. *The Constitution of Society: Outline of the Theory of Structuration.* Cambridge: Polity.

Giles, David C. 2002. 'Parasocial Interaction: A Review of the Literature and a Model for Future Research'. *Media Psychology* 4 (3): 279–305.

Gilroy, Paul. 2005. 'Could You Be Loved? Bob Marley, Anti-Politics and Universal Sufferation'. *Critical Quarterly* 47 (1–2): 226–45.

Gitlin, Todd. 1980. *The Whole World is Watching: Mass Media in the Making and Unmaking of the New Left.* Berkeley: University of California Press.

Glasser, Theodore L., and James S. Ettema. 1993. "When the Facts Don't Speak for Themselves: A Study of the Use of Irony in Daily Journalism'. *Critical Studies in Media Communication* 10 (4): 322–38.

Gleason, Benjamin. 2013. 'Occupy Wall Street: Exploring Informal Learning about a Social Movement on Twitter'. *American Behavioral Scientist* 57 (7): 966–82.

Gleason, Tim. 2015. 'If We Are All Journalists, Can Journalistic Privilege Survive?' *Javnost – The Public* 22 (4): 375–86.

Gledhill, Christine. 1988. 'Pleasurable Negotiations'. In *Female Spectators: Looking at Film and Television,* edited by E. Deidre Pribram, 64–89. London: Verso.

Godwin, Mike. 1995. 'Godwin's Law of Nazi Analogies (and Corollaries)'. EFF.org

Goffman, Erving. 1959. *The Presentation of Self in Everyday Life.* Garden City, NY: Doubleday.

Goffman, Erving. 1963. *Behaviour in Public Places: Notes on the Social Organization of Gatherings.* New York: Free Press.

Goodwin, Jeff. 2011. 'Why We Were Surprised (Again) by the Arab Spring'. *Swiss Political Science Review* 17 (4): 452–56.

Graeber, David. 2009. *Direct Action: An Ethnography.* Edinburgh: AK Press.

Gramsci, Antonio. 1971. *Selections from the Prison Notebooks of Antonio Gramsci.* London: International Publishers.

Granovetter, Mark. 1992. 'Economic Institutions as Social Constructions: A Framework for Analysis'. *Acta Sociologica* 35 (1): 3–11.

Grant, John. 2014. 'On the Critique of Political Imaginaries'. *European Journal of Political Theory* 13 (4): 408–26.

Greene, Ronald Walter, and Kevin Douglas Kuswa. 2012. '"From the Arab Spring to Athens, Occupy Wall Street to Moscow": Regional Accents and the Rhetorical Cartography of Power'. *Rhetoric Society Quarterly* 42 (3): 271–88.

Gregg, Melissa, and Gregory J. Seigworth. 2010. *The Affect Theory Reader.* Durham, NC: Duke University Press.

Gregory, Sam. 2015. 'Ubiquitous Witnesses: Who Creates the Evidence and the Live(d) Experience of Human Rights Violations'. *Information, Communication & Society* 18 (11): 1378–92.

Griffin, Michael. 2010. 'Media Images of War'. *Media, War & Conflict* 3 (1): 7–41.

Grusin, Richard A. 2010. *Premediation: Affect and Mediality after 9/11.* Basingstoke: Palgrave Macmillan.

Guaaybess, Tourya. 2008. 'Orientalism and the Economics of Arab Broadcasting'. In *Arab Media: Power and Weakness,* edited by Kai Hafez, 199–216. New York: Continuum.

Gunkel, David J., and Paul A. Taylor. 2014. *Heidegger and the Media.* Cambridge: Polity.

Gunter, Barrie, and Roger Dickinson. 2013. *News Media in the Arab World: A Study of 10 Arab and Muslim Countries.* London: Bloomsbury.

Guzman-Concha, Cesar. 2012. 'The Students' Rebellion in Chile: Occupy Protest or Classic Social Movement'. *Social Movement Studies* 11 (3–4): 408–15.

Hafez, Kai. 2008. *Arab Media: Power and Weakness.* New York: Continuum.

Hall, Stuart. 1973. *Encoding and Decoding in the Television Discourse.* Birmingham: University of Birmingham.

Hallin, Daniel C. 1992. 'The Passing of the "High Modernism" of American Journalism'. *Journal of Communication* 42 (3): 14–25.

Hamdy, Naila, and Ehab H. Gomaa. 2012. 'Framing the Egyptian Uprising in Arabic Language Newspapers and Social Media'. *Journal of Communication* 62 (2): 195–211.

Hammond, Phil. 2007. *Media, War, and Postmodernity.* London: Routledge.
Hammoudi, Abdellah. 1997. *Master and Disciple: The Cultural Foundations of Moroccan Authoritarianism.* Chicago: University of Chicago Press.
Hansen, Thomas Blom, and Finn Stepputat. 2001. *States of Imagination: Ethnographic Explorations of the Postcolonial State.* Durham, NC: Duke University Press.
Hänska-Ahy, Maximillian T., and Roxanna Shapour. 2013. 'Who's Reporting the Protests? Converging Practices of Citizen Journalists and Two BBC World Service Newsrooms, from Iran's Election Protests to the Arab Uprisings'. *Journalism Studies* 14 (1): 29–45.
Hanusch, Folker. 2013. 'Journalists in Times of Change: Evidence from a New Survey of Australia's Journalistic Workforce'. *Australian Journalism Review* 35 (1): 29–42.
Hardt, Michael, and Antonio Negri. 2000. *Empire.* Cambridge, MA: Harvard University Press.
Hariman, Robert, and John Louis Lucaites. 2007. *No Caption Needed: Iconic Photographs, Public Culture, and Liberal Democracy.* Chicago: University of Chicago Press.
Harlow, Summer, and Thomas J. Johnson. 2011. 'Overthrowing the Protest Paradigm? How the New York Times, Global Voices and Twitter Covered the Egyptian Revolution'. *International Journal of Communication* 5: 1359–74.
Harman, Graham. 2002. *Tool-Being: Heidegger and the Metaphysics of Objects.* Chicago, IL: Open Court.
Harman, Graham. 2011. *The Quadruple Object.* Winchester: Zero Books.
Harman, Graham. 2017. 'McLuhan and Phenomenology'. In *Conditions of Mediation: Phenomenological Perspectives on Media*, edited by Tim Markham and Scott Rodgers. Oxford: Peter Lang.
Hay, James. 2011. '"Popular Culture": A Critique of the New Political Reason'. *Cultural Studies* 25 (4–5): 659–84.
Hegel, Georg Wilhelm Friedrich. 1979. *Phenomenology of Spirit.* Oxford: Oxford University Press. First published in 1807.
Heidegger, Martin. 1962. *Being and Time.* Oxford: Basil Blackwell.
Hemmingway, Emma. 2007. *Into the Newsroom: Exploring the Digital Production of Regional Television News.* London: Routledge.
Herman, Edward S., and Noam Chomsky. 1988. *Manufacturing Consent: The Political Economy of the Mass Media.* New York: Pantheon.
Hermida, Alfred. 2012. 'Tweets and Truth: Journalism as a Discipline of Collaborative Verification'. *Journalism Practice* 6 (5–6): 659–68.
Hermida, Alfred, Seth C. Lewis and Rodrigo Zamith. 2014. 'Sourcing the Arab Spring: A Case Study of Andy Carvin's Sources on Twitter during the Tunisian and Egyptian Revolutions'. *Journal of Computer-Mediated Communication* 19 (3): 479–99.
Hesmondhalgh, David. 2006. 'Bourdieu, the Media and Cultural Production'. *Media, Culture & Society* 28 (2): 211–31.

Hesmondhalgh, David, and Sarah Baker. 2008. 'Creative Work and Emotional Labour in the Television Industry'. *Theory, Culture & Society* 25 (7–8): 97–118.

Hirst, Martin. 2011. *News 2.0: Can Journalism Survive the Internet?* London: Allen & Unwin.

Hjarvard, Stig. 2013. *The Mediatization of Culture and Society.* London: Routledge.

Hobson, John M., and Leonard Seabrooke. 2007. *Everyday Politics of the World Economy.* Cambridge: Cambridge University Press.

Hofheinz, Albrecht. 2011. 'Nextopia? Beyond Revolution 2.0'. *Oriente Moderno* 91 (1): 23–39.

Hollis, Rosemary. 2012. 'No Friend of Democratization: Europe's Role in the Genesis of the "Arab Spring"'. *International Affairs* 88 (1): 81–94.

Horkheimer, Max, and Theodor W. Adorno. 1973. *Dialectic of Enlightenment.* London: Allen Lane. First published in 1944.

Howard, Philip N., Aiden Duffy, Deen Freelon, Muzammil M. Hussain, Will Mari and Marwa Mazaid. 2011. 'Opening Closed Regimes: What Was the Role of Social Media during the Arab Spring?' *Project on Information Technology and Political Islam.* http://dx.doi.org/10.2139/ssrn.2595096.

Howard, Philip N., and Muzammil M. Hussain. 2011. 'The Role of Digital Media'. *Journal of Democracy* 22 (3): 35–48.

Huntington, Samuel P. 1993. 'The Clash of Civilizations'. *Foreign Affairs* 72 (3): 22–49.

Husserl, Edmund. 1931. *Ideas: General Introduction to Pure Phenomenology.* London: Allen & Unwin.

Husserl, Edmund. 1970. *The Crisis of European Sciences and Transcendental Phenomenology: An Introduction to Phenomenological Philosophy.* Evanston, IL: Northwestern University Press.

Husted, Emil. 2015. 'From Creation to Amplification: Occupy Wall Street's Transition into an Online Populist Movement'. In *Civic Engagement and Social Media: Political Participation beyond Protest,* edited by Julie Uldam and Anne Vestergaard, 131–52. Basingstoke: Palgrave Macmillan.

Ibrahim, Yasmin. 2015. 'Self-Representation and the Disaster Event: Self-Imaging, Morality and Immortality'. *Journal of Media Practice* 16 (3): 211–27.

Inbar, Efraim. 2013. *The Arab Spring, Democracy and Security: Domestic and International Ramifications.* London: Routledge.

Isin, Engin F. 2002. *Being Political: Genealogies of Citizenship.* Minneapolis: University of Minnesota Press.

Ismail, Salwa. 2011. 'Authoritarian Government, Neoliberalism and Everyday Civilities in Egypt'. *Third World Quarterly* 32 (5): 845–62.

Jeffery, Bob, Joseph Ibrahim and David Waddington. 2015. 'Politics, Consumption or Nihilism: Protest and Disorder after the Global Crash'. *Contention: The Multidisciplinary Journal of Social Protest* 2 (2): 1–4.

Jenkins, Henry. 2006. *Convergence Culture: Where Old and New Media Collide.* New York: NYU Press.

Jennings, Will, and Gerry Stoker. 2016. 'The Bifurcation of Politics: Two Englands'. *The Political Quarterly.* http://dx.doi.org/10.1111/1467-923X.12228.

Johnson-Cartee, Karen S. 2005. *News Narratives and News Framing: Constructing Political Reality.* Oxford: Rowman & Littlefield.

Johnson, Terence James. 1972. *Professions and Power.* London: Macmillan.

Juris, Jeffrey Scott. 2012. 'Reflections on #Occupy Everywhere: Social Media, Public Space, and Emerging Logics of Aggregation'. *American Ethnologist* 39 (2): 259–79.

Juris, Jeffrey Scott, Michelle Ronayne, Firuzeh Shokooh-Valle and Robert Wengronowitz. 2012. 'Negotiating Power and Difference within the 99%'. *Social Movement Studies* 11 (3–4): 434–40.

Juris, Jeffrey Scott, and Geoffrey Henri Pleyers. 2009. 'Alter-Activism: Emerging Cultures of Participation among Young Global Justice Activists'. *Journal of Youth Studies* 12 (1): 57–75.

Khalaf, Samir. 2012. *Lebanon Adrift: From Battleground to Playground.* London: Saqi Books.

Khamis, Sahar. 2009. 'Modern Egyptian Media: Transformations, Paradoxes, Debates and Comparative Perspectives'. *Journal of Arab & Muslim Media Research* 1 (3): 259–77.

Khamis, Sahar, Paul B. Gold and Katherine Vaughn. 2012. 'Beyond Egypt's "Facebook Revolution" and Syria's "YouTube Uprising": Comparing Political Contexts, Actors and Communication Strategies'. *Arab Media & Society* 15. http://www.arabmediasociety.com/?article=791.

Khondker, Habibul Haque. 2011. 'Role of the New Media in the Arab Spring'. *Globalizations* 8 (5): 675–79.

Kian, Edward M., and Matthew H. Zimmerman. 2012. 'The Medium of the Future: Top Sports Writers Discuss Transitioning from Newspapers to Online Journalism'. *International Journal of Sports Communication* 5 (3): 285–304.

Klikauer, Thomas. 2016. 'Negative Recognition Master and Slave in the Workplace'. *Thesis Eleven* 132 (1): 39–49. First published in 2015.

Knightley, Phillip. 1975. *The First Casualty: The War Correspondent as Hero, Propagandist, and Myth Maker from the Crimea to Vietnam.* London: Deutsch.

Koffman, Ofra, Shani Orgad and Rosalind Gill. 2015. 'Girl Power and "Selfie Humanitarianism"'. *Continuum* 29 (2): 157–68.

Krastev, Ivan. 2014. *Democracy Disrupted: The Politics of Global Protest.* Philadelphia: University of Pennsylvania Press.

Krumpal, Ivar. 2013. 'Determinants of Social Desirability Bias in Sensitive Surveys: A Literature Review'. *Quality & Quantity* 47 (4): 2025–47.

Kuebler, Johanne. 2011. 'Overcoming the Digital Divide: The Internet and Political Mobilization in Egypt and Tunisia'. *CyberOrient* 5 (1). http://www.cyberorient.net/article.do?articleId=6212.

Kuhn, Raymond, and Erik Neveu. 2013. *Political Journalism: New Challenges, New Practices.* London: Routledge.

Kuran, Timur. 1991. 'Now Out of Never: The Element of Surprise in the East European Revolution of 1989'. *World Politics* 44 (1): 7–48.

Kurtz, Mariam M. 2015. 'The Egyptian Revolution Empowers Women'. In *Women, War, and Violence,* edited by Mariam M. Kurtz and Lester R. Kurtz, 343–48. Westport, CT: Praeger.

Kyriakidou, Myria. 2014. 'Distant Suffering in Audience Memory: The Moral Hierarchy of Remembering'. *International Journal of Communication* 8: 1474–94.

Laclau, Ernesto, and Chantal Mouffe. 1985. *Hegemony and Socialist Strategy: Towards a Radical Democratic Politics.* London: Verso.

Larsson, Anders Olof, and Hallvard Moe. 2012. 'Studying Political Microblogging: Twitter Users in the 2010 Swedish Election Campaign'. *New Media & Society* 14 (5): 729–47.

Lasch, Christopher. 1978. *The Culture of Narcissism: American Life in an Age of Diminishing Expectations.* New York: Norton.

Lash, Scott. 2010. *Intensive Culture: Social Theory, Religion and Contemporary Capitalism.* Los Angeles, CA; London: Sage.

Lash, Scott, and Celia Lury. 2007. *Global Culture Industry: The Mediation of Things.* Cambridge: Polity.

Lasorsa, Dominic L., Seth C. Lewis and Avery E. Holton. 2012. 'Normalizing Twitter: Journalism Practice in an Emerging Communication Space'. *Journalism Studies* 13 (1): 19–36. First published in 2011.

Lee, Ching Kwan, and Yonghong Zhang. 2013. 'The Power of Instability: Unraveling the Microfoundations of Bargained Authoritarianism in China'. *American Journal of Sociology* 118 (6): 1475–508.

Lefebvre, Henri. 1991. *The Production of Space.* Oxford: Blackwell.

Levi, Margaret, and Laura Stoker. 2000. 'Political Trust and Trustworthiness'. *Annual Review of Political Science* 3 (1): 475–507.

Lewiński, Marcin, and Dima Mohammed. 2012. 'Deliberate Design or Unintended Consequences: The Argumentative Uses of Facebook during the Arab Spring'. *Journal of Public Deliberation* 8 (1): Article 11.

Leys, Ruth. 2011. 'The Turn to Affect: A Critique'. Critical Inquiry 37 (3): 434–72.

Liberati, Nicola. 2016. 'Technology, Phenomenology and the Everyday World: A Phenomenological Analysis on How Technologies Mould Our World'. *Human Studies* 39 (2): 189–216. First published in 2015.

Lim, Merlyna. 2012. 'Clicks, Cabs, and Coffee Houses: Social Media and Oppositional Movements in Egypt, 2004–2011'. *Journal of Communication* 62 (2): 231–48.

Litt, Eden. 2012. 'Knock, Knock. Who's There? The Imagined Audience'. *Journal of Broadcasting & Electronic Media* 56 (3): 330–45.

Loader, Brian, and Dan Mercea. 2012. *Social Media and Democracy: Innovations in Participatory Politics.* London: Routledge.

Lotan, Gilad, Erhardt Graeff, Mike Ananny, Devin Gaffney, Ian Pearce and danah boyd. 2011. 'The Revolutions Were Tweeted: Information Flows during the 2011 Tunisian and Egyptian Revolutions'. *International Journal of Communication* 5. http://ijoc.org/index.php/ijoc/article/view/1246/643.

Lynch, Marc. 2003. 'Beyond the Arab Street: Iraq and the Arab Public Sphere'. *Politics & Society* 31 (1): 55–91.

Lynch, Marc. 2006. *Voices of the New Arab Public: Iraq, Al-Jazeera, and Middle East Politics Today.* New York: Columbia University Press.

Lynch, Marc. 2011. 'After Egypt: The Limits and Promise of Online Challenges to the Authoritarian Arab State'. *Perspectives on Politics* 9 (2): 301–10.

Madianou, Mirca, and Daniel Miller. 2012. *Migration and New Media: Transnational Families and Polymedia.* London: Routledge.

Maguire, Jennifer Smith, and Julian Matthews. 2010. 'Cultural Intermediaries and the Media'. *Sociology Compass* 4 (7): 405–16.

Maier, Scott R. 2015. 'Compassion Fatigue and the Elusive Quest for Journalistic Impact a Content and Reader-Metrics Analysis Assessing Audience Response'. *Journalism & Mass Communication Quarterly* 92 (3): 700–22.

Malešević, Siniša. 2010. *The Sociology of War and Violence.* Cambridge: Cambridge University Press.

Maltby, Sarah. 2014. 'Broadcasting Graphic War Violence: The Moral Face of Channel 4'. *Journalism* 15 (3): 289–306.

Mannheim, Karl. 2013. *Ideology and Utopia.* London: Routledge. First published in 1929.

Mark, D. Clifton. 2014. 'Recognition and Honor: A Critique of Axel Honneth's and Charles Taylor's Histories of Recognition'. *Constellations* 21 (1): 16–31.

Markham, Tim. 2011a. 'The Political Phenomenology of War Reporting'. *Journalism* 12 (5): 567–85.

Markham, Tim. 2011b. *The Politics of War Reporting: Authority, Authenticity and Morality.* Manchester: Manchester University Press.

Marlière, Philippe. 1998. 'The Rules of the Journalistic Field: Pierre Bourdieu's Contribution to the Sociology of the Media'. *European Journal of Communication* 13 (2): 219–34.

Marlière, Philippe. 2001. 'The Impact of Market Journalism: Pierre Bourdieu on the Media'. *The Sociological Review* 49 (1): 199–211.

Marzouki, Yousri, Ines Skandrani-Marzouki, Moez Béjaoui, Haythem Hammoudi and Tarek Bellaj. 2012. 'The Contribution of Facebook to the 2011 Tunisian Rev olution: A Cyberpsychological Insight'. *Cyberpsychology, Behavior, and Social Networking* 15 (5): 237–44.

Mason, Corinne Lysandra. 2016. 'Tinder and Humanitarian Hook-Ups: The Erotics of Social Media Racism'. *Feminist Media Studies.* http://www.tandfonline.com/doi/abs/10.1080/14680777.2015.1137339.

Mason, Paul. 2012. *Why It's Kicking Off Everywhere: The New Global Revolutions.* London: Verso.

Matheson, Donald. 2003. 'Scowling at Their Notebooks: How British Journalists Understand Their Writing'. *Journalism* 4 (2): 165–83.

McCall, Leslie. 2005. 'The Complexity of Intersectionality'. *Signs* 30 (3): 1771–800.

McCarthy, Anna. 2001. *Ambient Television: Visual Culture and Public Space.* Durham, NC: Duke University Press.

McChesney, Robert W. 2003. 'The Problem of Journalism: A Political Economic Contribution to an Explanation of the Crisis in Contemporary Us Journalism'. *Journalism Studies* 4 (3): 299–329.

McDowell, Linda, Esther Rootham and Abby Hardgrove. 2014. 'Politics, Anti-Politics, Quiescence and Radical Unpolitics: Young Men's Political Participation in an "Ordinary" English Town'. *Journal of Youth Studies* 17 (1): 42–62.

McLaren, Margaret A. 2002. *Feminism, Foucault, and Embodied Subjectivity.* New York: SUNY Press.

McLuhan, Marshall. 1964. *Understanding Media: The Extensions of Man.* London: Routledge & Kegan Paul.

McNair, Brian. 2000. *Journalism and Democracy: An Evaluation of the Political Public Sphere.* London: Routledge.

McNair, Brian. 2003. 'From Control to Chaos: Towards a New Sociology of Journalism'. *Media, Culture & Society* 25 (4): 547–55.

McNay, Lois. 2000. *Gender and Agency: Reconfiguring the Subject in Feminist and Social Theory.* Cambridge: Polity.

McNay, Lois. 2008. *Against Recognition.* Cambridge: Polity.

McRobbie, Angela, and Sarah L. Thornton. 1995. 'Rethinking "Moral Panic" for Multi-Mediated Social Worlds'. *British Journal of Sociology* 46 (4): 559–74.

Meek, David. 2012. 'YouTube and Social Movements: A Phenomenological Analysis of Participation, Events and Cyberplace'. *Antipode* 44 (4): 1429–48.

Mellor, Noha. 2005. *The Making of Arab News.* Oxford: Rowman & Littlefield.

Mellor, Noha. 2007. *Modern Arab Journalism: Problems and Prospects.* Edinburgh: Edinburgh University Press.

Mellor, Noha. 2008. 'Arab Journalists as Cultural Intermediaries'. *International Journal of Press/Politics* 13 (4): 465–83.

Mellor, Noha. 2011. *Arab Media: Globalization and Emerging Media Industries.* Cambridge: Polity.

Mihai, Mihaela. 2016. 'Theorizing Change: Between Reflective Judgment and the Inertia of Political Habitus'. *European Journal of Political Theory* 15 (1): 22–42. First published in 2014.

Miller, Jason. 2016. 'The Role of Aesthetics in Hegelian Theories of Recognition'. *Constellations* 23 (1): 96–109.

Min, Seong-Jae. 2016. 'Conversation through Journalism: Searching for Organizing Principles of Public and Citizen Journalism'. *Journalism* 17 (5): 567–82. First published in 2015.

Mindich, David T. Z. 2005. *Tuned Out: Why Americans under 40 Don't Follow the News.* Oxford: Oxford University Press.

Moeller, Susan D. 1999. *Compassion Fatigue: How the Media Sell Disease, Famine, War, and Death.* New York: Routledge.

Moghadam, Valentine M. 2013. 'What is Democracy? Promises and Perils of the Arab Spring'. *Current Sociology* 61 (4): 393–408.

Moores, Shaun. 2017.'Digital Orientations: Movement, Dwelling and Media Use'. In *Conditions of Mediation: Phenomenological Perspectives on Media*, edited by Tim Markham and Scott Rodgers. Oxford: Peter Lang.

Morell, Mayo Fuster. 2012. 'The Free Culture and 15M Movements in Spain: Composition, Social Networks and Synergies'. *Social Movement Studies* 11 (3–4): 386–92.

Mortensen, Mette. 2015. 'Connective Witnessing: Reconfiguring the Relationship between the Individual and the Collective'. *Information, Communication & Society* 18 (11): 1393–406.

Mouffe, Chantal. 2013. *Agonistics: Thinking the World Politically.* London: Verso.

Mudde, Cas, and Cristóbal Rovira Kaltwasser. 2012. *Populism in Europe and the Americas: Threat or Corrective for Democracy.* Cambridge: Cambridge University Press.

Mulhall, Stephen. 2005. 'Human Mortality: Heidegger on How to Portray the Impossible Possibility of Dasein'. In *A Companion to Heidegger,* edited by Jubert L. Dreyfus and Mark A. Wrathall, 297–310. Oxford: Blackwell.

Mungiu-Pippidi, Alina. 2013. 'Controlling Corruption through Collective Action'. *Journal of Democracy* 24 (1): 101–15.

Murthy, Dhiraj. 2013. *Twitter: Social Communication in the Twitter Age.* Cambridge: Polity.

Mustafa Tagma, Halit. 2011. 'Model, Event, Context: Globalization, Arab Social Movements, and the Modeling of Global Order'. *Globalizations* 8 (5): 623–28.

Naef, Michael, and Jürgen Schupp. 2009. 'Measuring Trust: Experiments and Surveys in Contrast and Combination'. *SOEP Working Paper* 167.

Neal, Sarah. 2015. 'Researching the Everyday: An Interview with Amanda Wise'. *Sociology* 49 (5): 988–1000.

Negus, Keith. 2002. 'The Work of Cultural Intermediaries and the Enduring Distance between Production and Consumption'. *Cultural Studies* 16 (4): 501–15.

Neilson, Brett, and Ned Rossiter. 2005. 'From Precarity to Precariousness and Back Again: Labour, Life and Unstable Networks'. *Fibreculture* 5: 10–13.

Nerone, John. 2015. 'Journalism's Crisis of Hegemony'. *Javnost – The Public* 22 (4): 313–27.

Neuman, W. Russell. 1991. *The Future of the Mass Audience.* Cambridge: Cambridge University Press.

Neveu, Erik. 2002. 'Four Generations of Political Journalism'. In *Political Journalism: New Challenges, New Practices,* edited by Raymond Kuhn and Erik Neveu, 22–43. London: Routledge.

Newman, Nic. 2009. 'The Rise of Social Media and its Impact on Mainstream Journalism' (working paper, Reuters Institute for the Study of Journalism).

Newsom, Victoria Ann, Lara Lengel and Catherine Cassara. 2011. 'The Arab Spring – Local Knowledge and the Revolutions: A Framework for Social Media Information Flow'. *International Journal of Communication* 5: 1301–12.

Nilsson, Bo, and Eric Carlsson. 2014. 'Swedish Politicians and New Media: Democracy, Identity and Populism in a Digital Discourse'. *New Media & Society* 16 (4): 655–71.

Nixon, Sean, and Paul Du Gay. 2002. 'Who Needs Cultural Intermediaries?' *Cultural Studies* 16 (4): 495–500.

Nye, Joseph S., Philip Zelikow and David C. King. 1997. *Why People Don't Trust Government.* Cambridge, MA: Harvard University Press.

O'Leary, Timothy. 2002. *Foucault: The Art of Ethics.* London: Continuum.

O'Donnell, Guillermo, Philippe C. Schmitter, Cynthia J. Arnson and Abraham F. Lowenthal. 2013. *Transitions from Authoritarian Rule: Tentative Conclusions about Uncertain Democracies.* Baltimore, MD: John Hopkins University Press.

O'Donnell, Penny. 2009. 'Journalism, Change and Listening Practices'. *Continuum: Journal of Media & Cultural Studies* 23 (4): 503–17.

O'Donnell, Penny, Justine Lloyd and Tanja Dreher. 2009. 'Listening, Pathbuilding and Continuations: A Research Agenda for the Analysis of Listening'. *Continuum* 23 (4): 423–39.

Ong, Jonathan Corpus. 2014. '"Witnessing" or "Mediating" Distant Suffering? Ethical Questions across Moments of Text, Production, and Reception'. *Television & New Media* 15 (3): 179–96.

Orgad, Shani. 2011. 'Proper Distance from Ourselves: The Potential for Estrangement in the Mediapolis'. *International Journal of Cultural Studies* 14 (4): 401–21.

Orgad, Shani. 2012. *Media Representation and the Global Imagination.* Cambridge: Polity.

Örnebring, Henrik. 2013. 'Journalistic Ideals versus Journalistic Practice: The Relationship between Role Perception and Valued Skills among Journalists in Six European Countries'. *ICA 63rd Annual Conference: Challenging Communication Research, London*, 17–21 June.

Pace, Michelle, and Francesco Cavatorta. 2012. 'The Arab Uprisings in Theoretical Perspective: An Introduction'. *Mediterranean Politics* 17 (2): 125–38.

Palmer, Lindsay. 2015. 'Outsourcing Authority in the Digital Age: Television News Networks and Freelance War Correspondents'. *Critical Studies in Media Communication* 32 (4): 225–39.

Papacharissi, Zizi. 2010. *A Private Sphere: Democracy in a Digital Age.* Cambridge: Polity.

Papacharissi, Zizi. 2015. *Affective Publics: Sentiment, Technology, and Politics.* Oxford: Oxford University Press.

Papacharissi, Zizi, and Maria de Fatima Oliveira. 2012. 'Affective News and Networked Publics: The Rhythms of News Storytelling on# Egypt'. *Journal of Communication* 62 (2): 266–82.

Papacharissi, Zizi, and Emily Easton. 2013. 'In the Habitus of the New'. In *A Companion to New Media Dynamics,* edited by John Hartley, Jean Burgess and Axel Bruns, 167–84. Oxford: Wiley-Blackwell.

Pasquino, Gianfranco. 2007. 'The Five Faces of Silvio Berlusconi: The Knight of Anti-Politics'. *Modern Italy* 12 (1): 39–54.

Pasti, Svetlana, Mikhail Chernysh and Luiza Svitich. 2012. 'Russian Journalists and Their Profession'. In *The Global Journalist in the 21st Century,* edited by David H. Weaver and Lars Willnat, 267–82. London: Routledge.

Pavlik, John V. 2013. 'Innovation and the Future of Journalism'. *Digital Journalism* 1 (2): 181–93.

Peters, John Durham. 2001. 'Witnessing'. *Media, Culture & Society* 23 (6): 707–23.

Phillips, John W. P. 2010. 'Art, Politics and Philosophy Alain Badiou and Jacques Rancière'. *Theory, Culture & Society* 27 (4): 146–60.

Phillips, Mike, and Chris Speed. 2012. 'Ubiquity: A Paranoid Manifesto'. *Ubiquity: The Journal of Pervasive Media* 1 (1): 3–6.

Picard, Robert G. 2004. 'Commercialism and Newspaper Quality'. *Newspaper Research Journal* 25 (1): 54–65.

Picard, Robert G. 2015. *Journalists' Perceptions of the Future of Journalistic Work.* Oxford: Reuters Institute for the Study of Journalism. http://reutersinstitute.politics.ox.ac.uk/sites/default/files/Journalists.

Pickerill, Jenny, and John Krinsky. 2012. 'Why Does Occupy Matter?' *Social Movement Studies* 11 (3–4): 279–87.

Pies, Judith. 2008. 'Agents of Change? Journalism Ethics in Lebanese and Jordanian Journalism Education'. In *Arab Media: Power and Weakness,* edited by Kai Hafez, 165–84. London: Continuum.

Pink, Sarah, Jolynna Sinanan, Larissa Hjorth and Heather Horst. 2016. 'Tactile Digital Ethnography: Researching Mobile Media through the Hand'. *Mobile Media & Communication* 4 (2): 237–51. First published in 2015.

Pintak, Lawrence. 2008. 'Satellite TV News and Arab Democracy'. *Journalism Practice* 2 (1): 15–26.

Pintak, Lawrence. 2011. *The New Arab Journalist: Mission and Identity in a Time of Turmoil.* London: I. B. Tauris.

Pintak, Lawrence, and Jeremy Ginges. 2008. 'The Mission of Arab Journalism: Creating Change in a Time of Turmoil'. *International Journal of Press/Politics* 13 (3): 193–227.

Pontari, Beth A., and Barry R. Schlenker. 2000. 'The Influence of Cognitive Load on Self-Presentation: Can Cognitive Busyness Help as Well as Harm Social Performance'. *Journal of Personality and Social Psychology* 78 (6): 1092–108.

Poster, Mark. 2001. *What's the Matter with the Internet?* Minneapolis: University of Minnesota Press.

Powers, Devon. 2015. 'First! Cultural Circulation in the Age of Recursivity'. *New Media & Society*. http://nms.sagepub.com/content/early/2015/08/17/1461444815600280.abstract.

Protess, David L. 1992. *The Journalism of Outrage: Investigative Reporting and Agenda Building in America.* New York: Guilford Press.

Putnam, Robert D. 2000. *Bowling Alone: The Collapse and Revival of American Community.* New York: Simon & Schuster.

Quandt, Thorsten. 2012. 'What's Left of Trust in a Network Society? An Evolutionary Model and Critical Discussion of Trust and Societal Communication'. *European Journal of Communication* 27 (1): 7–21.

Rahimi, Babak. 2011a. 'Affinities of Dissent: Cyberspace, Performative Networks and the Iranian Green Movement'. *CyberOrient* 5 (2). http://www.cyberorient.net/article.do?articleId=7357.

Rahimi, Babak. 2011b. 'The Agonistic Social Media: Cyberspace in the Formation of Dissent and Consolidation of State Power in Postelection Iran'. *The Communication Review* 14 (3): 158–78.

Ramadan, Walaa. 2014. 'Media Coverage of the Arab Spring and the New Middle East'. *Middle East Monitor.* https://www.middleeastmonitor.com/20140510-media-coverage-of-the-arab-spring-and-the-new-middle-east/.

Rancière, Jacques. 1998. *Disagreement: Politics and Philosophy.* Minneapolis: University of Minnesota Press.

Rancière, Jacques. 2004. *The Politics of Aesthetics: The Distribution of the Sensible.* London: Continuum.

Rancière, Jacques. 2009. *The Emancipated Spectator.* London: Verso.

Rancière, Jacques. 2010. *Dissensus: On Politics and Aesthetics.* London: Continuum.

Rantanen, Terhi. 2004. *The Media and Globalization.* London: Sage.

Rantanen, Terhi. 2009. *When News Was New.* Chichester: Wiley-Blackwell.

Reinardy, Scott. 2011. 'Newspaper Journalism in Crisis: Burnout on the Rise, Eroding Young Journalists' Career Commitment'. *Journalism* 12 (1): 33–50.

Rice, Paige. 2013. 'Women Spring: Reclaiming Resistance as the Ultimate Other'. *Global Societies Journal* 1: 54–64.

Rinke, Eike M., and Maria Röder. 2011. 'Media Ecologies, Communication Culture, and Temporal-Spatial Unfolding: Three Components in a Communication Model of the Egyptian Regime Change'. *International Journal of Communication* 5: 1273–85.

Robbins, Derek. 2015. 'Pierre Bourdieu and Jacques Rancière on Art/aesthetics and Politics: The Origins of Disagreement, 1963–1985'. *The British Journal of Sociology* 66 (4): 738–58.

Robertson, Alexa. 2010. *Mediated Cosmopolitanism: The World of Television News.* Cambridge: Polity.

Robertson, Alexa. 2013. 'Connecting in Crisis: "Old" and "New" Media and the Arab Spring'. *International Journal of Press/Politics* 18 (3): 325–41.

Robinson, Michael. 1975. 'American Political Legitimacy in an Era of Electronic Journalism: Reflections on the Evening News'. In *Television as a Social Force,* edited by Douglass Cater and Richard Adler. New York: Praeger.

Rodgers, James. 2012. *Reporting Conflict.* Basingstoke: Palgrave Macmillan.

Ross, Daniel. 2009. 'Politics and Aesthetics, or, Transformations of Aristotle in Bernard Stiegler'. *Transformations Journal of Media & Culture* 17.

Ruddock, Andy. 2006. 'Invisible Centers: Boris Johnson, Authenticity, Cultural Citizenship and a Centrifugal Model of Media Power'. *Social Semiotics* 16 (2): 263–82.

Rugh, William A. 2004. *The Arab Mass Media: Newspapers, Radio, and Television in Arab Politics.* Westport, CT: Greenwood.

Russell, Adrienne. 2011. 'Extra-National Information Flows, Social Media and the 2011 Egyptian Uprising'. *International Journal of Communication* 5: 1238–47.

Russial, John, Peter Laufer and Janet Wasko. 2015. 'Journalism in Crisis?' *Javnost – The Public* 22 (4): 299–312.

Sabry, Tarik. 2010. *Cultural Encounters in the Arab World: On Media, the Modern and the Everyday.* London: I. B. Tauris.

Said, Edward W. 1978. *Orientalism.* London: Routledge & Kegan Paul.

Saikal, Amin. 2013. 'Iraq: Elite Fragmentation, Islam and Democracy'. In *American Democracy Promotion in the Changing Middle East,* edited by Shahram Akbarzadeh, Benjamin MacQueen, James Piscatori and Amin Saikal, 101–13. London: Routledge.

Sakr, Naomi. 2010. 'News, Transparency and the Effectiveness of Reporting from Inside Arab Dictatorships'. *International Communication Gazette* 72 (1): 35–50.

Sakr, Naomi. 2013. *Transformations in Egyptian Journalism.* London: I. B. Tauris.

Salamey, Imad. 2009. 'Failing Consociationalism in Lebanon and Integrative Options'. *International Journal of Peace Studies* 14 (2): 83–105.

Salamey, Imad, and Muzammil Hussain. 2013. 'The Challenge of Media Fragmentation and Political Sectarianism after the Arab Spring'. IEMed Mediterranean

Yearbook: 64–70. http://www.iemed.org/observatori-en/arees-danalisi/documents/anuari/iemed-2013/the-challenge-of-media-fragmentation-and-political-sectarianism-after-the-arab-spring.

Saleh, Ibrahim. 2013. 'Understanding the Minds, Problems and Aspirations: An Untold Story about the Egyptian Dilemma'. *African Journal of Political Science and International Relations* 7 (4): 172–81.

Sassen, Saskia. 2011. 'The Global Street: Making the Political'. *Globalizations* 8 (5): 573–79.

Sauter, Theresa. 2014. '"What's on Your Mind?" Writing on Facebook as a Tool for Self-Formation'. *New Media & Society* 16 (5): 823–39. First published in 2013.

Seeck, Hannele, and Terhi Rantanen. 2015. 'Media Events, Spectacles and Risky Globalization: A Critical Review and Possible Avenues for Future Research'. *Media, Culture & Society* 37 (2): 163–79.

Scannell, Paddy. 1996. *Radio, Television, and Modern Life: A Phenomenological Approach.* Oxford: Blackwell.

Scannell, Paddy. 2014. *Television and the Meaning of "Live": An Enquiry into the Human Situation.* Cambridge: Polity.

Schatz, Edward, ed. 2013. Political Ethnography: What Immersion Contributes to the Study of Power. Chicago: University of Chicago Press.

Scheuer, Jeffrey. 2008. *The Big Picture: Why Democracies Need Journalistic Excellence.* London: Routledge.

Schlesinger, Philip. 1981. 'Between Sociology and Journalism'. *The Sociological Review* 29 (S1): 341–69.

Schrøder, Kim Christian, and Louise Phillips. 2007. 'Complexifying Media Power: A Study of the Interplay between Media and Audience Discourses on Politics'. *Media, Culture & Society* 29 (6): 890–915.

Schudson, Michael. 2003. *The Sociology of News.* New York: W. W. Norton.

Schultz, Ida. 2007. 'The Journalistic Gut Feeling'. *Journalism Practice* 1 (2): 190–207.

Scott, Martin. 2015. 'Distant Suffering Online: The Unfortunate Irony of Cyber-Utopian Narratives'. *International Communication Gazette* 77 (7): 637–53.

Seib, Philip M. 2002. *The Global Journalist: News and Conscience in a World of Conflict.* Oxford: Rowman & Littlefield.

Sennett, Richard. 1977. *The Fall of Public Man.* Cambridge: Cambridge University Press.

Sharkey, Jacqueline. 2000. 'Collective Amnesia'. *American Journalism Review* 22 (8). http://ajrarchive.org/article.asp?id=788.

Silva, Elizabeth B. 2016. 'Unity and Fragmentation of the Habitus'. *The Sociological Review* 64 (1): 166–83.

Silverstone, Roger. 2006. *Media and Morality: On the Rise of the Mediapolis.* Cambridge: Polity.

Singer, Jane. 2005. 'The Political J-blogger: "Normalizing" a New Media Form to Fit Old Norms and Practices'. *Journalism* 6 (2): 173–98.

Singer, Jane B., David Domingo, Ari Heinonen, Alfred Hermida, Steve Paulussen, Thorsten Quandt, Zvi Reich and Marina Vujnovic. 2011. *Participatory Journalism: Guarding Open Gates at Online Newspapers.* Oxford: John Wiley & Sons.

Skovsgaard, Morten. 2014. 'Watchdogs on a Leash? The Impact of Organisational Constraints on Journalists' Perceived Professional Autonomy and Their Relationship with Superiors'. *Journalism* 15 (3): 344–63.

Smith, Jonathan A., Michael Howard Larkin and Paul Flowers. 2009. *Interpretative Phenomenological Analysis: Theory, Method and Research.* London: Sage.

Soguk, Nevzat. 2011. 'Uprisings in "Arab Streets", Revolutions in "Arab Minds"! A Provocation'. *Globalizations* 8 (5): 595–99.

Sontag, Susan. 2003. *Regarding the Pain of Others*. London: Penguin.

Sparks, Colin. 2007. 'Extending and Refining the Propaganda Model'. *Westminster Papers in Communication and Culture* 4 (2): 68–84.

Springborg, Robert. 2011. 'The Precarious Economics of Arab Springs'. *Survival* 53 (6): 85–104.

Starbird, Kate, and Leysia Palen. 2012. '(How) Will the Revolution be Retweeted?: Information Diffusion and the 2011 Egyptian Uprising'. *Proceedings of the ACM 2012 Conference on Computer Supported Cooperative Work,* 7–16.

Stassen, Wilma. 2010. 'Your News in 140 Characters: Exploring the Role of Social Media in Journalism'. *Global Media Journal: African Edition* 4 (1): 116–31.

Staudigl, Michael. 2007. 'Towards a Phenomenological Theory of Violence: Reflections Following Merleau-Ponty and Schutz'. *Human Studies* 30 (3): 233–53.

Steensen, Steen. 2014. 'Conversing the Audience: A Methodological Exploration of How Conversation Analysis Can Contribute to the Analysis of Interactive Journalism'. *New Media & Society* 16 (8): 1197–213.

Stepan, Alfred, and Juan J. Linz. 2013. 'Democratization Theory and the "Arab Spring"'. *Journal of Democracy* 24 (2): 15–30.

Stephenson, Niamh, and Dimitris Papadopoulos. 2006. *Analysing Everyday Experience: Social Research and Political Change.* Basingstoke: Palgrave Macmillan.

Stiegler, Bernard. 1998. *Technics and Time: The Fault of Epimetheus.* Stanford: Stanford University Press.

Stiegler, Bernard. 2011. 'Suffocated Desire or How the Cultural Industry Destroys the Individual: Contribution to a Theory of Mass Consumption'. *Parrhesia* 13: 52–61.

Stiegler, Bernard. 2013a. *Disbelief and Discredit.* Cambridge: Polity.

Stiegler, Bernard. 2013b. 'The Most Precious Good in the Era of Social Technologies'. In *Unlike Us Reader,* edited by Geert Lovink and Miriam Rasch, 16–30. Amsterdam: Institute of Network Cultures.

Stoker, Gerry, B. Guy Peters and Jon Pierre. 2015. *The Relevance of Political Science.* Basingstoke: Palgrave Macmillan.

Strömbäck, Jesper. 2008. 'Four Phases of Mediatization: An Analysis of the Mediatization of Politics'. *International Journal of Press/Politics* 13 (3): 228–46.

Sutherland, Thomas. 2013. 'Liquid Networks and the Metaphysics of Flux: Ontologies of Flow in an Age of Speed and Mobility'. *Theory, Culture & Society* 30 (5): 3–23.

Tadros, Mariz. 2015. 'Contentious and Prefigurative Politics: Vigilante Groups' Struggle against Sexual Violence in Egypt (2011–2013)'. *Development and Change* 46 (6): 1345–68.

Taylor, Charles. 1994. *Multiculturalism.* Princeton: Princeton University Press.

Taylor, Charles. 2004. *Modern Social Imaginaries.* Durham, NC: Duke University Press.

Tejerina, Benjamín, Ignacia Perugorría, Tova Benski and Lauren Langman. 2013. 'From Indignation to Occupation: A New Wave of Global Mobilization'. *Current Sociology* 61 (4): 377–92.

Tester, Keith. 1994. *Compassion, Morality and the Media.* Buckingham: Open University.

Thompson, Paul. 2005. 'Foundation and Empire: A Critique of Hardt and Negri'. *Capital & Class* 29 (2): 73–98.

Thornborrow, Joanna, and Martin Montgomery. 2010. 'Special Issue on Personalization in the Broadcast News Interview'. *Discourse & Communication* 4 (2): 99–104.

Throop, C. Jason, and Keith M. Murphy. 2002. 'Bourdieu and Phenomenology: A Critical Assessment'. *Anthropological Theory* 2 (2): 185–207.

Thurman, Neil, Steve Schifferes, Richard Fletcher, Nic Newman, Stephen Hunt and Aljosha Karim Schapals. 2016. 'Giving Computers a Nose for News: Exploring the Limits of Story Detection and Verification'. *Digital Journalism* 4 (7): 838–48.

Tilly, Charles. 2007. 'Mechanisms of the Middle Range'. Paper given at SSRC conference in honour of Robert K.Merton at Columbia University, 9–10 August 2007. http://essays.ssrc.org/tilly/wp-content/uploads/2008/06/tilly-mechanisms-middle-range.pdf.

Todorov, Tzvetan. 1990. *Genres in Discourse.* Cambridge: Cambridge University Press. First published in 1978.

Tremayne, Mark, and Andrew Clark. 2014. 'New Perspectives from the Sky: Unmanned Aerial Vehicles and Journalism'. *Digital Journalism* 2 (2): 232–46.

Trombetta, Lorenzo. 2012. 'Altering Courses in Unknown Waters: Interaction between Traditional and New Media during the First Months of the Syrian Uprising'. *Global Media Journal – German Edition* 2 (1). https://www.db-thueringen.de/servlets/MCRFileNodeServlet/dbt_derivate_00025454/GMJ3_Trombetta_final.pdf.

Tufekci, Zeynep, and Christopher Wilson. 2012. 'Social Media and the Decision to Participate in Political Protest: Observations from Tahrir Square'. *Journal of Communication* 62 (2): 363–79.

Tumber, Howard, and Frank Webster. 2006. *Journalists under Fire: Information War and Journalistic Practices.* London: Sage.

Turner, Graeme. 2010. *Ordinary People and the Media: The Demotic Turn.* London: Sage.

Uldam, Julie, and Anne Vestergaard. 2015. *Civic Engagement and Social Media: Political Participation beyond the Protest.* Basingstoke: Palgrave Macmillan.

UNICEF. 2013. 'Eddie Izzard in Iraq: Help the Children of Syria'. https://www.youtube.com/watch?v=_RSE7Xgw2ZE.

Van Dijck, José. 2013. *The Culture of Connectivity: A Critical History of Social Media.* Oxford: Oxford University Press.

Van Zoonen, Liesbet. 1994. *Feminist Media Studies.* London: Sage.

Van Zoonen, Liesbet. 2013. 'From Identity to Identification: Fixating the Fragmented Self'. *Media, Culture & Society* 35 (1): 44–51.

Virilio, Paul. 2000. *The Information Bomb.* London: Verso.

Virilio, Paul. 2006. *Speed and Politics.* Los Angeles, CA: Semiotext(e).

Virilio, Paul. 2012. *Great Accelerator.* Cambridge: Polity.

Vobič, Igor, and Ana Milojević. 2014. ' "What We Do is Not Actually Journalism": Role Negotiations in Online Departments of Two Newspapers in Slovenia and Serbia'. *Journalism* 15 (8): 1023–40.

Volpi, Frédéric. 2011. 'Framing Civility in the Middle East: Alternative Perspectives on the State and Civil Society'. *Third World Quarterly* 32 (5): 827–43.

Von Engelhardt, Johannes. 2015. 'Studying Western Audiences Vis-À-Vis Mediated Distant Suffering. A Call to Venture beyond Media Studies'. *International Communication Gazette* 77 (7): 695–707.

Wacquant, Loïc. 2014. 'Homines in Extremis: What Fighting Scholars Teach Us about Habitus'. *Body & Society* 20 (2): 3–17.

Waisbord, Silvio. 2013. *Reinventing Professionalism: Journalism and News in Global Perspective.* Oxford: John Wiley & Sons.

Wajcman, Judy. 2004. *Technofeminism.* Cambridge: Polity.

Wall, Melissa, and Sahar El Zahed. 2011. ' "I'll be Waiting for You Guys": A YouTube Call to Action in the Egyptian Revolution'. *International Journal of Communication* 5: 1333–43.

Wapner, Paul. 2002. 'Horizontal Politics: Transnational Environmental Activism and Global Cultural Change'. *Global Environmental Politics* 2 (2): 37–62.

Watenpaugh, Keith David. 2014. *Being Modern in the Middle East: Revolution, Nationalism, Colonialism, and the Arab Middle Class.* Princeton: Princeton University Press.

Weaver, David H., Randal A. Beam, Bonnie J. Brownlee, Paul S. Voakes and G. Cleveland Wilhoit. 2009. *The American Journalist in the 21st Century: U.S. News People at the Dawn of a New Millennium.* London: Routledge.

Weaver, David H., and Lars Willnat. 2012. *The Global Journalist in the 21st Century.* London: Routledge.

Weber, Max. 1978. *Economy and Society: An Outline of Interpretive Sociology.* Oakland, CA: University of California Press.

Wehrle, Maren. 2016. 'Normative Embodiment. The Role of the Body in Foucault's Genealogy. A Phenomenological Re-Reading'. *Journal of the British Society for Phenomenology* 47 (1): 56–71.

Wellman, Barry, and Caroline A. Haythornthwaite. 2002. *The Internet in Everyday Life.* Oxford: Blackwell.

Wiik, Jenny. 2010. 'Journalism in Transition. The Professional Identity of Swedish Journalists'. PhD diss., University of Gothenburg. http://hdl.handle.net/2077/21853.

Wilkins, Lee. 2016. 'Affirmative Duties: The Institutional and Individual Capabilities Required in Disaster Coverage'. *Journalism Studies* 17 (2): 216–30. First published in 2014.

Williams, Clare, Jenny Kitzinger and Lesley Henderson. 2003. 'Envisaging the Embryo in Stem Cell Research: Rhetorical Strategies and Media Reporting of the Ethical Debates'. *Sociology of Health & Illness* 25 (7): 793–814.

Wilson, Christopher, and Alexandra Dunn. 2011. 'Media in the Egyptian Revolution: Descriptive Analysis from the Tahrir Data Set'. *International Journal of Communication* 5: 1248–72.

Wilson, Japhy, and E. Swyngedouw, eds. 2014. *The Post-Political and Its Discontents: Spaces of Depoliticization, Spectres of Radical Politics.* Edinburgh: Edinburgh University Press.

Withy, Katherine. 2014. 'Situation and Limitation: Making Sense of Heidegger on Thrownness'. *European Journal of Philosophy* 22 (1): 61–81. First published in 2011.

Wizda, Sharyn. 1997. 'Parachute Journalism'. *American Journalism Review* 19 (6): 40–45.

Wodak, Ruth. 2013. *Right-Wing Populism in Europe: Politics and Discourse.* London: Bloomsbury.

Wodak, Ruth. 2015. *The Politics of Fear: What Right-Wing Populist Discourses Mean.* London: Sage.

Wright, Joseph, and Abel Escriba-Folch. 2012. 'Authoritarian Institutions and Regime Survival: Transitions to Democracy and Subsequent Autocracy'. *British Journal of Political Science* 42 (2): 283–309.

Ytre-Arne, Brita. 2011. '"I Want to Hold it in My Hands": Readers' Experiences of the Phenomenological Differences Between Women's Magazines Online and in Print'. *Media, Culture & Society* 33 (3): 467–77.

Ytreberg, Espen. 2002. 'Erving Goffman as a Theorist of the Mass Media'. *Critical Studies in Media Communication* 19 (4): 481–97.

Zelizer, Barbie. 2010. *About to Die: How News Images Move the Public.* Oxford: Oxford University Press.

Žižek, Slavoj. 2011. 'For Egypt, This is the Miracle of Tahrir Square'. *The Guardian*, 10 February. https://www.theguardian.com/global/2011/feb/10/egypt-miracle-tahrir-square.

Index

Lightning Source UK Ltd.
Milton Keynes UK
UKOW04n1616050917
308561UK00001BA/18/P

9 781786 604217